JEWISH HISTORY ATLAS

Jewish History Atlas

REVISED EDITION

Martin Gilbert

Cartography by ARTHUR BANKS and T. A. BICKNELL

Macmillan Publishing Co., Inc.
New York

Macmillan Publishing Co., Inc.
866 Third Avenue, New York, N.Y. 10022

Library of Congress Cataloging in Publication Data
Gilbert, Martin, 1936-
   Jewish history atlas.
   1. Jews—Historical geography—Maps.   2. Israel—
Historical geography—Maps.   I. Title.
G1030.G5   1977   912′.19′74924   77-8252
ISBN 0-02-543260-5

First American Printing of Revised Edition 1977

10   9   8   7   6   5   4   3

Printed in the United States of America

You may say you have been oppressed
and persecuted – that has been your
power! You have been hammered into
very fine steel, and that is why you
have never been broken.

LLOYD GEORGE IN 1925

Preface

This atlas traces the world-wide Jewish migrations from ancient
Mesopotamia to modern Israel. It seeks to follow the diverse—and sometimes
obscure—path of a far-ranging people, and to map their strange experiences
in good times and bad.

My original concern was to avoid undue emphasis upon the many horrific
aspects of Jewish history. I wished to portray with equal force the
construction, achievements and normalities of Jewish life through almost
four thousand years. In part I believe that I have succeeded; for there are many
maps of traders, philosophers, financiers, settlers and sages. But as my
research into Jewish history progressed, I was surprised, depressed, and to
some extent overwhelmed by the perpetual and irrational violence which
pursued the Jews in every century and to almost every corner of the globe.
If, therefore, persecution, expulsion, torture, humiliation, and mass murder
haunt these pages, it is because they also haunt the Jewish story.

But not all terrors are unmitigated; and I have felt a great relief in being
able also to map the other side of the coin—the Jewish revolts against
Roman, Chinese and Persian oppression—the often repeated pattern of mutual
self-help and communal charity, the self-defence leagues organized against
the Russian and Ukrainian pogroms, the brave if hopeless risings in ghetto
and concentration camp during the Nazi era, and the stubborn resistance to
Arab pressures by modern Israel.

If this Atlas can help to answer even a small portion of the questions which
Jews so often ask about themselves, or can tell Christians something more
about the varied experiences of their neighbours, it will have served a
purpose. In particular, I hope that the maps succeed in portraying the complex
comings and goings of many different sorts of Jews, and the extraordinary
diversity of the Jewish saga.

In this Atlas I have tried to look at the role of the Jews in their
different national settings, and show their reaction to persecution, whether by
dispersal, acceptance or defence. Both in resisting the continual pressure of
hostile societies and in braving the dangers of flight and exile, the Jewish people
have shown high courage and a keen capacity to rise again; "trampled into the

dust" as Cardinal Manning described it, "and yet never combining with the dust into which it is trampled."

For those who wish to follow up some of the themes covered by the maps, I have provided a short bibliography. In it I have included a few general books, together with a number of specialist works in which I found information for remote or neglected topics.

Many of my maps are intended to make certain obscure episodes in Jewish history better known, if only in outline. There are many equally fascinating problems on which no detailed research has yet been done; and the history of the Jews which most people know is primarily the history of those episodes on which books or monographs have been written. There are still many areas of darkness. But as I hope this Atlas shows, those aspects of Jewish history which can be mapped are full of unusual details and dramatic moments, ranging over every continent and every civilization, and adding a unique dimension to the story of mankind.

I should like to thank all those who have offered me advice, or scrutinized the maps at different stages. I am particularly grateful to Mr. Joshua Sherman and Dr. Harry Shukman of St. Antony's College, Oxford, to Miss Joanna Kaye, and to Mr. Jonathan Zamit, each of whom gave me valuable advice and criticism.

In asking for corrections, and suggestions for further maps, I realize that I am risking a spate of correspondence. On a subject so wide, so controversial, and in some areas so uncertain, error is perhaps inevitable, and omission unavoidable. Nevertheless, in the hope of being able to improve on the maps with each edition, and to enlarge on the range of maps, I invite the reader to send on all corrections or suggestions that seem necessary.

MARTIN GILBERT

Merton College, Oxford

List of Maps

JEWISH HISTORY ATLAS

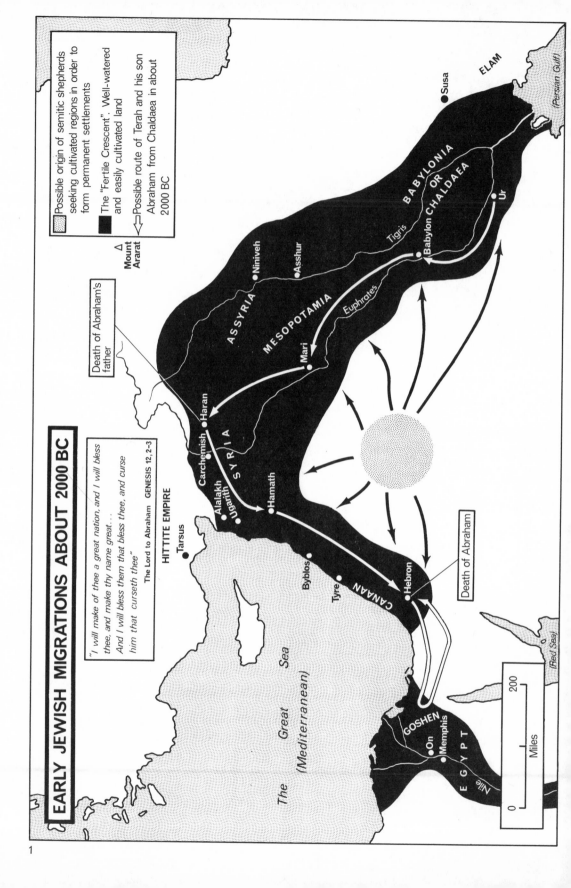

EARLY JEWISH MIGRATIONS ABOUT 2000 BC

"I will make of thee a great nation, and I will bless thee, and make thy name great...
And I will bless them that bless thee, and curse him that curseth thee"

The Lord to Abraham GENESIS 12, 2-3

Possible origin of semitic shepherds seeking cultivated regions in order to form permanent settlements

The "Fertile Crescent". Well-watered and easily cultivated land

Possible route of Terah and his son Abraham from Chaldaea in about 2000 BC

△ Mount Ararat

Death of Abraham's father

Death of Abraham

ELAM

(Persian Gulf)

Susa

BABYLONIA OR CHALDAEA

Ur

Tigris

Babylon

Euphrates

Nineveh

Asshur

ASSYRIA

MESOPOTAMIA

Mari

Haran

Carchemish

SYRIA

Alalakh
Ugarith

Hamath

HITTITE EMPIRE

Tarsus

Byblos

Tyre

CANAAN

Hebron

The Great Sea
(Mediterranean)

GOSHEN

On
Memphis

E G Y P T

Nile

(Red Sea)

0 Miles 200

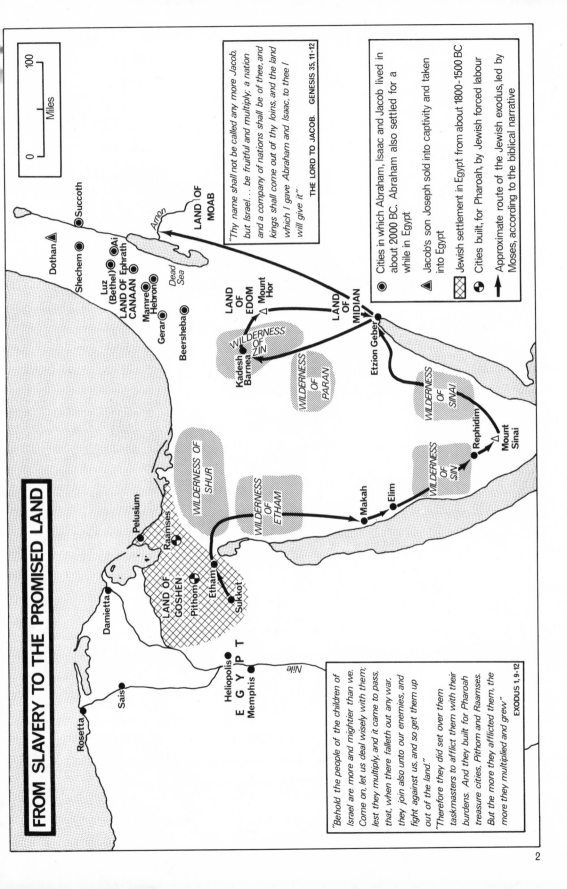

FROM SLAVERY TO THE PROMISED LAND

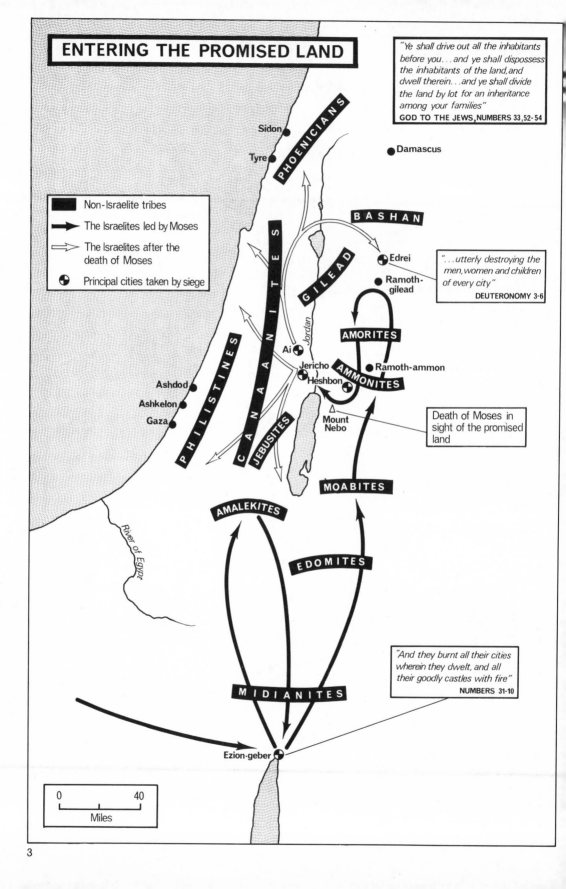

ENTERING THE PROMISED LAND

"Ye shall drive out all the inhabitants before you...and ye shall dispossess the inhabitants of the land, and dwell therein...and ye shall divide the land by lot for an inheritance among your families"
GOD TO THE JEWS, NUMBERS 33,52-54

● Damascus

Sidon

Tyre

PHOENICIANS

BASHAN

Non-Israelite tribes

The Israelites led by Moses

The Israelites after the death of Moses

● **Principal cities taken by siege**

GILEAD

⊕ Edrei

● Ramoth-gilead

"...utterly destroying the men, women and children of every city"
DEUTERONOMY 3-6

Jordan

P H I L I S T I N E S

C A N A A N I T E S

Ai ⊕

AMORITES

Jericho
Heshbon ⊕

AMMONITES

● Ramoth-ammon

Ashdod ●

Ashkelon ●

Gaza ●

J E B U S I T E S

△
Mount Nebo

Death of Moses in sight of the promised land

MOABITES

River of Egypt

AMALEKITES

EDOMITES

"And they burnt all their cities wherein they dwelt, and all their goodly castles with fire"
NUMBERS 31-10

M I D I A N I T E S

Ezion-geber ⊕

0   40
Miles

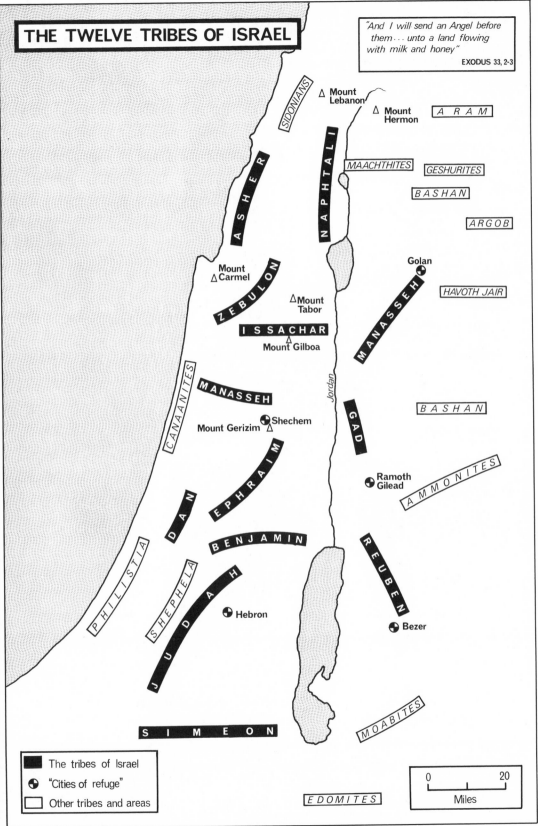

THE TWELVE TRIBES OF ISRAEL

"And I will send an Angel before
   them ... unto a land flowing
with milk and honey"

EXODUS 33, 2-3

SIDONIANS

△ Mount
Lebanon

△ Mount
Hermon

A R A M

MAACHTHITES

GESHURITES

ASHER

NAPHTALI

B A S H A N

ARGOB

Mount
△ Carmel

Golan ⊕

ZEBULON

△ Mount
Tabor

HAVOTH JAIR

MANASSEH

ISSACHAR

△
Mount Gilboa

Jordan

MANASSEH

B A S H A N

Mount Gerizim ⊕ Shechem
△

GAD

EPHRAIM

⊕ Ramoth
Gilead

A M M O N I T E S

C A N A A N I T E S

DAN

BENJAMIN

R E U B E N

P H I L I S T I A

S H E P H E L A

J U D A H

⊕ Hebron

⊕ Bezer

S I M E O N

M O A B I T E S

■ The tribes of Israel
⊕ "Cities of refuge"
☐ Other tribes and areas

0   20
|————|————|
   Miles

E D O M I T E S

4

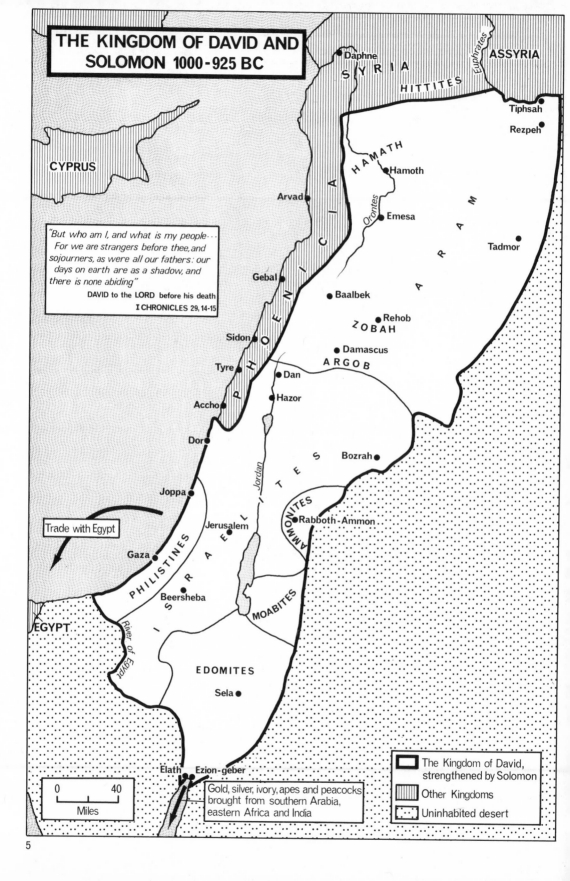

THE KINGDOM OF DAVID AND SOLOMON 1000-925 BC

ASSYRIA

SYRIA

HITTITES

Euphrates

Daphne

Tiphsah

Rezpeh

HAMATH

Hamoth

Arvad

P H O E N I C I A

Emesa

Orontes

A R A M

Tadmor

"But who am I, and what is my people...
For we are strangers before thee, and
sojourners, as were all our fathers: our
days on earth are as a shadow, and
there is none abiding"

DAVID to the LORD before his death
I CHRONICLES 29, 14-15

Gebal

Baalbek

Rehob

Z O B A H

Sidon

Damascus

Tyre

A R G O B

Dan

Accho

Hazor

Dor

Bozrah

Joppa

A M M O N I T E S

Jordan

Rabboth-Ammon

Trade with Egypt

Jerusalem

Gaza

P H I L I S T I N E S

I S R A E L I T E S

Beersheba

MOABITES

EGYPT

River of Egypt

E D O M I T E S

Sela

Elath Ezion-geber

0   40
Miles

Gold, silver, ivory, apes and peacocks
brought from southern Arabia,
eastern Africa and India

CYPRUS

	The Kingdom of David, strengthened by Solomon
	Other Kingdoms
	Uninhabited desert

5

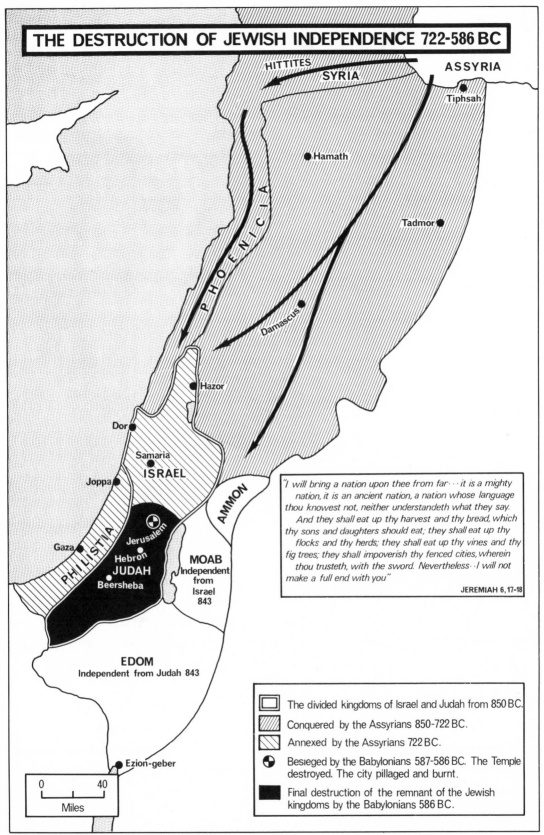

THE DESTRUCTION OF JEWISH INDEPENDENCE 722-586 BC

HITTITES
SYRIA
ASSYRIA
● Tiphsah

● Hamath

● Tadmor

P H O E N I C I A

Damascus ●

● Hazor

Dor ●

Samaria ●
ISRAEL

Joppa ●

AMMON

Gaza ●
Jerusalem ⊕
Hebron ●
JUDAH
Beersheba ●

MOAB
Independent
from
Israel
843

PHILISTIA

EDOM
Independent from Judah 843

Ezion-geber ●

"*I will bring a nation upon thee from far··· it is a mighty nation, it is an ancient nation, a nation whose language thou knowest not, neither understandeth what they say. And they shall eat up thy harvest and thy bread, which thy sons and daughters should eat; they shall eat up thy flocks and thy herds; they shall eat up thy vines and thy fig trees; they shall impoverish thy fenced cities, wherein thou trusteth, with the sword. Nevertheless··· I will not make a full end with you*"

JEREMIAH 6, 17-18

0   40
Miles

The divided kingdoms of Israel and Judah from 850 BC.

Conquered by the Assyrians 850-722 BC.

Annexed by the Assyrians 722 BC.

⊕ Besieged by the Babylonians 587-586 BC. The Temple destroyed. The city pillaged and burnt.

Final destruction of the remnant of the Jewish kingdoms by the Babylonians 586 BC.

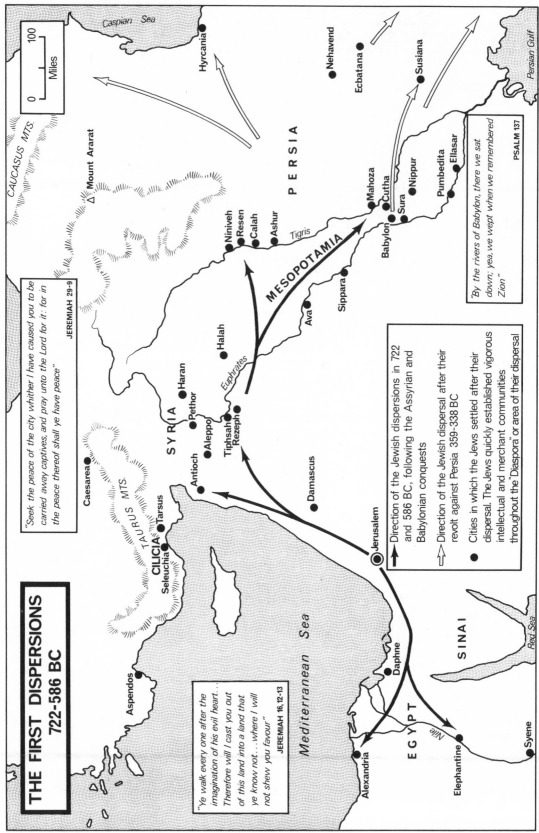

THE FIRST DISPERSIONS
722-586 BC

Caspian Sea

CAUCASUS MTS.

Hyrcania

△ Mount Ararat

Nehavend

Ecbatana

Susiana

Persian Gulf

P E R S I A

Nineveh
Resen
Calah
Ashur

Tigris

Mahoza
Cutha
Sura
Babylon

Pumbedita
Ellasar
Nippur

MESOPOTAMIA

Sippara

Ava

Halah

Euphrates

Haran
Pethor

S Y R I A

Aleppo
Tiphsah
Rezeph

Antioch

Damascus

Caesarea

TAURUS MTS.

Tarsus
CILICIA
Seleuchia

Aspendos

Mediterranean Sea

Jerusalem

Daphne

SINAI

Red Sea

Alexandria

E G Y P T

Nile

Elephantine

Syene

100
Miles
0

Direction of the Jewish dispersions in 722 and 586 BC, following the Assyrian and Babylonian conquests

Direction of the Jewish dispersal after their revolt against Persia 359-338 BC

● Cities in which the Jews settled after their dispersal. The Jews quickly established vigorous intellectual and merchant communities throughout the "Diaspora" or area of their dispersal

7

THE IMPERIAL POWERS 586–165 BC

THE PERSIAN EMPIRE 550–333 BC

Jerusalem

0 ___ 300
Miles

THE BABYLONIAN EMPIRE 586–550 BC

"The virgin of Israel is fallen,
She shall no more rise;
She is cast down upon the ground,
There is none to raise her up."
AMOS 5–2

Jerusalem

THE PTOLEMAIC EMPIRE 270 BC

"Our inheritance is turned to strangers,
Our houses to aliens.
We are orphans and fatherless,
Our mothers are as widows.
Our necks are under persecution,
We labour, and have no rest."
LAMENTATIONS 5, 2–5

Jerusalem

THE EMPIRE OF ALEXANDER THE GREAT 323 BC

Jerusalem

○ Empires controlling Jerusalem after the Assyrian conquest. The Jews gradually settled throughout the territory of the imperial powers.

■ ○

THE JEWS OF THE EASTERN MEDITERRANEAN BOTH BEFORE AND AFTER THE ARAB CONQUEST

0   20
Miles

For more than three thousand years Jews lived in the principal towns of the Eastern Mediterranean. The longest single overlordship of the area was that of Rome (677 years). Jewish rule in Judaea and Samaria in ancient times lasted a total of 641 years. Other rulers of the area included the Arabs (447 years), the Ottoman Turks (401 years) and the Crusaders (192 years)

Make war upon those who have been given scripture... until they pay the tribute readily, having been brought low
KORAN, SURA No 9, 29

ALEPPO

Jews lived here from biblical times. In 1173 AD there were 1,500 Jews; in 1900 more than 10,000 forced to pay an annual poll tax

ANTIOCH

In Roman times, a centre of Jewish settlement, whose Jews were granted equal citizenship rights with Greeks. In 600 AD, after attempts to forcible conversion, the Jews rebelled, and many were killed. In 1171 only 10 Jewish families still remained; in 1750 about 40; in 1894 about 80; in 1928 about 10

TRIPOLI

At the time of the Arab conquest, the Arab Governor established a garrison of Jewish troops to guard the town against Byzantine attack. Early in the 11th century Jews were persecuted, their synagogue turned into a mosque, and several houses destroyed. In the 16th century Jewish refugees from Spain settled and prospered. Early in the 17th century there were further persecutions and many Jews fled. In 1939 there were only four Jewish families left

BEIRUT

In 500 AD there was a flourishing Jewish community, but in 1173 Benjamin of Tudela found only 50 Jews. In 1889 there were 1,500 Jews out of a total population of 20,000, in 1913 5,000 out of 150,000

GAZA

Some Jews settled here in Talmudic times. In 1481 AD Meshullam of Volterra found 60 Jewish householders. From 1600-1799 the Jewish community flourished, but in 1799 it fled the city on the eve of Napoleon's arrival. Resettled in the 1880's, some 90 Jews were recorded in 1903

DAMASCUS

Contained some 10,000 Jewish inhabitants in Roman times, and over 3,000 when visited by Benjamin of Tudela in 1173 AD. In 1840 a ritual murder charge was brought against the Jews, and in 1880 they were falsely accused of taking part in a massacre of Christians. In 1901 there were eight synagogues, and as many as 20,000 Jews

RAFAH

A flourishing Jewish community lived here both before and after the Arab conquest, but in 1080 AD the Jews were driven out after nearly a thousand years of continuous settlement

⊙ Towns with Jewish inhabitants in Byzantine times, in which Jews were still living both before and after the Arab conquest in the seventh century AD

Mediterranean Sea

Antioch · Aleppo · Latakia · Baniyas · Hama · Masyaf · Homs · Tripoli · Jubail · Baalbek · Beirut · Sidon · Damascus · Tyre · Golan Heights · Safed · Naveh · Acre · Haifa · Tiberias · Nazareth · Ajlun · SAMARIA · R. Jordan · Salt · Jaffa · Lod · Ramleh · Amman · Jericho · JUDAEA · Jerusalem · Hebron · Dead Sea · Gaza · Juttah · Rafah · Ayn-al-Yahudiyya · Punon

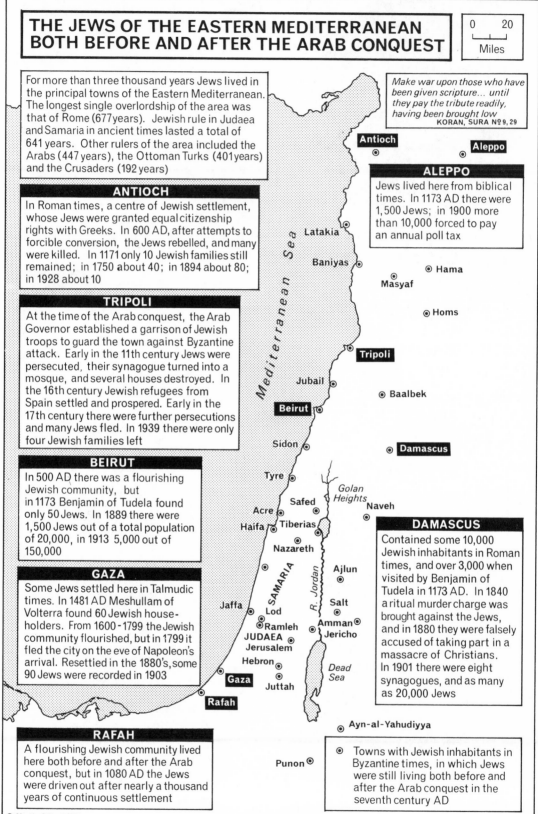

9

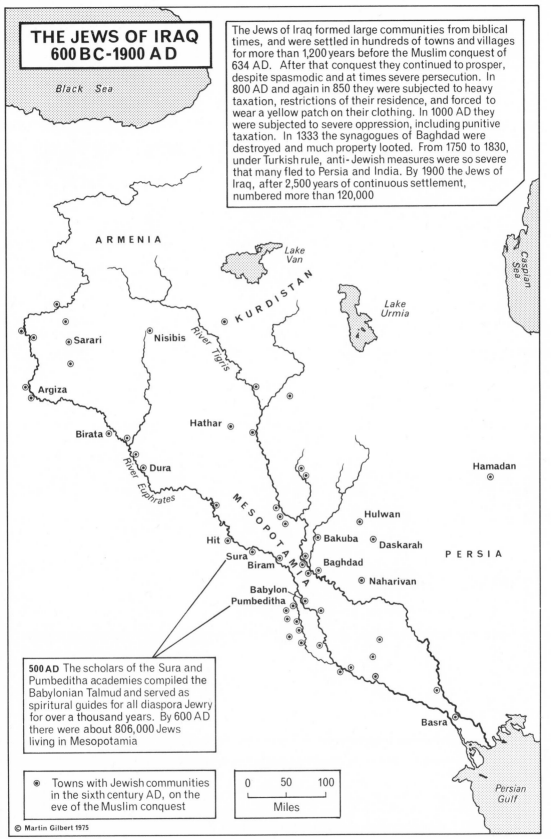

THE JEWS OF IRAQ
600 BC-1900 AD

The Jews of Iraq formed large communities from biblical times, and were settled in hundreds of towns and villages for more than 1,200 years before the Muslim conquest of 634 AD. After that conquest they continued to prosper, despite spasmodic and at times severe persecution. In 800 AD and again in 850 they were subjected to heavy taxation, restrictions of their residence, and forced to wear a yellow patch on their clothing. In 1000 AD they were subjected to severe oppression, including punitive taxation. In 1333 the synagogues of Baghdad were destroyed and much property looted. From 1750 to 1830, under Turkish rule, anti-Jewish measures were so severe that many fled to Persia and India. By 1900 the Jews of Iraq, after 2,500 years of continuous settlement, numbered more than 120,000

Black Sea

ARMENIA

Lake Van

K U R D I S T A N

Lake Urmia

Caspian Sea

Sarari

Nisibis

River Tigris

Argiza

Hathar

Birata

River Euphrates

Dura

Hamadan

M E S O P O T A M I A

Hulwan

Hit

Bakuba

Daskarah

Sura

PERSIA

Biram

Baghdad

Babylon
Pumbeditha

Naharivan

500 AD The scholars of the Sura and Pumbeditha academies compiled the Babylonian Talmud and served as spiritual guides for all diaspora Jewry for over a thousand years. By 600 AD there were about 806,000 Jews living in Mesopotamia

Basra

⊙   Towns with Jewish communities in the sixth century AD, on the eve of the Muslim conquest

0	50	100

Miles

Persian Gulf

© Martin Gilbert 1975

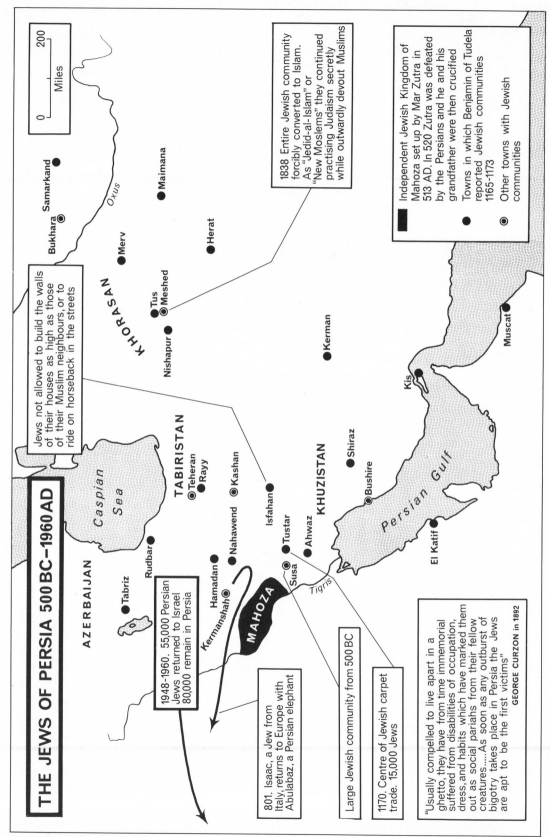

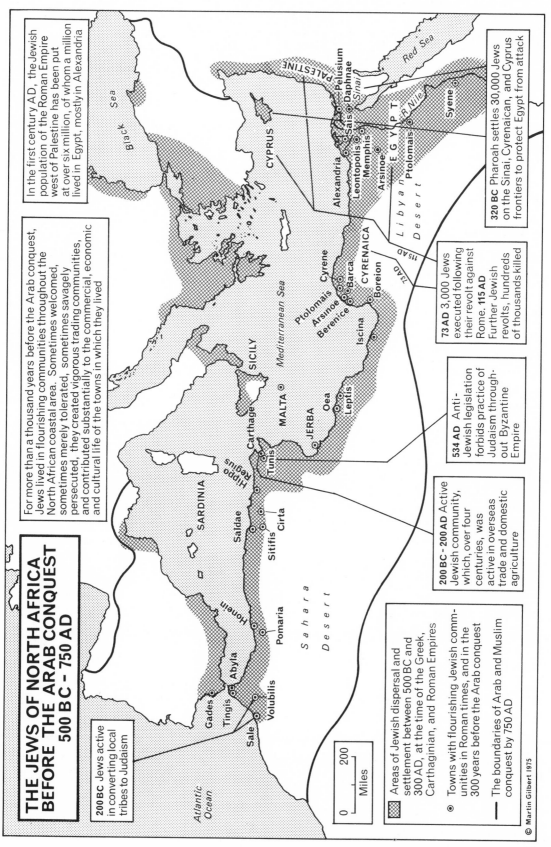

THE JEWS OF NORTH AFRICA BEFORE THE ARAB CONQUEST 500 BC – 750 AD

In the first century AD, the Jewish population of the Roman Empire west of Palestine has been put at over six million, of whom a million lived in Egypt, mostly in Alexandria

320 BC Pharoah settles 30,000 Jews on the Sinai, Cyrenaican, and Cyprus frontiers to protect Egypt from attack

73 AD 3,000 Jews executed following their revolt against Rome. 115 AD Further Jewish revolts, hundreds of thousands killed

For more than a thousand years before the Arab conquest, Jews lived in flourishing communities throughout the North African coastal area. Sometimes welcomed, sometimes merely tolerated, sometimes savagely persecuted, they created vigorous trading communities, and contributed substantially to the commercial, economic and cultural life of the towns in which they lived

534 AD Anti-Jewish legislation forbids practice of Judaism throughout Byzantine Empire

200 BC – 200 AD Active Jewish community, which, over four centuries, was active in overseas trade and domestic agriculture

200 BC Jews active in converting local tribes to Judaism

Areas of Jewish dispersal and settlement between 500 BC and 300 AD, at the time of the Greek, Carthaginian, and Roman Empires

◉ Towns with flourishing Jewish communities in Roman times, and in the 300 years before the Arab conquest

— The boundaries of Arab and Muslim conquest by 750 AD

0   200

Miles

© Martin Gilbert 1975

Atlantic Ocean

Sale
Volubilis
Tingis
Gades
Abyla
Pomaria
Honein
Saldae
Sitifis
Cirta
SARDINIA
Hippo Regius
Carthage
Tunis
JERBA
MALTA ◉
Oea
Leptis
Iscina
Boreion
Berenice
Arsinoe
Ptolomais
Barca
Cyrene
CYRENAICA
SICILY
Mediterranean Sea
Sahara Desert
Libyan Desert
EGYPT
Syene
R. Nile
Ptolomais
Arsinoe
Memphis
Sais
Leontopolis
Alexandria
Pelusium
Daphnae
Sinai
PALESTINE
Red Sea
CYPRUS
Black Sea

132 AD
115 AD

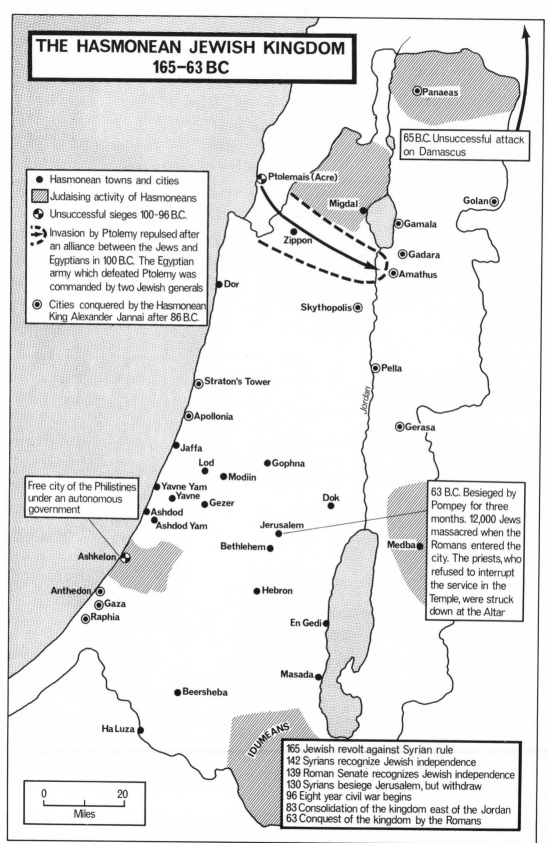

THE HASMONEAN JEWISH KINGDOM 165–63 BC

65 B.C. Unsuccessful attack on Damascus

- ● Hasmonean towns and cities
- ▨ Judaising activity of Hasmoneans
- ⊕ Unsuccessful sieges 100–96 B.C.
- ⬆⟶ Invasion by Ptolemy repulsed after an alliance between the Jews and Egyptians in 100 B.C. The Egyptian army which defeated Ptolemy was commanded by two Jewish generals
- ◉ Cities conquered by the Hasmonean King Alexander Jannai after 86 B.C.

●Panaeas

Golan◉

Ptolemais (Acre)⊕

Migdal

●Gamala

Zippon

●Gadara

●Amathus

Dor●

Skythopolis◉

●Pella

Straton's Tower◉

Apollonia◉

●Gerasa

Jaffa●

Lod●

●Gophna

●Modiin

Yavne Yam◉
Yavne●   Gezer●

●Dok

Free city of the Philistines under an autonomous government

Ashdod●

Jerusalem●

Ashdod Yam●

Bethlehem●

Medba●

63 B.C. Besieged by Pompey for three months. 12,000 Jews massacred when the Romans entered the city. The priests, who refused to interrupt the service in the Temple, were struck down at the Altar

Ashkelon⊗

Anthedon◉

●Hebron

●Gaza

◉Raphia

En Gedi●

Masada●

●Beersheba

Ha Luza●

IDUMEANS

Jordan

0 — 20
Miles

165 Jewish revolt against Syrian rule
142 Syrians recognize Jewish independence
139 Roman Senate recognizes Jewish independence
130 Syrians besiege Jerusalem, but withdraw
96 Eight year civil war begins
83 Consolidation of the kingdom east of the Jordan
63 Conquest of the kingdom by the Romans

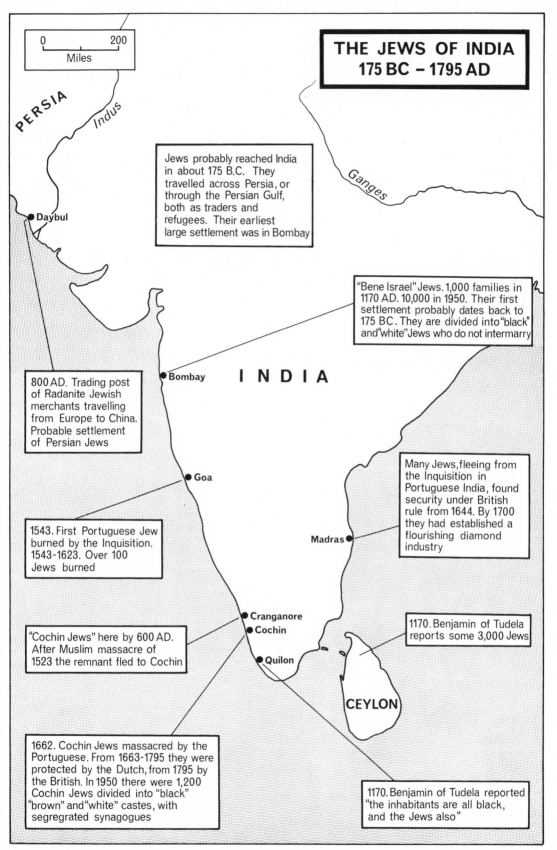

THE JEWS OF INDIA
175 BC – 1795 AD

0   200
Miles

PERSIA

Indus

Ganges

Jews probably reached India in about 175 B.C. They travelled across Persia, or through the Persian Gulf, both as traders and refugees. Their earliest large settlement was in Bombay

● Daybul

"Bene Israel" Jews. 1,000 families in 1170 AD. 10,000 in 1950. Their first settlement probably dates back to 175 BC. They are divided into "black" and "white" Jews who do not intermarry

● Bombay

INDIA

800 AD. Trading post of Radanite Jewish merchants travelling from Europe to China. Probable settlement of Persian Jews

● Goa

Many Jews, fleeing from the Inquisition in Portuguese India, found security under British rule from 1644. By 1700 they had established a flourishing diamond industry

1543. First Portuguese Jew burned by the Inquisition. 1543-1623. Over 100 Jews burned

Madras ●

● Cranganore
● Cochin

1170. Benjamin of Tudela reports some 3,000 Jews

"Cochin Jews" here by 600 AD. After Muslim massacre of 1523 the remnant fled to Cochin

● Quilon

CEYLON

1662. Cochin Jews massacred by the Portuguese. From 1663-1795 they were protected by the Dutch, from 1795 by the British. In 1950 there were 1,200 Cochin Jews divided into "black" "brown" and "white" castes, with segregrated synagogues

1170. Benjamin of Tudela reported "the inhabitants are all black, and the Jews also"

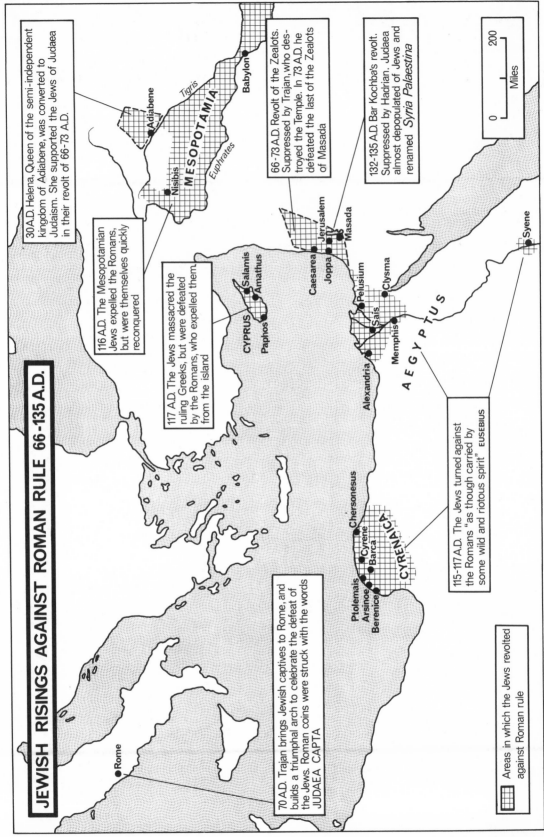

JEWISH RISINGS AGAINST ROMAN RULE 66-135 A.D.

30 A.D. Helena, Queen of the semi-independent kingdom of Adiabene, was converted to Judaism. She supported the Jews of Judaea in their revolt of 66-73 A.D.

116 A.D. The Mesopotamian Jews expelled the Romans, but were themselves quickly reconquered

66-73 A.D. Revolt of the Zealots. Suppressed by Trajan, who destroyed the Temple. In 73 A.D. he defeated the last of the Zealots of Masada

132-135 A.D. Bar Kochba's revolt. Suppressed by Hadrian. Judaea almost depopulated of Jews and renamed *Syria Palaestina*

117 A.D. The Jews massacred the ruling Greeks, but were defeated by the Romans, who expelled them from the island

115-117 A.D. The Jews turned against the Romans "as though carried by some wild and riotous spirit" EUSEBIUS

70 A.D. Trajan brings Jewish captives to Rome, and builds a triumphal arch to celebrate the defeat of the Jews. Roman coins were struck with the words JUDAEA CAPTA

MESOPOTAMIA

Tigris

Euphrates

Babylon

Adiabene

Nisibis

Jerusalem

Masada

Caesarea

Joppa

Pelusium

Clysma

Sais

Memphis

Alexandria

A E G Y P T U S

Syene

CYPRUS

Salamis

Amathus

Paphos

Chersonesus

Cyrene

Barca

CYRENAICA

Ptolemais

Arsinoe

Berenice

Rome

0   200

Miles

Areas in which the Jews revolted against Roman rule

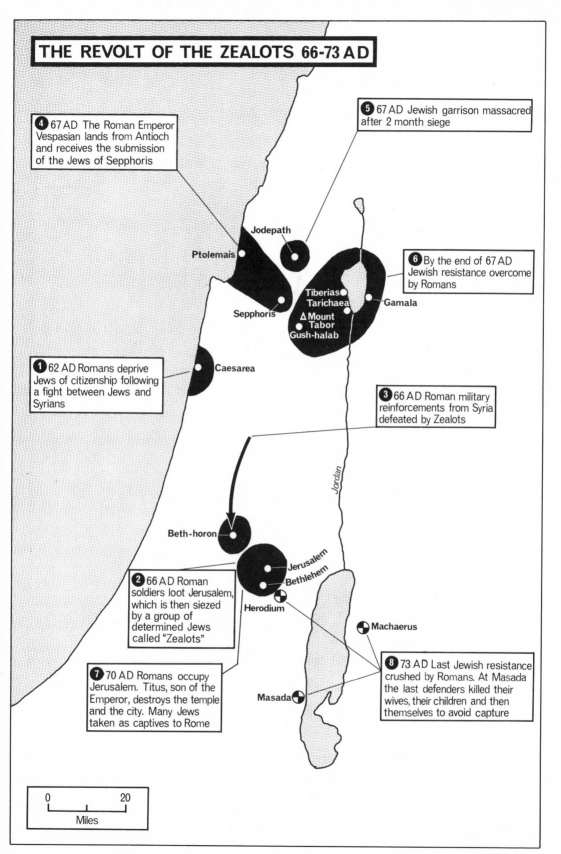

THE REVOLT OF THE ZEALOTS 66-73 AD

5 67 AD Jewish garrison massacred after 2 month siege

4 67 AD The Roman Emperor Vespasian lands from Antioch and receives the submission of the Jews of Sepphoris

6 By the end of 67 AD Jewish resistance overcome by Romans

Jodepath

Ptolemais

Tiberias
Tarichaea
△ Mount Tabor
Gush-halab

Gamala

Sepphoris

1 62 AD Romans deprive Jews of citizenship following a fight between Jews and Syrians

Caesarea

3 66 AD Roman military reinforcements from Syria defeated by Zealots

Jordan

Beth-horon

Jerusalem
Bethlehem

2 66 AD Roman soldiers loot Jerusalem, which is then siezed by a group of determined Jews called "Zealots"

Herodium

Machaerus

8 73 AD Last Jewish resistance crushed by Romans. At Masada the last defenders killed their wives, their children and then themselves to avoid capture

7 70 AD Romans occupy Jerusalem. Titus, son of the Emperor, destroys the temple and the city. Many Jews taken as captives to Rome

Masada

```
0          20
  Miles
```

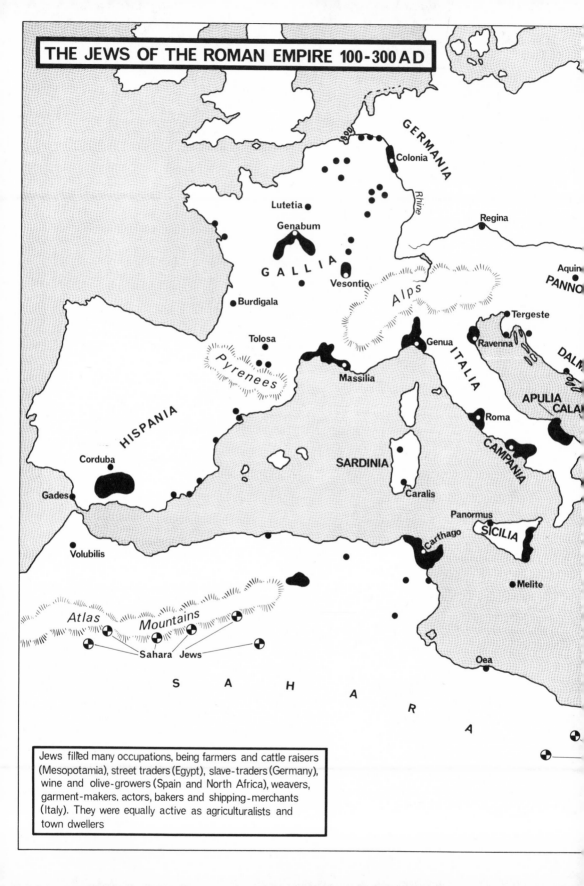

THE JEWS OF THE ROMAN EMPIRE 100-300 A.D.

GERMANIA

Colonia

Rhine

Lutetia

Regina

Genabum

GALLIA

Vesontio

Aquin

Alps

PANNO

Burdigala

Genua

Tergeste

Tolosa

Ravenna

ITALIA

DALM

Massilia

Roma

APULIA

CALA

HISPANIA

Pyrenees

SARDINIA

CAMPANIA

Corduba

Caralis

Gades

Panormus

SICILIA

Volubilis

Carthago

Melite

Atlas   Mountains

Sahara   Jews

S   A   H   A   R   A

Oea

Jews filled many occupations, being farmers and cattle raisers (Mesopotamia), street traders (Egypt), slave-traders (Germany), wine and olive-growers (Spain and North Africa), weavers, garment-makers, actors, bakers and shipping-merchants (Italy). They were equally active as agriculturalists and town dwellers

By 300 A.D., the Jews had settled in every part of the Roman Empire except Britain. They were guaranteed freedom of religion and were allowed to practice Jewish law in disputes between Jews. They were exempt from military service.

There were probably at least three million Jews in 300 A.D., a million of whom lived west of Macedonia

0   200
Miles

Don

Tanais

Olbia

Phanagoria

Panticapaeum

Mountain Jews

Caucasus Mts.

Danube

Serdica   MOESIA

Trapezus

Amisus

Byzantium

Prusa

Ancyra

Melitene

Tigris

ASSYRIA

PHRYGIA

MESOPOTAMIA

MACEDONIA

Euphrates

Tarsus

CILICIA

Sura

Ephesus

Delos

LYCIA   CYPRUS

SYRIA

Pumbedita
Babylon

ACHAIA

Damascus

Hierosolyma
(Jerusalem)

Cyrene

Alexandria

Pelusium

Berenice

Aelana

CYRENAICA

AEGYPTUS

welling
vs

The 40,000 Jews of Cyprus were expelled after rebelling against Roman rule in 115 A.D.

■ Areas of widespread Jewish settlement

● Towns with large Jewish communities

✠ Isolated Jewish communities established after the Roman conquest of Palestine and surviving to this day

17

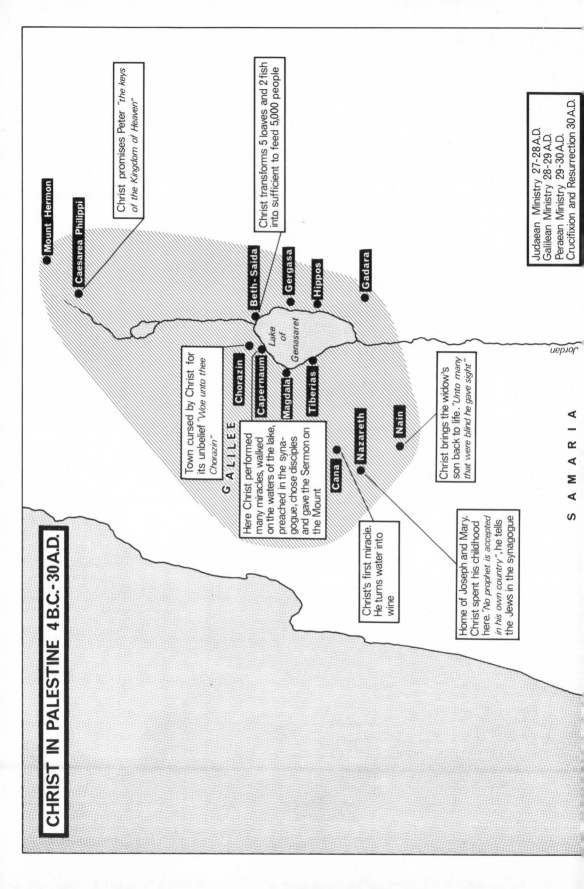

CHRIST IN PALESTINE 4 B.C.-30 A.D.

Christ promises Peter *"the keys of the Kingdom of Heaven"*

Christ transforms 5 loaves and 2 fish into sufficient to feed 5,000 people

● Mount Hermon

● Caesarea Philippi

● Beth-Saida

● Gergasa

● Hippos

● Gadara

Lake of Genasaret

Town cursed by Christ for its unbelief *'Woe unto thee Chorazin'*

● Chorazin

● Capernaum

● Magdala

● Tiberias

G A L I L E E

Here Christ performed many miracles, walked on the waters of the lake, preached in the synagogue, chose disciples and gave the Sermon on the Mount

● Nain

Christ brings the widow's son back to life. *"Unto many that were blind he gave sight"*

Jordan

● Cana

● Nazareth

Christ's first miracle. He turns water into wine

Home of Joseph and Mary. Christ spent his childhood here. *"No prophet is accepted in his own country"*, he tells the Jews in the synagogue

S A M A R I A

Judaean Ministry 27-28 A.D.
Galilean Ministry 28-29 A.D.
Peraean Ministry 29-30 A.D.
Crucifixion and Resurrection 30 A.D.

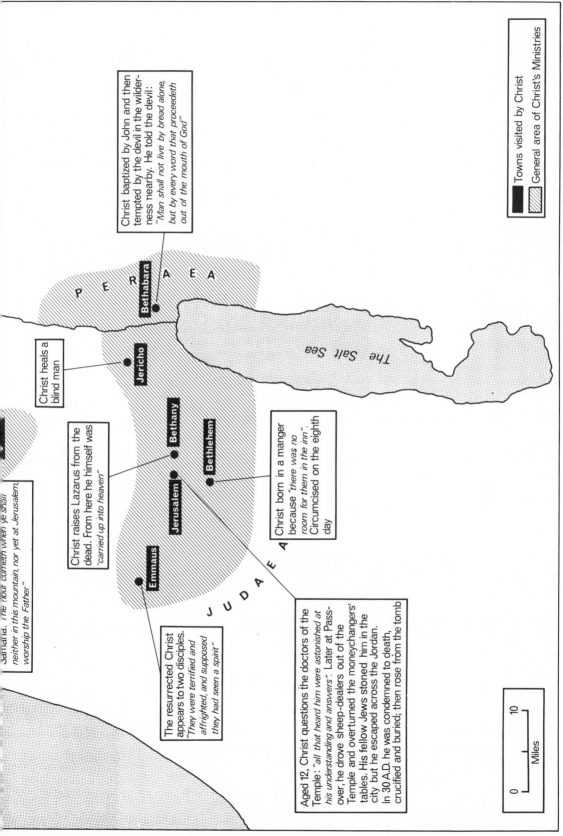

Christ baptized by John and then tempted by the devil in the wilderness nearby. He told the devil: *"Man shall not live by bread alone, but by every word that proceedeth out of the mouth of God"*

Christ heals a blind man

Samaria. The *"hour cometh when ye shall neither in this mountain, nor yet at Jerusalem, worship the Father"*

Christ raises Lazarus from the dead. From here he himself was *"carried up into heaven"*

Christ born in a manger because *"there was no room for them in the inn"*. Circumcised on the eighth day

The resurrected Christ appears to two disciples. *"They were terrified and affrighted, and supposed they had seen a spirit"*

Aged 12, Christ questions the doctors of the Temple: *"all that heard him were astonished at his understanding and answers"*. Later at Passover, he drove sheep-dealers out of the Temple and overturned the moneychangers' tables. His fellow Jews stoned him in the city but he escaped across the Jordan. In 30 A.D. he was condemned to death, crucified and buried; then rose from the tomb

P E R A E A

Bethabara

Jericho

Bethany

Jerusalem

Bethlehem

Emmaus

J U D A E A

The Salt Sea

◾ Towns visited by Christ

▨ General area of Christ's Ministries

0   10
Miles

18

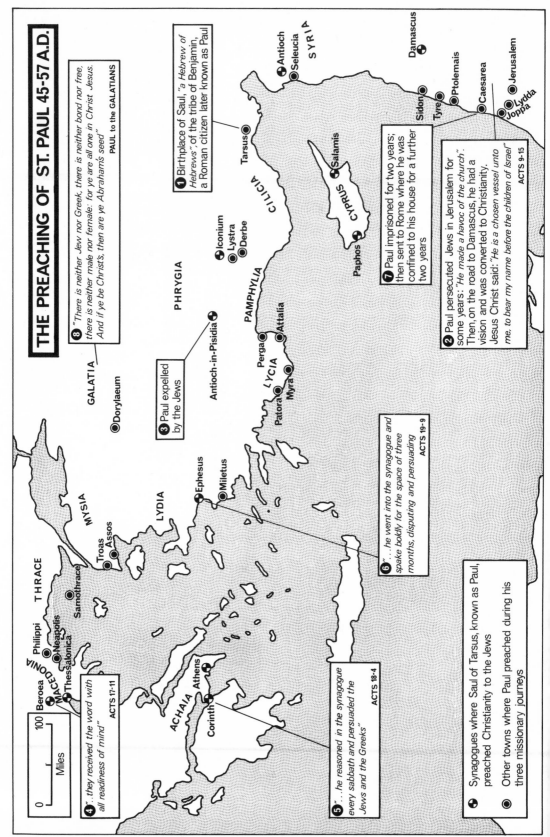

THE PREACHING OF ST. PAUL 45-57 A.D.

8 *"There is neither Jew nor Greek, there is neither bond nor free, there is neither male nor female: for ye are all one in Christ Jesus. And if ye be Christ's, then are ye Abraham's seed"*

PAUL to the GALATIANS

1 Birthplace of Saul, *"a Hebrew of Hebrews"*, of the tribe of Benjamin, a Roman citizen later known as Paul

7 Paul imprisoned for two years; then sent to Rome where he was confined to his house for a further two years

2 Paul persecuted Jews in Jerusalem for some years: *"He made a havoc of the church"*. Then, on the road to Damascus, he had a vision and was converted to Christianity. Jesus Christ said: *"He is a chosen vessel unto me, to bear my name before the children of Israel"*

ACTS 9-15

3 Paul expelled by the Jews

6 *"...he went into the synagogue and spake boldly for the space of three months, disputing and persuading"*

ACTS 19-9

5 *"...he reasoned in the synagogue every sabbath and persuaded the Jews and the Greeks"*

ACTS 18-4

4 *"...they received the word with all readiness of mind"*

ACTS 17-11

⊕ Synagogues where Saul of Tarsus, known as Paul, preached Christianity to the Jews

◉ Other towns where Paul preached during his three missionary journeys

0 100
Miles

SYRIA
Damascus
Antioch
Seleucia
Sidon
Tyre
Ptolemais
Caesarea
Lydda
Joppa
Jerusalem

Tarsus
CILICIA
CYPRUS
Salamis
Paphos

PHRYGIA
Iconium
Lystra
Derbe

GALATIA
Dorylaeum

Antioch-in-Pisidia
PAMPHYLIA
Perga
Attalia
LYCIA
Patara
Myra

MYSIA
LYDIA
Ephesus
Miletus
Troas
Assos

THRACE
Samothrace
Neapolis
Philippi
MACEDONIA
Thessalonica
Beroea

ACHAIA
Athens
Corinth

19

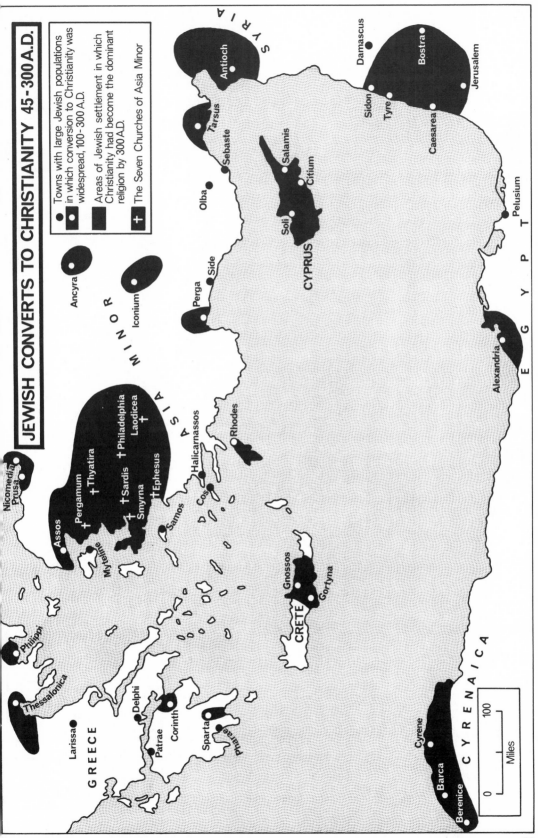

JEWISH CONVERTS TO CHRISTIANITY 45-300 A.D.

● Towns with large Jewish populations in which conversion to Christianity was widespread, 100-300 A.D.

■ Areas of Jewish settlement in which Christianity had become the dominant religion by 300 A.D.

✝ The Seven Churches of Asia Minor

SYRIA

Antioch
Tarsus
Sebaste
Damascus
Bostra
Jerusalem
Sidon
Tyre
Caesarea
Pelusium

Olba

Side
Perga

Salamis
Citium
Soli
CYPRUS

EGYPT

Alexandria

ASIA MINOR

Ancyra
Iconium

✝Pergamum
✝Thyatira
✝Philadelphia
✝Sardis   ✝Laodicea
✝Smyrna
✝Ephesus

Assos
Mytelite
Samos
Cos
Halicarnassos
Rhodes

Nicomedia
Prusa

Larissa

GREECE

Thessalonica
Philippi

Delphi
Corinth
Patrae
Sparta
Phanae

Cnossos
Gortyna
CRETE

CYRENAICA

Cyrene
Barca
Berenice

0   100
Miles

20

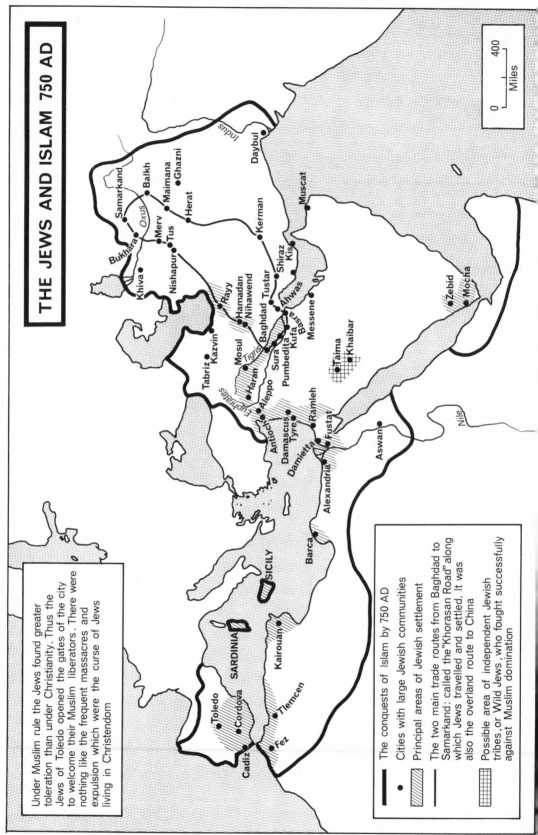

THE JEWS AND ISLAM 750 AD

Under Muslim rule the Jews found greater toleration than under Christianity. Thus the Jews of Toledo opened the gates of the city to welcome their Muslim liberators. There were nothing like the frequent massacres and expulsion which were the curse of Jews living in Christendom

0   400

Miles

─── The conquests of Islam by 750 AD

● Cities with large Jewish communities

▨ Principal areas of Jewish settlement

─── The two main trade routes from Baghdad to Samarkand: called the "Khorasan Road" along which Jews travelled and settled. It was also the overland route to China

▦ Possible area of independent Jewish tribes, or Wild Jews, who fought successfully against Muslim domination

Samarkand
Balkh
Bukhara
Oxus
Merv
Tus
Khiva
Nishapur
Maimana
Ghazni
Herat
Kerman
Daybul
Indus
Muscat
Rayy
Hamadan
Nihawend
Baghdad Tustar
Shiraz
Kis
Tabriz
Kazvin
Mosul
Harran
Sura
Ahwas
Kufa Basra
Pumbedita
Messene
Tigris
Aleppo
Euphrates
Antioch
Damascus
Tyre
Ramleh
Fustat
Damietta
Alexandria
Aswan
Nile
Barca
Zebid
Mocha
Taima
Khaibar
SICILY
SARDINIA
Kairouan
Toledo
Cordova
Tlemcen
Cadiz
Fez

21

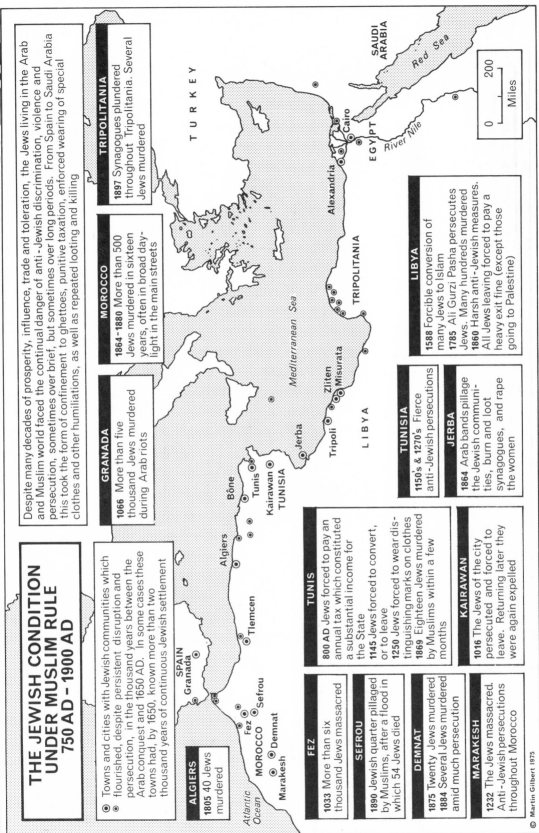

THE JEWISH CONDITION UNDER MUSLIM RULE 750 AD – 1900 AD

Despite many decades of prosperity, influence, trade and toleration, the Jews living in the Arab and Muslim world faced the continual danger of anti-Jewish discrimination, violence and persecution, sometimes over brief, but sometimes over long periods. From Spain to Saudi Arabia this took the form of confinement to ghettoes, punitive taxation, enforced wearing of special clothes and other humiliations, as well as repeated looting and killing

- Towns and cities with Jewish communities which
- flourished, despite persistent disruption and persecution, in the thousand years between the Arab conquest and 1650 AD. In some cases these towns had, by 1650, known more than two thousand years of continuous Jewish settlement

TRIPOLITANIA

1897 Synagogues plundered throughout Tripolitania. Several Jews murdered

MOROCCO

1864–1880 More than 500 Jews murdered in sixteen years, often in broad daylight in the main streets

GRANADA

1066 More than five thousand Jews murdered during Arab riots

LIBYA

1588 Forcible conversion of many Jews to Islam
1785 Ali Gurzi Pasha persecutes Jews. Many hundreds murdered
1860 Harsh anti-Jewish measures. All Jews leaving forced to pay a heavy exit fine (except those going to Palestine)

TUNISIA

1150's & 1270's Fierce anti-Jewish persecutions

JERBA

1864 Arab bands pillage the Jewish communities, burn and loot synagogues, and rape the women

ALGIERS

1805 40 Jews murdered

FEZ

1033 More than six thousand Jews massacred

SEFROU

1890 Jewish quarter pillaged by Muslims, after a flood in which 54 Jews died

DEMNAT

1875 Twenty Jews murdered
1884 Several Jews murdered amid much persecution

MARAKESH

1232 The Jews massacred. Anti-Jewish persecutions throughout Morocco

TUNIS

800 AD Jews forced to pay an annual tax which constituted a substantial income for the State
1145 Jews forced to convert, or to leave
1250 Jews forced to wear distinguishing marks on clothes
1869 Eighteen Jews murdered by Muslims within a few months

KAIRAWAN

1016 The Jews of the city persecuted and forced to leave. Returning later they were again expelled

TURKEY

SAUDI ARABIA

Red Sea

Cairo

EGYPT

River Nile

Alexandria

Mediterranean Sea

TRIPOLITANIA

Ziliten
Misurata
Tripoli
Jerba

LIBYA

Tunis
Kairawan
TUNISIA

Bône

Algiers

Tlemcen

SPAIN
Granada

Fez
Sefrou
MOROCCO
Demnat
Marakesh

Atlantic Ocean

0   200
Miles

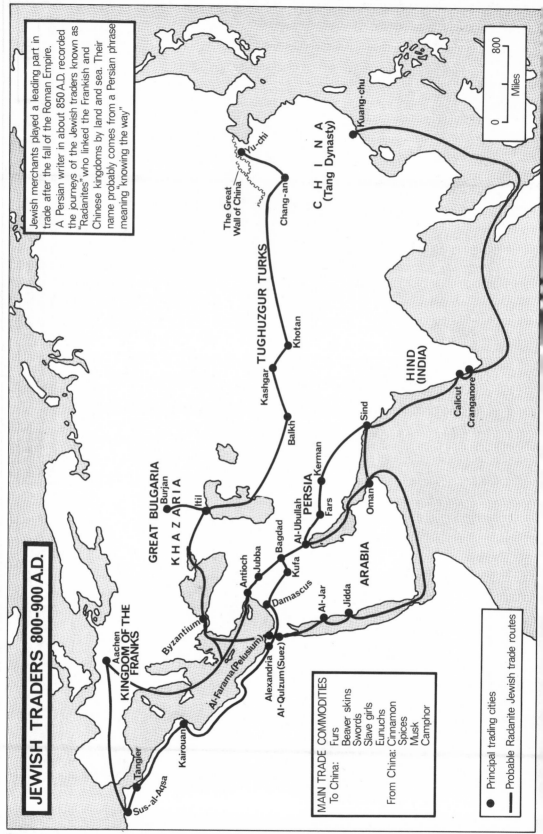

JEWISH TRADERS 800-900 A.D.

Jewish merchants played a leading part in trade after the fall of the Roman Empire. A Persian writer in about 850 A.D. recorded the journeys of the Jewish traders known as "Radanites" who linked the Frankish and Chinese kingdoms by land and sea. Their name probably comes from a Persian phrase meaning "knowing the way"

The Great Wall of China

KINGDOM OF THE FRANKS

GREAT BULGARIA

KHAZARIA

TUGHUZGUR TURKS

C H I N A (Tang Dynasty)

PERSIA

ARABIA

HIND (INDIA)

Aachen
Tangier
Sus-al-Aqsa
Kairouan
Byzantium
Antioch
Jubba
Damascus
Al-Jar
Jidda
Alexandria
Al-Farama(Pelusium)
Al-Quizum (Suez)
Kufa
Bagdad
Al-Ubullah
Fars
Kerman
Oman
Sind
Itil
Burjan
Balkh
Kashgar
Khotan
Chang-an
Yu-chi
Kuang-chu
Calicut
Cranganore

MAIN TRADE COMMODITIES
To China: Furs
Beaver skins
Swords
Slave girls
Eunuchs
From China: Cinnamon
Spices
Musk
Camphor

• Principal trading cities
— Probable Radanite Jewish trade routes

800
0
Miles

23

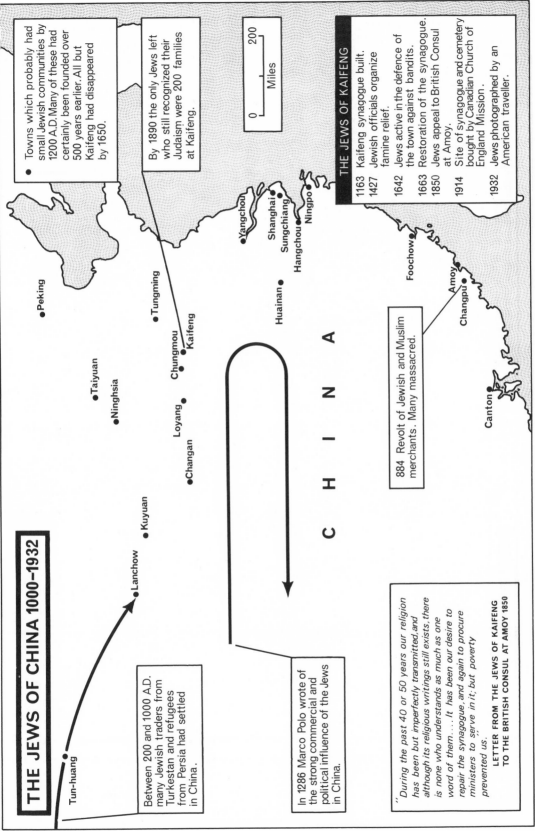

THE JEWS OF CHINA 1000-1932

Towns which probably had small Jewish communities by 1200 A.D. Many of these had certainly been founded over 500 years earlier. All but Kaifeng had disappeared by 1650.

By 1890 the only Jews left who still recognized their Judaism were 200 families at Kaifeng.

0   200

Miles

THE JEWS OF KAIFENG

1163	Kaifeng synagogue built.
1427	Jewish officials organize famine relief.
1642	Jews active in the defence of the town against bandits.
1663	Restoration of the synagogue.
1850	Jews appeal to British Consul at Amoy.
1914	Site of synagogue and cemetery bought by Canadian Church of England Mission.
1932	Jews photographed by an American traveller.

•Peking

•Tungming

•Taiyuan

Chungmou
•Kaifeng

•Ninghsia

Loyang
•

•Changan

•Kuyuan

•Lanchow

•Tun-huang

Yangchou•
Shanghai•
Sungchiang•
Hangchou• Ningpo•

Huainan•

Foochow•

Amoy•
Changpu•

Canton•

C H I N A

884 Revolt of Jewish and Muslim merchants. Many massacred.

Between 200 and 1000 A.D. many Jewish traders from Turkestan and refugees from Persia had settled in China.

In 1286 Marco Polo wrote of the strong commercial and political influence of the Jews in China.

"During the past 40 or 50 years our religion has been but imperfectly transmitted, and although its religious writings still exists, there is none who understands as much as one word of them.... It has been our desire to repair the synagogue, and again to procure ministers to serve in it; but poverty prevented us."

LETTER FROM THE JEWS OF KAIFENG TO THE BRITISH CONSUL AT AMOY 1850

THE KHAZAR JEWISH KINGDOM 700-1016 AD

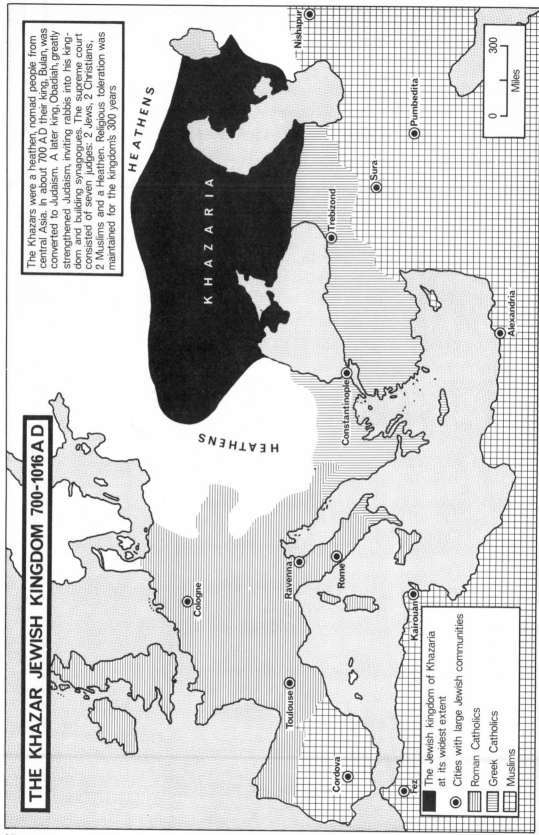

The Khazars were a heathen, nomad people from central Asia. In about 700 AD their king, Bulan, was converted to Judaism. A later king, Obadiah, greatly strengthened Judaism, inviting rabbis into his kingdom and building synagogues. The supreme court consisted of seven judges: 2 Jews, 2 Christians, 2 Muslims and a Heathen. Religious toleration was maintained for the kingdoms 300 years

HEATHENS

KHAZARIA

HEATHENS

Nishapur

Pumbedita

Sura

Trebizond

Constantinople

Alexandria

Cologne

Ravenna

Rome

Toulouse

Kairouan

Cordova

Fez

0   300
Miles

The Jewish kingdom of Khazaria at its widest extent

Cities with large Jewish communities

Roman Catholics

Greek Catholics

Muslims

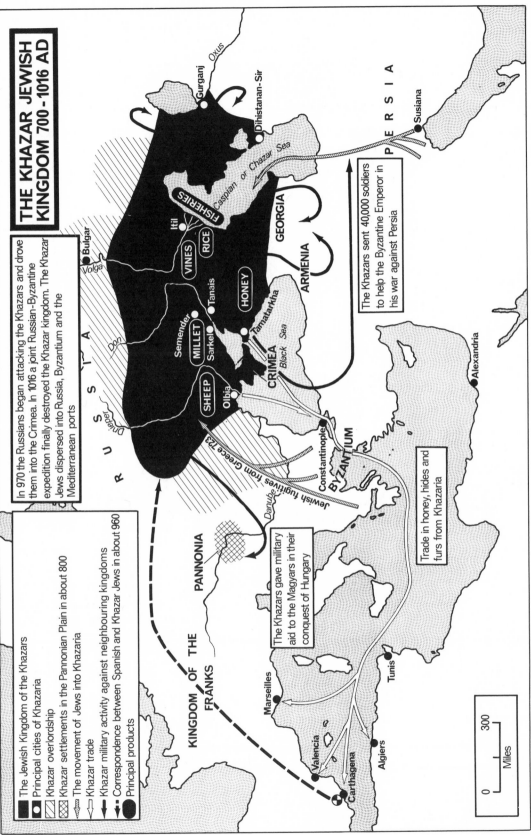

THE KHAZAR JEWISH KINGDOM 700 - 1016 AD

In 970 the Russians began attacking the Khazars and drove them into the Crimea. In 1016 a joint Russian-Byzantine expedition finally destroyed the Khazar kingdom. The Khazar Jews dispersed into Russia, Byzantium and the Mediterranean ports

The Khazars sent 40,000 soldiers to help the Byzantine Emperor in his war against Persia

Trade in honey, hides and furs from Khazaria

The Khazars gave military aid to the Magyars in their conquest of Hungary

- ■ The Jewish Kingdom of the Khazars
- ○ Principal cities of Khazaria
- Khazar overlordship
- Khazar settlements in the Pannonian Plain in about 800
- The movement of Jews into Khazaria
- Khazar trade
- Khazar military activity against neighbouring kingdoms
- Correspondence between Spanish and Khazar Jews in about 960
- Principal products

PERSIA

Susiana

Gurganj

Dihistanan- Sir

Oxus

Caspian or Chazar Sea

FISHERIES

Itil

VINES

RICE

Volga

Bulgar

HONEY

GEORGIA

ARMENIA

Semender

MILLET

Tanais

Sarkel

Tamatarkha

CRIMEA

Black Sea

Don

SHEEP

Olbia

Dnieper

R U S S I A

Jewish fugitives from Greece 723

Danube

Constantinople

BYZANTIUM

Alexandria

PANNONIA

KINGDOM OF THE FRANKS

Marseilles

Valencia

Carthagena

Algiers

Tunis

0   300

Miles

26

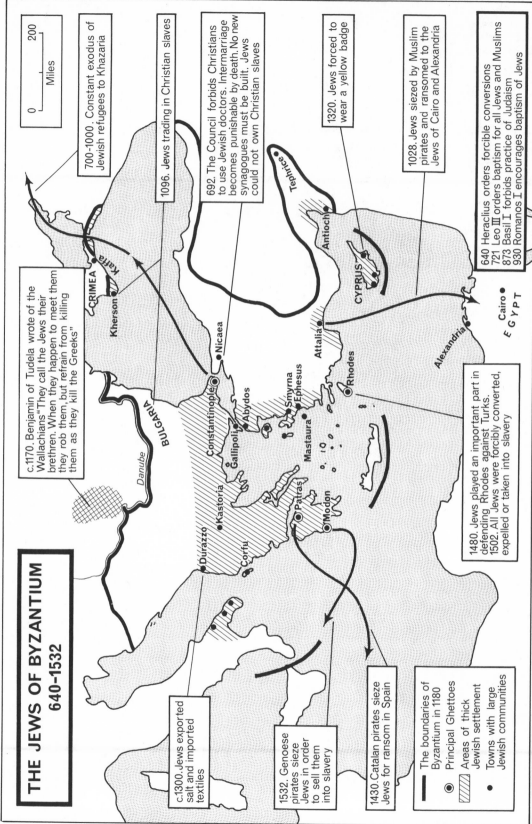

THE JEWS OF BYZANTIUM 640-1532

200 — Miles — 0

700-1000. Constant exodus of Jewish refugees to Khazaria

1096. Jews trading in Christian slaves

692. The Council forbids Christians to use Jewish doctors. Intermarriage becomes punishable by death. No new synagogues must be built. Jews could not own Christian slaves

1320. Jews forced to wear a yellow badge

1028. Jews siezed by Muslim pirates and ransomed to the Jews of Cairo and Alexandria

640 Heraclius orders forcible conversions
721 Leo III orders baptism for all Jews and Muslims
873 Basil I forbids practice of Judaism
930 Romanos I encourages baptism of Jews

c.1170. Benjamin of Tudela wrote of the Wallachians "They call the Jews their brethren. When they happen to meet them they rob them, but refrain from killing them as they kill the Greeks"

1480. Jews played an important part in defending Rhodes against Turks.
1502. All Jews were forcibly converted, expelled or taken into slavery

c.1300. Jews exported salt and imported textiles

1532. Genoese pirates sieze Jews in order to sell them into slavery

1430. Catalan pirates sieze Jews for ransom in Spain

CRIMEA
Kaffa
Kherson
BULGARIA
Danube
Durazzo
Corfu
Kastoria
Constantinople
Gallipoli
Abydos
Patras
Modon
Mastaura
Smyrna
Ephesus
Nicaea
Attalia
Rhodes
Tephrice
Antioch
CYPRUS
Alexandria
Cairo
EGYPT

── The boundaries of Byzantium in 1180
⊙ Principal Ghettoes
▨ Areas of thick Jewish settlement
• Towns with large Jewish communities

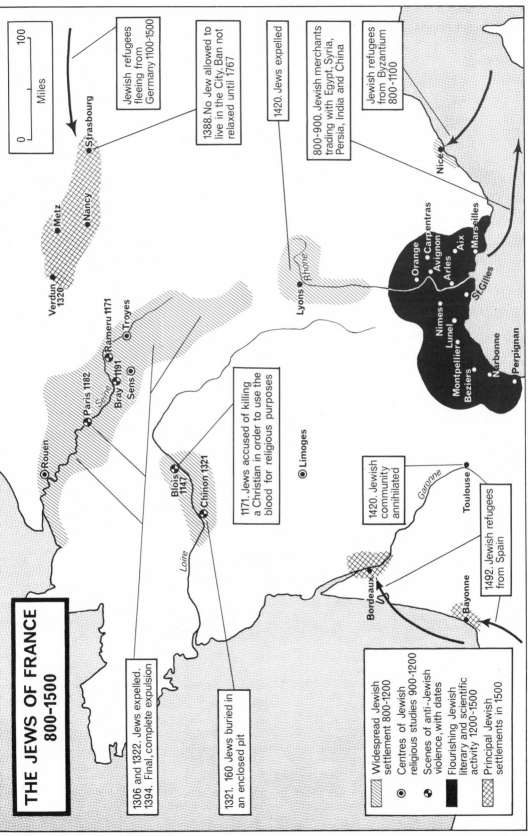

THE JEWS OF FRANCE 800–1500

Jewish refugees fleeing from Germany 1100-1500

1388. No Jew allowed to live in the City. Ban not relaxed until 1767

1420. Jews expelled

800-900. Jewish merchants trading with Egypt, Syria, Persia, India and China

Jewish refugees from Byzantium 800-1100

1306 and 1322. Jews expelled. 1394. Final, complete expulsion

1321. 160 Jews buried in an enclosed pit

1171. Jews accused of killing a Christian in order to use the blood for religious purposes

1420. Jewish community annihilated

1492. Jewish refugees from Spain

Miles
0   100

Strasbourg

Metz

Nancy

Verdun
1320

Rameru 1171
Troyes

Paris 1182
Bray 1191
Sens

Rouen

Lyons

Rhône

Blois
1147
Chinon 1321

Loire

Limoges

Garonne

Toulouse

Bordeaux

Bayonne

Orange
Carpentras
Avignon
Arles
Aix
Marseilles
St-Gilles
Nîmes
Lunel
Montpellier
Béziers
Narbonne
Perpignan

Nice

Widespread Jewish settlement 800-1200

Centres of Jewish religious studies 900-1200

Scenes of anti-Jewish violence, with dates

Flourishing Jewish literary and scientific activity 1200-1500

Principal Jewish settlements in 1500

28

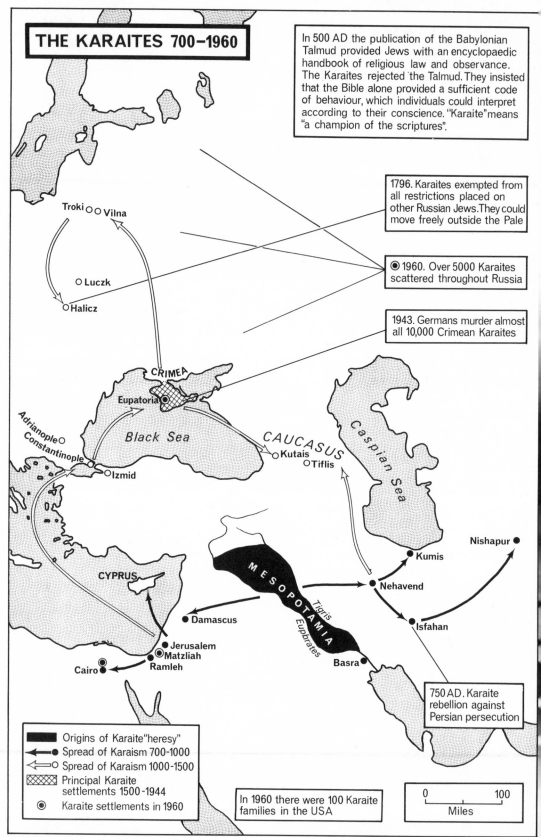

THE KARAITES 700-1960

In 500 AD the publication of the Babylonian Talmud provided Jews with an encyclopaedic handbook of religious law and observance. The Karaites rejected the Talmud. They insisted that the Bible alone provided a sufficient code of behaviour, which individuals could interpret according to their conscience. "Karaite" means "a champion of the scriptures".

1796. Karaites exempted from all restrictions placed on other Russian Jews. They could move freely outside the Pale

1960. Over 5000 Karaites scattered throughout Russia

1943. Germans murder almost all 10,000 Crimean Karaites

Troki ○○ Vilna

○ Luczk

○ Halicz

CRIMEA

Eupatoria ○

Adrianople ○
Constantinople ○
○ Izmid

Black Sea

CAUCASUS
○ Kutais
○ Tiflis

Caspian Sea

CYPRUS

Nishapur ●

○ Kumis

MESOPOTAMIA

Tigris
Euphrates

● Nehavend

● Damascus

● Isfahan

Jerusalem ●
● Matzliah
Cairo ◉ ● Ramleh

Basra ●

750 AD. Karaite rebellion against Persian persecution

Legend:
- ▬ Origins of Karaite "heresy"
- ←● Spread of Karaism 700-1000
- ⇐○ Spread of Karaism 1000-1500
- ▨ Principal Karaite settlements 1500-1944
- ◉ Karaite settlements in 1960

In 1960 there were 100 Karaite families in the USA

0   100
Miles

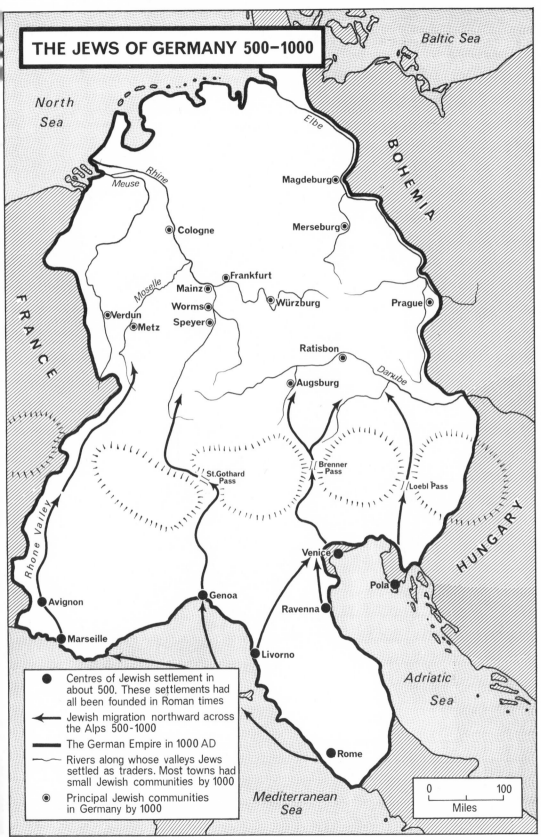

THE JEWS OF GERMANY 500–1000

North Sea

Baltic Sea

BOHEMIA

Elbe

Magdeburg ⊙

Merseburg ⊙

Rhine

Meuse

Cologne ⊙

FRANCE

Moselle

Frankfurt ⊙

Mainz ⊙

Würzburg ⊙

Prague ⊙

Worms ⊙

Verdun ⊙

Speyer ⊙

Metz ⊙

Ratisbon ⊙

Danube

Augsburg ⊙

St. Gothard Pass

Brenner Pass

Loebl Pass

Rhone Valley

HUNGARY

Venice ●

Pola ●

Genoa ●

Ravenna ●

Avignon ●

Marseille ●

Livorno ●

Adriatic Sea

Rome ●

Mediterranean Sea

● Centres of Jewish settlement in about 500. These settlements had all been founded in Roman times

← Jewish migration northward across the Alps 500–1000

━━ The German Empire in 1000 AD

∿ Rivers along whose valleys Jews settled as traders. Most towns had small Jewish communities by 1000

⊙ Principal Jewish communities in Germany by 1000

0   100
Miles

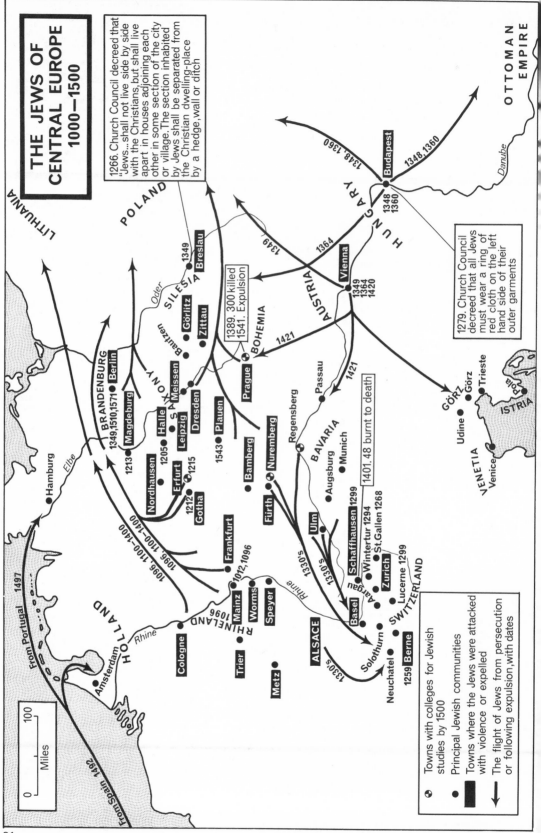

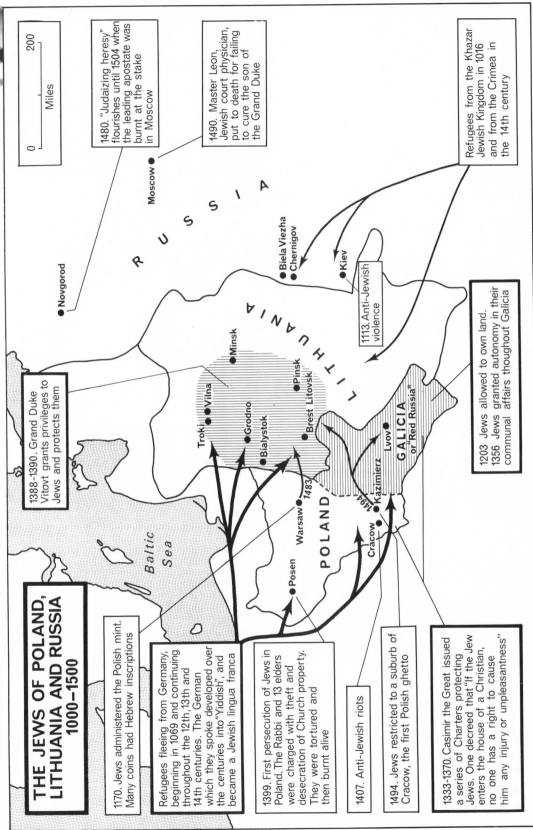

THE JEWS OF POLAND, LITHUANIA AND RUSSIA 1000–1500

0 — 200 Miles

1480. "Judaizing heresy" flourishes until 1504 when the leading apostate was burnt at the stake in Moscow

1490. Master Leon, Jewish court physician, put to death for failing to cure the son of the Grand Duke

Refugees from the Khazar Jewish Kingdom in 1016 and from the Crimea in the 14th century

1388–1390. Grand Duke Vitovt grants privileges to Jews and protects them

1113. Anti-Jewish violence

1203 Jews allowed to own land. 1356 Jews granted autonomy in their communal affairs throughout Galicia

1170. Jews administered the Polish mint. Many coins had Hebrew inscriptions

Refugees fleeing from Germany, beginning in 1069 and continuing throughout the 12th, 13th and 14th centuries. The German which they spoke developed over the centuries into "Yiddish", and became a Jewish lingua franca

1399. First persecution of Jews in Poland. The Rabbi and 13 elders were charged with theft and desecration of Church property. They were tortured and then burnt alive

1407. Anti-Jewish riots

1494. Jews restricted to a suburb of Cracow, the first Polish ghetto

1333–1370. Casimir the Great issued a series of Charters protecting Jews. One decreed that "If the Jew enters the house of a Christian, no one has a right to cause him any injury or unpleasantness"

RUSSIA

Moscow

Novgorod

Biela Viezha
Chernigov

Kiev

LITHUANIA

Minsk

Troki
Vilna

Grodno

Pinsk

Brest Litovsk

Bialystok

Baltic Sea

Posen

Warsaw 1483

POLAND

Cracow

Kazimierz 1494

Lvov

GALICIA or "Red Russia"

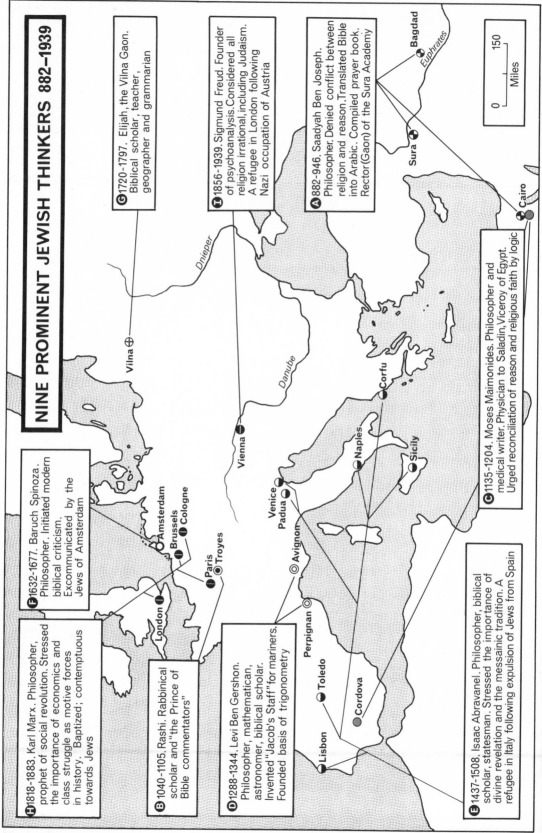

NINE PROMINENT JEWISH THINKERS 882–1939

G 1720-1797. Elijah, the Vilna Gaon. Biblical scholar, teacher, geographer and grammarian

H 1856-1939. Sigmund Freud. Founder of psychoanalysis. Considered all religion irrational, including Judaism. A refugee in London following Nazi occupation of Austria

A 882-946. Saadyah Ben Joseph. Philosopher. Denied conflict between religion and reason. Translated Bible into Arabic. Compiled prayer book. Rector (Gaon) of the Sura Academy

C 1135-1204. Moses Maimonides. Philosopher and medical writer. Physician to Saladin, Viceroy of Egypt. Urged reconciliation of reason and religious faith by logic

F 1632-1677. Baruch Spinoza. Philosopher. Initiated modern biblical criticism. Excommunicated by the Jews of Amsterdam

H 1818-1883. Karl Marx. Philosopher, prophet of social revolution. Stressed the importance of economics and class struggle as motive forces in history. Baptized; contemptuous towards Jews

B 1040-1105. Rashi. Rabbinical scholar and "the Prince of Bible commentators"

D 1288-1344. Levi Ben Gershon. Philosopher, mathematician, astronomer, biblical scholar. Invented "Jacob's Staff" for mariners. Founded basis of trigonometry

E 1437-1508. Isaac Abravanel. Philosopher, biblical scholar, statesman. Stressed the importance of divine revelation and the messainic tradition. A refugee in Italy following expulsion of Jews from Spain

0   150
Miles

Bagdad
Euphrates
Sura
Cairo
Dnieper
Danube
Vilna
Vienna
Corfu
Naples
Sicily
Venice
Padua
Avignom
Perpignan
Toledo
Cordova
Lisbon
Paris
Troyes
London
Amsterdam
Brussels
Cologne

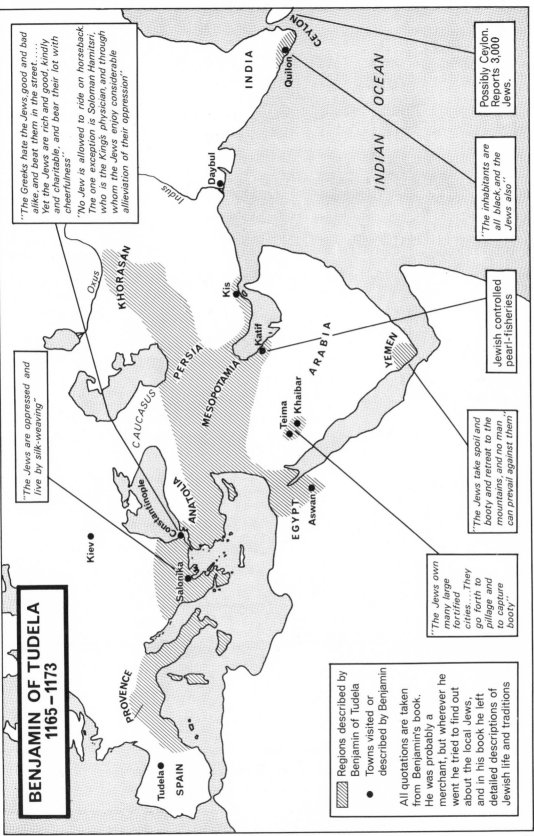

BENJAMIN OF TUDELA
1165 – 1173

"The Greeks hate the Jews, good and bad alike, and beat them in the street.......Yet the Jews are rich and good, kindly and charitable, and bear their lot with cheerfulness."

"No Jew is allowed to ride on horseback. The one exception is Soloman Hamitsri, who is the Kings physician, and through whom the Jews enjoy considerable alleviation of their oppression"

Possibly Ceylon. Reports 3,000 Jews.

"The inhabitants are all black, and the Jews also"

Jewish controlled pearl-fisheries

"The Jews are oppressed and live by silk-weaving"

"The Jews take spoil and booty and retreat to the mountains, and no man can prevail against them"

"The Jews own many large fortified cities....They go forth to pillage and to capture booty"

▨ Regions described by Benjamin of Tudela

● Towns visited or described by Benjamin

All quotations are taken from Benjamin's book. He was probably a merchant, but wherever he went he tried to find out about the local Jews, and in his book he left detailed descriptions of Jewish life and traditions

CEYLON
INDIA
Quilon
INDIAN OCEAN
Daybul
Indus
Oxus
KHORASAN
Kis
PERSIA
Katif
ARABIA
MESOPOTAMIA
YEMEN
CAUCASUS
Teima Khaibar
ANATOLIA
Constantinople
EGYPT
Aswan
Kiev
Salonika
PROVENCE
Tudela SPAIN

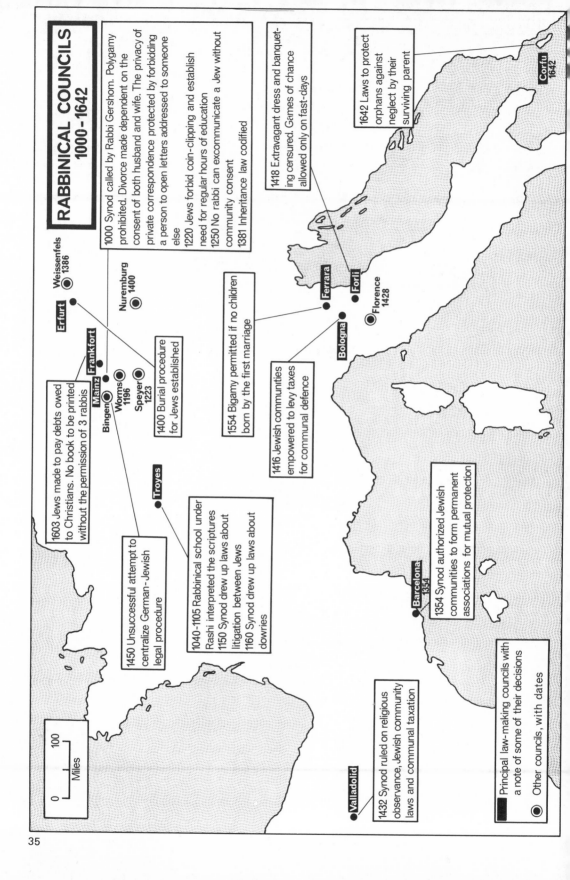

RABBINICAL COUNCILS
1000-1642

1000 Synod called by Rabbi Gershom. Polygamy prohibited. Divorce made dependent on the consent of both husband and wife. The privacy of private correspondence protected by forbidding a person to open letters addressed to someone else
1220 Jews forbid coin-clipping and establish need for regular hours of education
1250 No rabbi can excommunicate a Jew without community consent
1381 Inheritance law codified

1642 Laws to protect orphans against neglect by their surviving parent

Corfù 1642

1418 Extravagant dress and banqueting censured. Games of chance allowed only on fast-days

Weissenfels 1386

Nuremburg 1400

Erfurt

Frankfort

Mainz
Worms 1196
Speyer 1223
Bingen

1400 Burial procedure for Jews established

1603 Jews made to pay debts owed to Christians. No book to be printed without the permission of 3 rabbis

1450 Unsuccessful attempt to centralize German-Jewish legal procedure

Troyes

1040-1105 Rabbinical school under Rashi interpreted the scriptures
1150 Synod drew up laws about litigation between Jews
1160 Synod drew up laws about dowries

Ferrara
Forlì
Florence 1428
Bologna

1554 Bigamy permitted if no children born by the first marriage

1416 Jewish communities empowered to levy taxes for communal defence

1354 Synod authorized Jewish communities to form permanent associations for mutual protection

Barcelona 1354

Valladolid

1432 Synod ruled on religious observance, Jewish community laws and communal taxation

0 — 100 Miles

■ Principal law-making councils with a note of some of their decisions

● Other councils, with dates

35

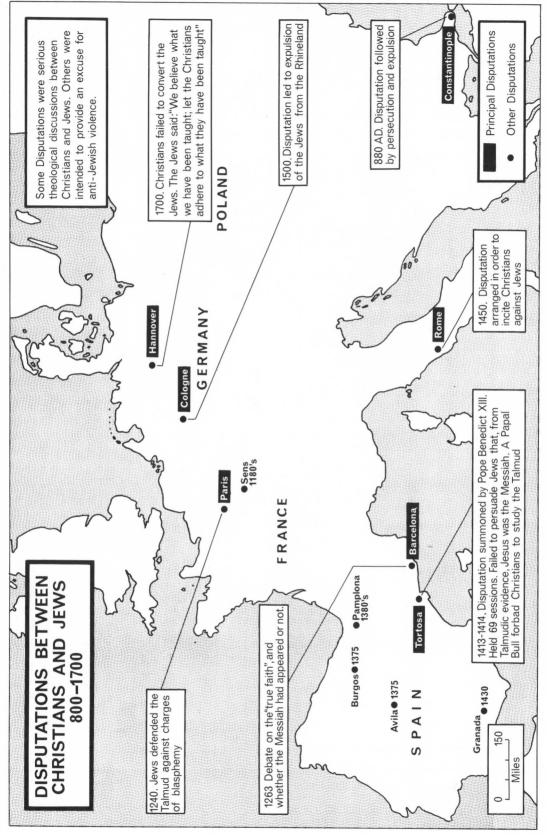

DISPUTATIONS BETWEEN
CHRISTIANS AND JEWS
800–1700

Some Disputations were serious theological discussions between Christians and Jews. Others were intended to provide an excuse for anti-Jewish violence.

1700. Christians failed to convert the Jews. The Jews said:"We believe what we have been taught; let the Christians adhere to what they have been taught"

1500. Disputation led to expulsion of the Jews from the Rhineland

880 AD. Disputation followed by persecution and expulsion

1450. Disputation arranged in order to incite Christians against Jews

1413-1414. Disputation summoned by Pope Benedict XIII. Held 69 sessions. Failed to persuade Jews that, from Talmudic evidence, Jesus was the Messiah. A Papal Bull forbad Christians to study the Talmud

1263 Debate on the"true faith", and whether the Messiah had appeared or not.

1240. Jews defended the Talmud against charges of blasphemy

POLAND

GERMANY

● Hannover

Cologne

FRANCE

Paris

● Sens
1180's

SPAIN

Burgos ● 1375

● Pamplona
1380's

Avila ● 1375

Granada ● 1430

Barcelona

Tortosa

Rome

Constantinople

Principal Disputations
Other Disputations

0   150
Miles

36

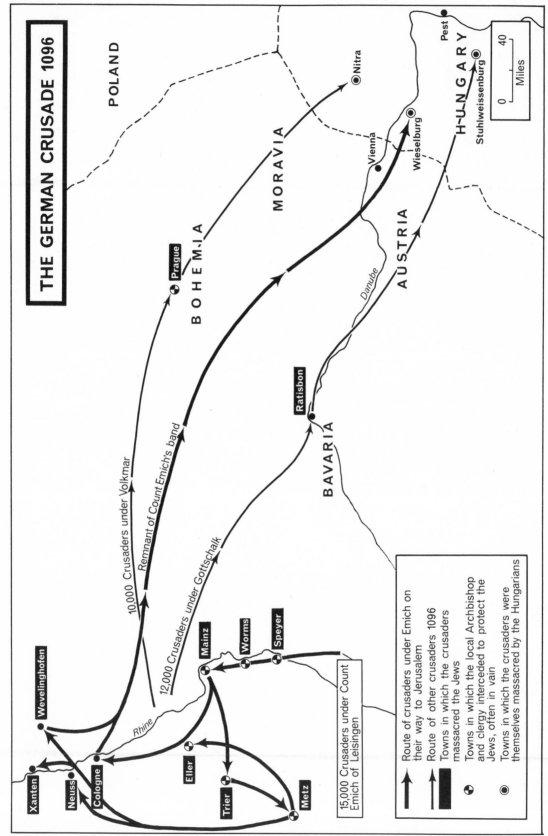

THE GERMAN CRUSADE 1096

POLAND

Nitra

H-U-N-G-A-R-Y

Pest

0   40
    Miles

Vienna

Wieselburg

Stuhlweissenburg

MORAVIA

AUSTRIA

BOHEMIA

Prague

Danube

10,000 Crusaders under Volkmar

Remnant of Count Emich's band

Ratisbon

BAVARIA

12,000 Crusaders under Gottschalk

Wevelinghofen

Rhine

Mainz

Worms

Speyer

Xanten

Neuss

Cologne

Eller

Trier

Metz

15,000 Crusaders under Count
Emich of Leisingen

Route of crusaders under Emich on
their way to Jerusalem

Route of other crusaders 1096

Towns in which the crusaders
massacred the Jews

Towns in which the local Archbishop
and clergy interceded to protect the
Jews, often in vain

Towns in which the crusaders were
themselves massacred by the Hungarians

37

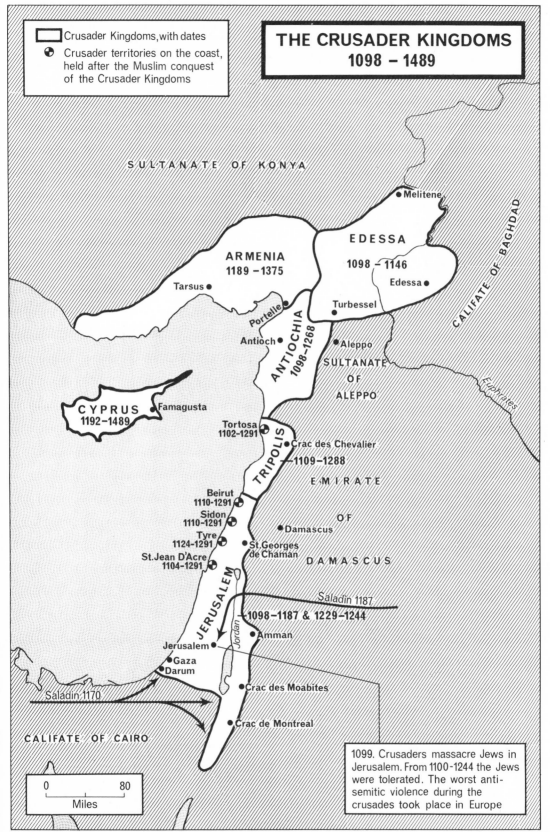

THE CRUSADER KINGDOMS
1098 – 1489

Crusader Kingdoms, with dates

Crusader territories on the coast,
held after the Muslim conquest
of the Crusader Kingdoms

SULTANATE OF KONYA

●Melitene

EDESSA
1098 – 1146

●Edessa

CALIFATE OF BAGHDAD

ARMENIA
1189 – 1375

Tarsus ●

Portelle●

●Turbessel

ANTIOCHIA
1098–1268

Antioch●

●Aleppo

SULTANATE
OF
ALEPPO

Euphrates

CYPRUS
1192–1489

Famagusta●

Tortosa
1102–1291

●Crac des Chevalier

TRIPOLIS

─1109–1288

EMIRATE

Beirut
1110-1291

Sidon
1110-1291

Tyre
1124-1291

St.Jean D'Acre
1104-1291

OF

●Damascus

●St.Georges
de Chaman

DAMASCUS

JERUSALEM

Jordan

Saladin 1187

─1098–1187 & 1229–1244

Jerusalem●

●Amman

●Gaza
Darum

●Crac des Moabites

Saladin 1170

●Crac de Montreal

CALIFATE OF CAIRO

0   80
Miles

1099. Crusaders massacre Jews in
Jerusalem. From 1100-1244 the Jews
were tolerated. The worst anti-
semitic violence during the
crusades took place in Europe

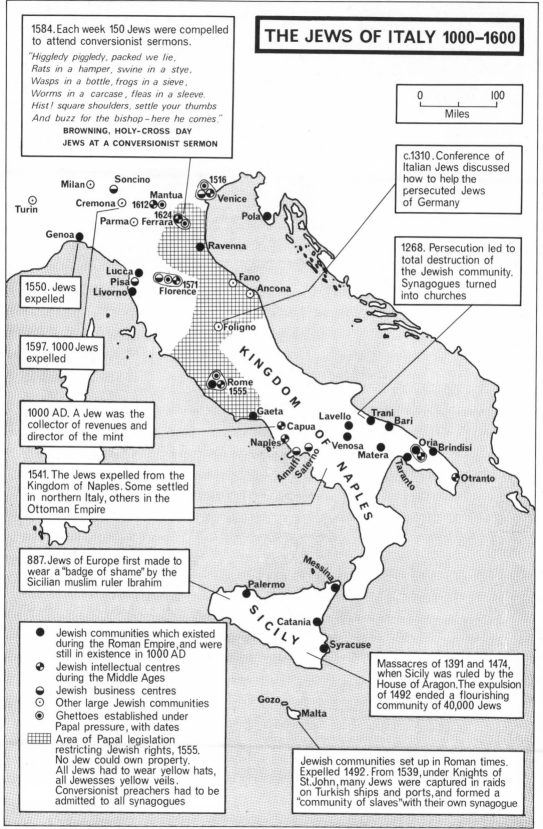

THE JEWS OF ITALY 1000–1600

1584. Each week 150 Jews were compelled to attend conversionist sermons.

"Higgledy piggledy, packed we lie,
Rats in a hamper, swine in a stye,
Wasps in a bottle, frogs in a sieve,
Worms in a carcase, fleas in a sleeve.
Hist! square shoulders, settle your thumbs
And buzz for the bishop – here he comes."
BROWNING, HOLY-CROSS DAY
JEWS AT A CONVERSIONIST SERMON

0   100
Miles

c.1310. Conference of Italian Jews discussed how to help the persecuted Jews of Germany

1268. Persecution led to total destruction of the Jewish community. Synagogues turned into churches

Milan
Soncino
Turin
Cremona
Mantua 1612
Parma
Ferrara 1624
1516
Venice
Pola
Genoa
Ravenna
Lucca
Pisa
Livorno
Florence 1571
Fano
Ancona
Foligno
1550. Jews expelled
1597. 1000 Jews expelled
Rome 1555

KINGDOM

1000 AD. A Jew was the collector of revenues and director of the mint

Gaeta
Capua
Lavello
Trani
Bari
Naples
Venosa
Oria
Brindisi
Amalfi
Salerno
Matera
Taranto
Otranto

OF NAPLES

1541. The Jews expelled from the Kingdom of Naples. Some settled in northern Italy, others in the Ottoman Empire

887. Jews of Europe first made to wear a "badge of shame" by the Sicilian muslim ruler Ibrahim

Messina
Palermo

SICILY

Catania
Syracuse

Massacres of 1391 and 1474, when Sicily was ruled by the House of Aragon. The expulsion of 1492 ended a flourishing community of 40,000 Jews

Gozo
Malta

Jewish communities set up in Roman times. Expelled 1492. From 1539, under Knights of St. John, many Jews were captured in raids on Turkish ships and ports, and formed a "community of slaves" with their own synagogue

● Jewish communities which existed during the Roman Empire, and were still in existence in 1000 AD

⊕ Jewish intellectual centres during the Middle Ages

⊖ Jewish business centres

⊙ Other large Jewish communities

◉ Ghettoes established under Papal pressure, with dates

▦ Area of Papal legislation restricting Jewish rights, 1555. No Jew could own property. All Jews had to wear yellow hats, all Jewesses yellow veils. Conversionist preachers had to be admitted to all synagogues

39

THE JEWS OF ENGLAND 1066–1290

- ◉ Towns with Archae, or official registers of Jewish financial transactions
- ● Other towns with Jewish communities, often of only three or four families
- ◑ Towns from which the Jews were expelled before 1290

"All Jews, wherever in the realm they are, must be under the King's protection.... nor can any of them put himself under the protection of any powerful person without the King's licence, because the Jews themselves and all their chattels are the Kings.... If anyone detain them or their money the King may claim them, if he so desire, as his own". **TWELFTH CENTURY LAW**

1190. Violent attack on Jews by crusaders. The Jews killed themselves rather than surrender

1255. Ritual murder charge 18 Jews executed

1281. Synod forbids Jews to hold public office

Newcastle

Lancaster

York
Beverley
Doncaster
Grimsby

Lincoln

Beaumaris
Newborough
Carnarvon
Criccieth
Harlech
Conway
Rhuddlan
Flint
Bala

Derby
Nottingham
King's Lynn
Norwich
Stamford
Leicester
Thetford
Bungay
Coventry
Eye
Huntingdon
Bury St. Edmunds
Warwick
Northampton
Cambridge
Worcester
Newport
Bedford
Ipswich
Sudbury
Hereford
Dunstable
Hitchin
Colchester
Oxford
Hertford
Gloucester
Berkhampsted
Cricklade
Wallingford
Wycombe
Marlborough
Reading
London
Faversham
Bristol
Windsor
Rochester
Devizes
Newbury
Canterbury
Guildford
Wells
Rye
Wilton
Winchester
Winchelsea
Romsey
Southampton
Arundel
Dorchester
Bosham
Chichester
Exeter

0   50
Miles

The first Jews came to England from Rouen with William the Conqueror. They were mostly moneylenders, dealing both with the King and his barons. After 1189, under the impetus of the crusades, they were much persecuted, fined, assaulted, and expelled from particular towns. In 1290 all 5000 were expelled, and crossed to France and Flanders, having had all their property confiscated.

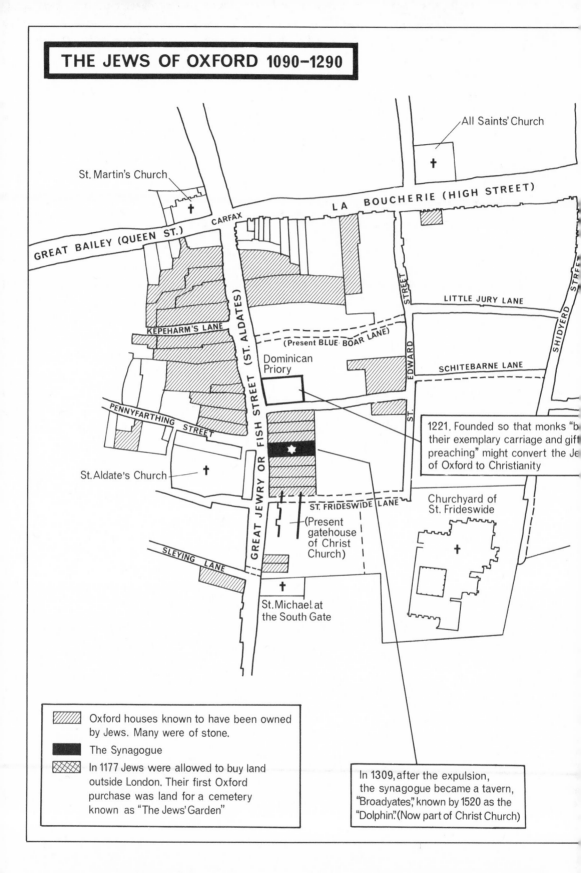

THE JEWS OF OXFORD 1090–1290

All Saints' Church

St. Martin's Church

LA BOUCHERIE (HIGH STREET)

GREAT BAILEY (QUEEN ST.)

CARFAX

LITTLE JURY LANE

KEPEHARM'S LANE

(Present BLUE BOAR LANE)

ST. EDWARD STREET

SHIDYERD STREET

SCHITEBARNE LANE

Dominican Priory

PENNYFARTHING STREET

GREAT JEWRY OR FISH STREET (ST. ALDATES)

St. Aldate's Church

1221. Founded so that monks "b
their exemplary carriage and gif
preaching" might convert the Je
of Oxford to Christianity

ST. FRIDESWIDE LANE

Churchyard of
St. Frideswide

(Present
gatehouse
of Christ
Church)

SLEYING LANE

St. Michael at
the South Gate

Oxford houses known to have been owned
by Jews. Many were of stone.

The Synagogue

In 1177 Jews were allowed to buy land
outside London. Their first Oxford
purchase was land for a cemetery
known as "The Jews' Garden"

In 1309, after the expulsion,
the synagogue became a tavern,
"Broadyates," known by 1520 as the
"Dolphin." (Now part of Christ Church)

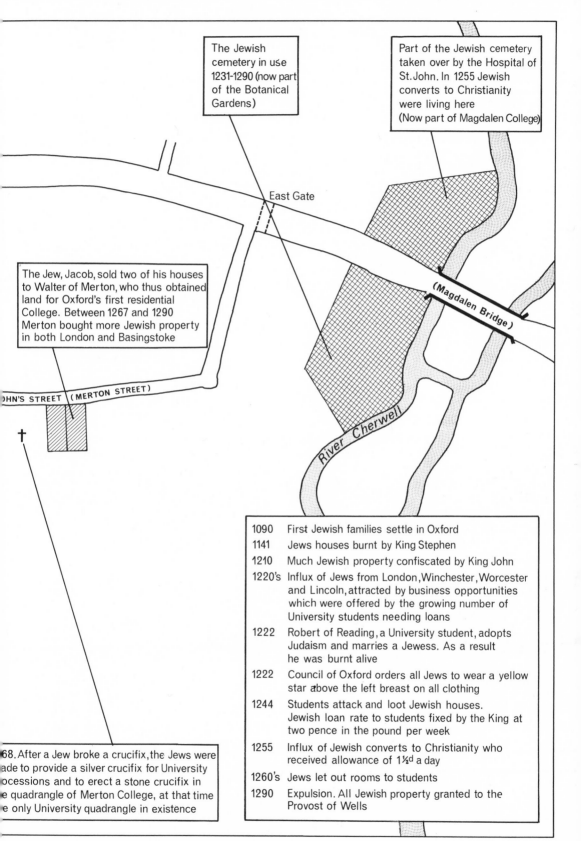

The Jewish cemetery in use 1231-1290 (now part of the Botanical Gardens)

Part of the Jewish cemetery taken over by the Hospital of St. John. In 1255 Jewish converts to Christianity were living here (Now part of Magdalen College)

East Gate

(Magdalen Bridge)

The Jew, Jacob, sold two of his houses to Walter of Merton, who thus obtained land for Oxford's first residential College. Between 1267 and 1290 Merton bought more Jewish property in both London and Basingstoke

)HN'S STREET (MERTON STREET)

River Cherwell

68. After a Jew broke a crucifix, the Jews were ade to provide a silver crucifix for University ocessions and to erect a stone crucifix in e quadrangle of Merton College, at that time e only University quadrangle in existence

1090	First Jewish families settle in Oxford
1141	Jews houses burnt by King Stephen
1210	Much Jewish property confiscated by King John
1220's	Influx of Jews from London, Winchester, Worcester and Lincoln, attracted by business opportunities which were offered by the growing number of University students needing loans
1222	Robert of Reading, a University student, adopts Judaism and marries a Jewess. As a result he was burnt alive
1222	Council of Oxford orders all Jews to wear a yellow star above the left breast on all clothing
1244	Students attack and loot Jewish houses. Jewish loan rate to students fixed by the King at two pence in the pound per week
1255	Influx of Jewish converts to Christianity who received allowance of 1½d a day
1260's	Jews let out rooms to students
1290	Expulsion. All Jewish property granted to the Provost of Wells

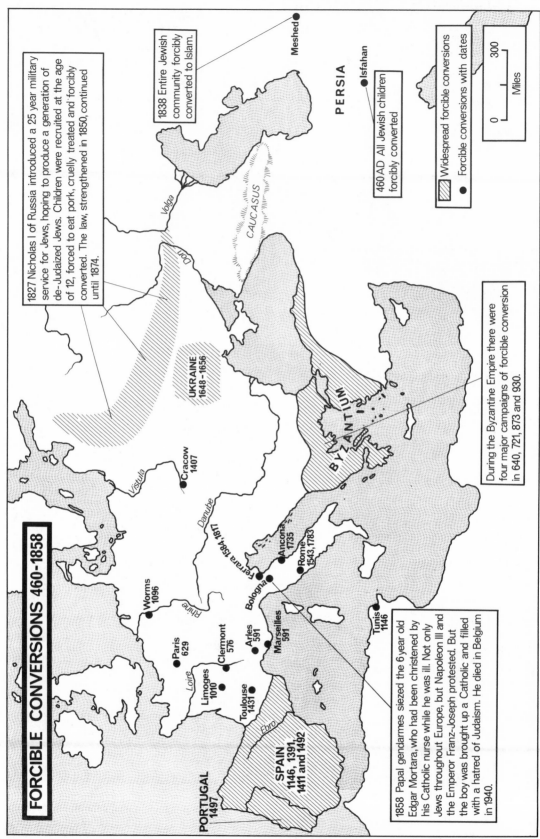

FORCIBLE CONVERSIONS 460-1858

1827 Nicholas I of Russia introduced a 25 year military service for Jews, hoping to produce a generation of de-Judaized Jews. Children were recruited at the age of 12, forced to eat pork, cruelly treated and forcibly converted. The law, strengthened in 1850, continued until 1874.

1838 Entire Jewish community forcibly converted to Islam.

Meshed

PERSIA

Isfahan

460 AD All Jewish children forcibly converted

Widespread forcible conversions

Forcible conversions with dates

0   300

Miles

Volga

CAUCASUS

Don

UKRAINE
1648 -1656

Vistula

Cracow
1407

Danube

BYZANTIUM

Rhine

Worms
1096

Paris
629

Loire

Clermont
576

Arles
591

Ferrara 1584,1817

Ancona
1735

Bologna

Rome
1543,1783

Marseilles
591

Tunis
1146

Limoges
1010

Toulouse
1431

Ebro

PORTUGAL
1497

SPAIN
1146, 1391,
1411 and 1492

During the Byzantine Empire there were four major campaigns of forcible conversion in 640, 721, 873 and 930.

1858 Papal gendarmes siezed the 6 year old Edgar Mortara, who had been christened by his Catholic nurse while he was ill. Not only Jews throughout Europe, but Napoleon III and the Emperor Franz-Joseph protested. But the boy was brought up a Catholic and filled with a hatred of Judaism. He died in Belgium in 1940.

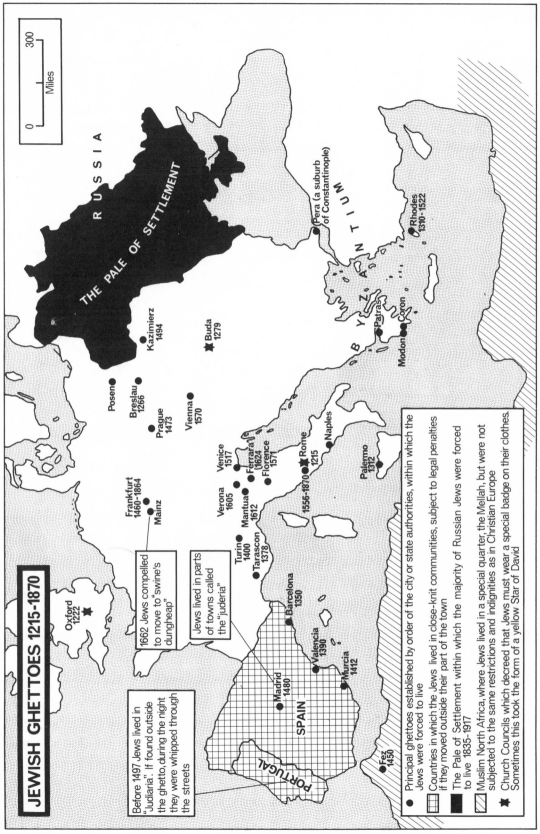

JEWISH GHETTOES 1215-1870

300 Miles

RUSSIA

THE PALE OF SETTLEMENT

Kazimierz 1494

★ Buda 1279

Posen●

Breslau 1266

Prague 1473

Vienna 1570

Frankfurt 1460-1864

Mainz●

Verona 1605

Mantua 1612

Venice 1517

Ferrara 1624

Florence 1571

Rome 1215

1556-1870 ★

Naples●

Palermo 1312

Turin 1400

Tarascon 1378

Oxford 1222 ★

Barcelona 1350

Valencia 1390

Madrid 1480

Murcia 1412

SPAIN

PORTUGAL

Fez 1450

(Pera (a suburb of Constantinople)

B Y Z A N T I U M

Patras●

Modon● ●Coron

Rhodes 1310-1522

1662 Jews compelled to move to "swine's dungheap"

Jews lived in parts of towns called the "juderia"

Before 1497 Jews lived in "Judiaria." If found outside the ghetto, during the night they were whipped through the streets

● Principal ghettoes established by order of the city or state authorities, within which the Jews were forced to live

▦ Countries in which the Jews lived in close-knit communities, subject to legal penalties if they moved outside their part of the town

■ The Pale of Settlement within which the majority of Russian Jews were forced to live 1835-1917

▨ Muslim North Africa, where Jews lived in a special quarter, the Mellah, but were not subjected to the same restrictions and indignities as in Christian Europe

★ Church Councils which decreed that Jews must wear a special badge on their clothes. Sometimes this took the form of a yellow Star of David

43

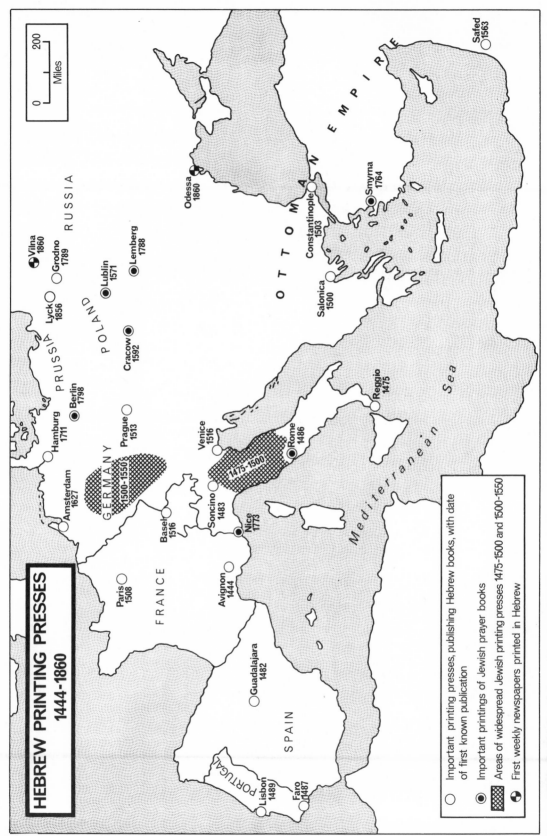

HEBREW PRINTING PRESSES 1444-1860

0 200 Miles

Legend:

○ Important printing presses, publishing Hebrew books, with date of first known publication

◉ Important printings of Jewish prayer books

▨ Areas of widespread Jewish printing presses 1475-1500 and 1500-1550

◓ First weekly newspapers printed in Hebrew

Locations:

Safed 1563

Smyrna 1764

Odessa 1860

Constantinople 1503

Vilna 1860

Grodno 1789

Lemberg 1788

Lublin 1571

Lyck 1856

Salonica 1500

Cracow 1592

Berlin 1798

Hamburg 1711

Prague 1513

Reggio 1475

Venice 1516

Rome 1486

Amsterdam 1627

Soncino 1483

Nice 1773

Basel 1516

Paris 1508

Avignon 1444

Guadalajara 1482

Lisbon 1489

Faro 1487

RUSSIA

PRUSSIA

POLAND

GERMANY (1500-1550)

FRANCE

SPAIN

PORTUGAL

OTTOMAN EMPIRE

Mediterranean Sea

1475-1500

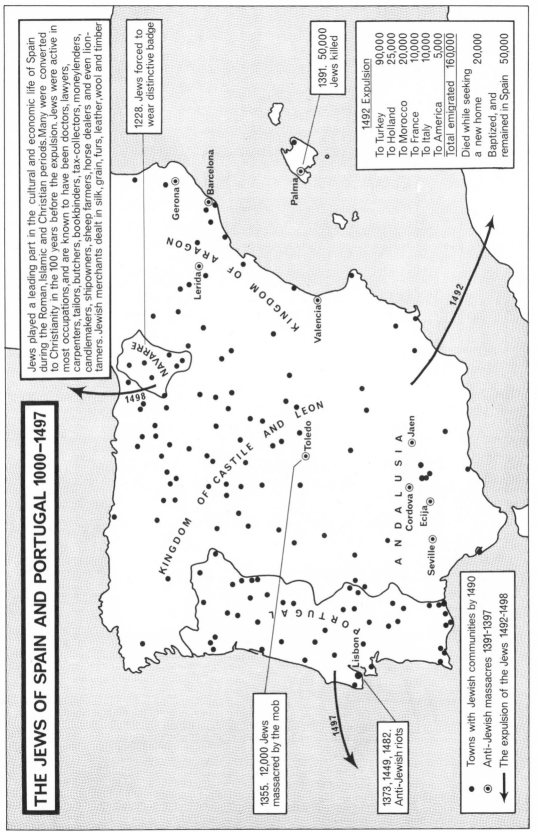

THE JEWS OF SPAIN AND PORTUGAL 1000–1497

Jews played a leading part in the cultural and economic life of Spain during the Roman, Islamic and Christian periods. Many were converted to Christianity in the 100 years before the expulsion. Jews were active in most occupations, and are known to have been doctors, lawyers, carpenters, tailors, butchers, bookbinders, tax-collectors, moneylenders, candlemakers, shipowners, sheep farmers, horse dealers and even lion-tamers. Jewish merchants dealt in silk, grain, furs, leather, wool and timber

1228. Jews forced to wear distinctive badge

1391. 50,000 Jews killed

1492 Expulsion	
To Turkey	90,000
To Holland	25,000
To Morocco	20,000
To France	10,000
To Italy	10,000
To America	5,000
Total emigrated	160,000
Died while seeking a new home	20,000
Baptized, and remained in Spain	50,000

KINGDOM OF ARAGON

NAVARRE

KINGDOM OF CASTILE AND LEON

ANDALUSIA

PORTUGAL

1492

1498

1497

Gerona
Barcelona
Palma
Lerida
Valencia
Toledo
Jaen
Cordova
Ecija
Seville
Lisbon

1355. 12,000 Jews massacred by the mob

1373, 1449, 1482. Anti-Jewish riots

- • Towns with Jewish communities by 1490
- ◉ Anti-Jewish massacres 1391–1397
- ↓ The expulsion of the Jews 1492–1498

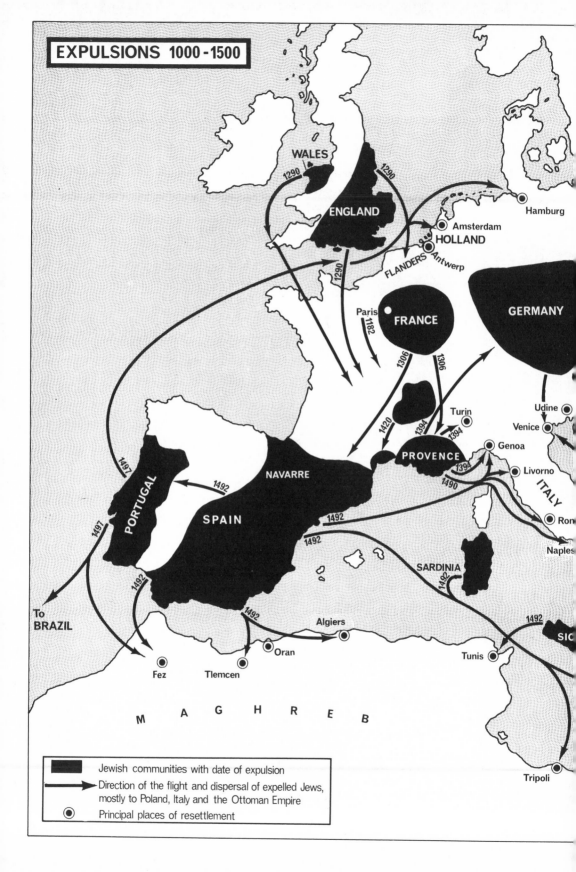

EXPULSIONS 1000-1500

WALES

ENGLAND

1290

1298

Hamburg

Amsterdam

HOLLAND

FLANDERS

Antwerp

Paris

1182

FRANCE

GERMANY

Udine

Venice

Turin

1306

1306

1394

1394

PROVENCE

1394

1420

Genoa

Livorno

ITALY

1490

Rom

NAVARRE

1497

1492

SPAIN

PORTUGAL

1497

1492

1492

Naples

SARDINIA

To
BRAZIL

1492

1492

1492

SIC

1492

Algiers

Tunis

Oran

Fez

Tlemcen

M A G H R E B

Tripoli

Jewish communities with date of expulsion

Direction of the flight and dispersal of expelled Jews,
mostly to Poland, Italy and the Ottoman Empire

Principal places of resettlement

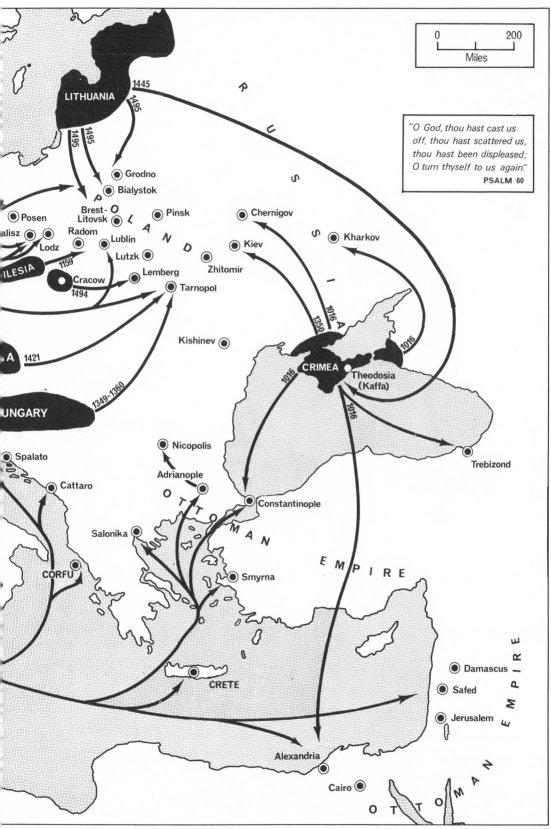

LITHUANIA

1445

1495

1495

1495

RUSSIA

⊙ Grodno

⊙ Bialystok

⊙ Posen
alisz ⊙ ⊙
Lodz ⊙
ILESIA

Radom ⊙
Lublin ⊙
1159
Cracow
1494
Lutzk ⊙

Brest-
Litovsk ⊙
⊙ Pinsk

POLAND

⊙ Chernigov

⊙ Kharkov

⊙ Kiev

Zhitomir ⊙

⊙ Lemberg
⊙ Tarnopol

Kishinev ⊙

1350

1016

1016

A 1421

1349-1360

UNGARY

CRIMEA ⊙
Theodosia
(Kaffa)

1016

1016

1016

⊙ Trebizond

⊙ Spalato

⊙ Cattaro

⊙ Nicopolis

Adrianople ⊙

OTTOMAN

⊙ Constantinople

CORFU ⊙

Salonika ⊙

⊙ Smyrna

EMPIRE

CRETE

OTTOMAN EMPIRE

⊙ Damascus

⊙ Safed

⊙ Jerusalem

Alexandria ⊙

Cairo ⊙

OTTOMAN EMPIRE

0   200
Miles

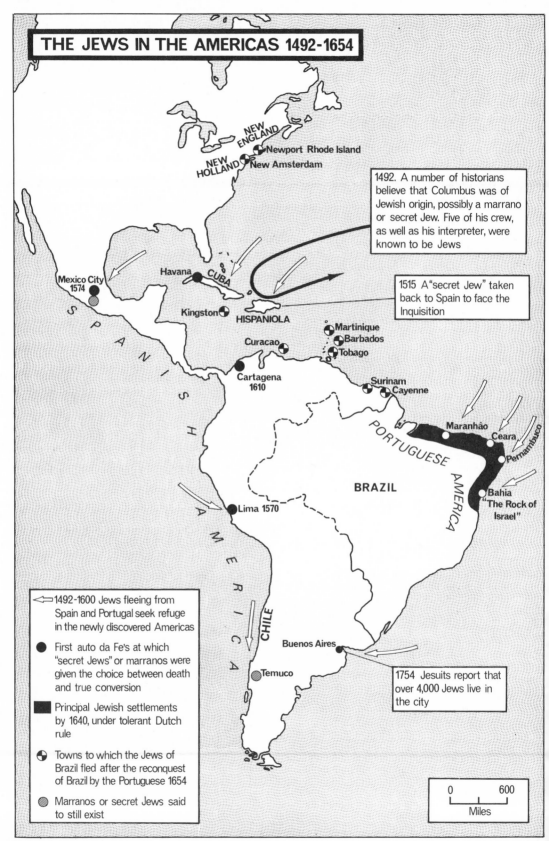

THE JEWS IN THE AMERICAS 1492-1654

NEW ENGLAND

NEW HOLLAND

Newport Rhode Island

New Amsterdam

1492. A number of historians believe that Columbus was of Jewish origin, possibly a marrano or secret Jew. Five of his crew, as well as his interpreter, were known to be Jews

Mexico City 1574

Havana

CUBA

1515 A "secret Jew" taken back to Spain to face the Inquisition

Kingston

HISPANIOLA

Martinique

Barbados

Tobago

Curacao

Cartagena 1610

Surinam

Cayenne

S P A N I S H   A M E R I C A

PORTUGUESE AMERICA

Maranhâo

Ceara

Pernambuco

BRAZIL

Bahia "The Rock of Israel"

Lima 1570

CHILE

Buenos Aires

Temuco

1754 Jesuits report that over 4,000 Jews live in the city

1492-1600 Jews fleeing from Spain and Portugal seek refuge in the newly discovered Americas

First auto da Fe's at which "secret Jews" or marranos were given the choice between death and true conversion

Principal Jewish settlements by 1640, under tolerant Dutch rule

Towns to which the Jews of Brazil fled after the reconquest of Brazil by the Portuguese 1654

Marranos or secret Jews said to still exist

0   600
Miles

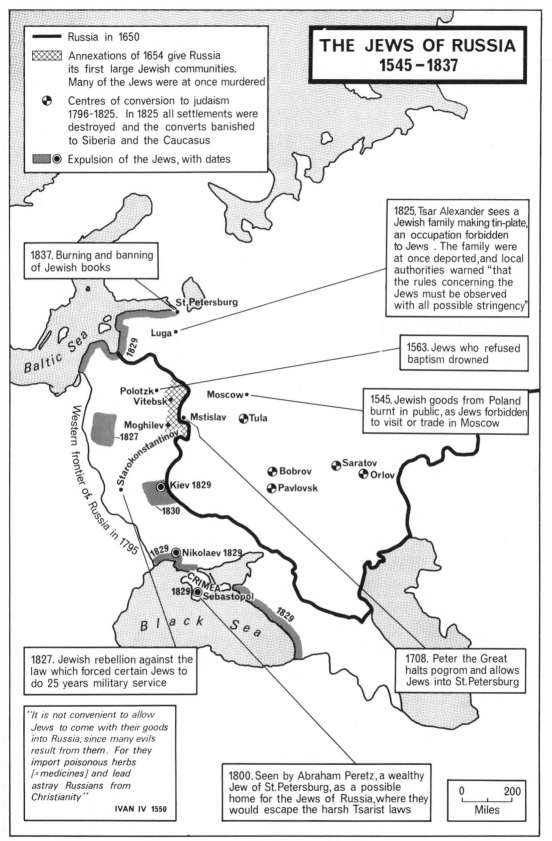

THE JEWS OF RUSSIA 1545 – 1837

— Russia in 1650

Annexations of 1654 give Russia its first large Jewish communities. Many of the Jews were at once murdered

Centres of conversion to judaism 1796-1825. In 1825 all settlements were destroyed and the converts banished to Siberia and the Caucasus

Expulsion of the Jews, with dates

1825. Tsar Alexander sees a Jewish family making tin-plate, an occupation forbidden to Jews. The family were at once deported, and local authorities warned "that the rules concerning the Jews must be observed with all possible stringency"

1837. Burning and banning of Jewish books

1563. Jews who refused baptism drowned

1545. Jewish goods from Poland burnt in public, as Jews forbidden to visit or trade in Moscow

St.Petersburg

Luga

Baltic Sea

1829

Polotzk
Vitebsk
Moghilev
1827
Starokonstantinov

Western frontier of Russia in 1795

Mstislav   Tula

Moscow

Saratov
Orlov

Bobrov

Pavlovsk

Kiev 1829

1830

1829   Nikolaev 1829

CRIMEA

1829   Sebastopol

1829

Black Sea

1827. Jewish rebellion against the law which forced certain Jews to do 25 years military service

1708. Peter the Great halts pogrom and allows Jews into St.Petersburg

"It is not convenient to allow Jews to come with their goods into Russia, since many evils result from them. For they import poisonous herbs [= medicines] and lead astray Russians from Christianity"

IVAN IV 1550

1800. Seen by Abraham Peretz, a wealthy Jew of St.Petersburg, as a possible home for the Jews of Russia, where they would escape the harsh Tsarist laws

0   200
Miles

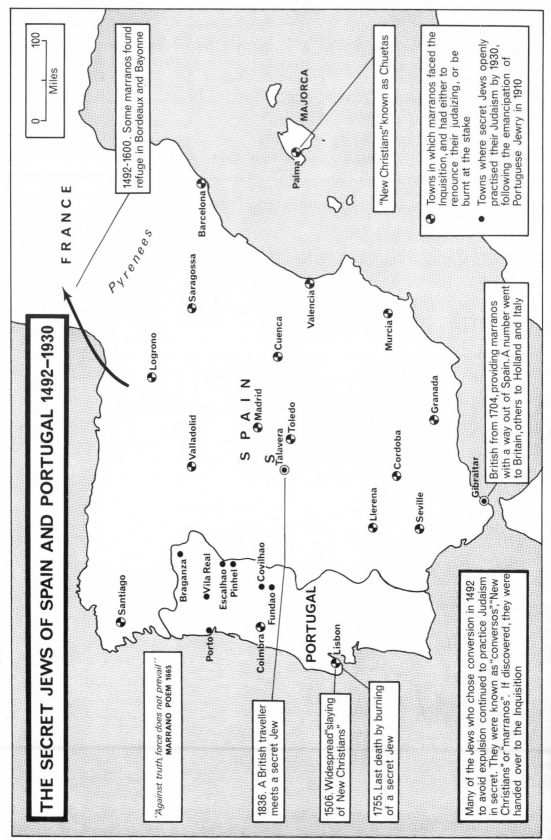

THE SECRET JEWS OF SPAIN AND PORTUGAL 1492–1930

"Against truth, force does not prevail"
MARRANO POEM 1665

1492–1600. Some marranos found refuge in Bordeaux and Bayonne

"New Christians"known as Chuetas

◗ Towns in which marranos faced the Inquisition, and had either to renounce their judaizing, or be burnt at the stake

● Towns where secret Jews openly practised their Judaism by 1930, following the emancipation of Portuguese Jewry in 1910

British from 1704, providing marranos with a way out of Spain. A number went to Britain, others to Holland and Italy

Many of the Jews who chose conversion in 1492 to avoid expulsion continued to practice Judaism in secret. They were known as "conversos", "New Christians" or "marranos". If discovered, they were handed over to the Inquisition

1836. A British traveller meets a secret Jew

1506. Widespread "slaying" of New Christians

1755. Last death by burning of a secret Jew

FRANCE

Pyrenees

MAJORCA

● Palma

◗ Barcelona

◗ Saragossa

◗ Valencia

◗ Murcia

◗ Logrono

◗ Cuenca

◗ Granada

S P A I N

S

◗ Madrid
◎ Talavera
◗ Toledo

◗ Valladolid

◗ Cordoba

◗ Llerena

◗ Seville

◗ Gibraltar

◗ Santiago

● Braganza
● Vila Real
● Escalhao
● Pinhel
● Covilhao
◗ Fundao
● Coimbra
● Porto

PORTUGAL

◗ Lisbon

0 ———— 100
Miles

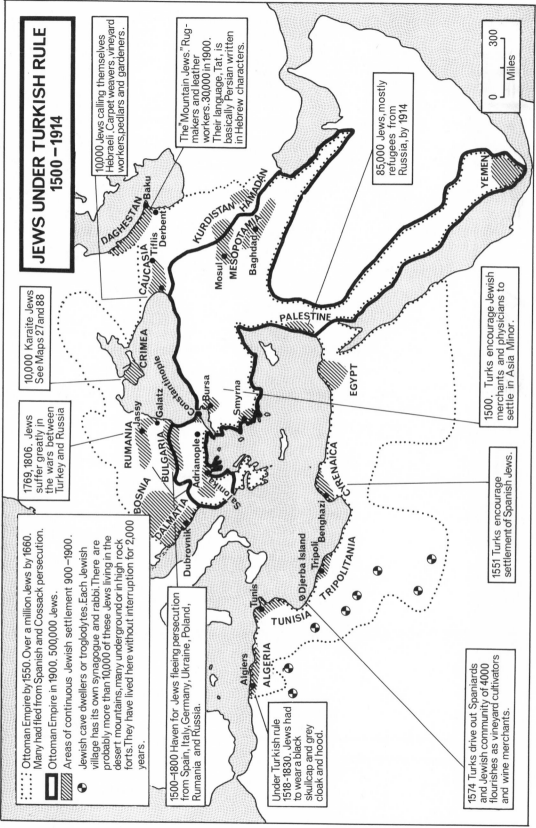

JEWS UNDER TURKISH RULE 1500–1914

300 Miles
0

10,000 Jews calling themselves Hebraeli. Carpet weavers, vineyard workers, pedlars and gardeners.

The "Mountain Jews." Rug-makers and leather workers. 30,000 in 1900. Their language, Tat, is basically Persian written in Hebrew characters.

85,000 Jews, mostly refugees from Russia, by 1914

YEMEN

DAGHESTAN
Baku
Derbent
Tiflis
KURDISTAN
HAMADAN
CAUCASIA
Mosul
MESOPOTAMIA
Baghdad
CRIMEA
PALESTINE
EGYPT

1500 Turks encourage Jewish merchants and physicians to settle in Asia Minor.

10,000 Karaite Jews See Maps 27 and 88

1769, 1806. Jews suffer greatly in the wars between Turkey and Russia

Jassy
Galatz
Bursa
Constantinople
Smyrna
RUMANIA
BULGARIA
Adrianople
Salonika
BOSNIA
DALMATIA
Dubrovnik

CYRENAICA
Benghazi
Tripoli
TRIPOLITANIA
Djerba Island

1551 Turks encourage settlement of Spanish Jews.

Ottoman Empire by 1550. Over a million Jews by 1660. Many had fled from Spanish and Cossack persecution.

Ottoman Empire in 1900. 500,000 Jews.

Areas of continuous Jewish settlement 900–1900.

Jewish cave dwellers or troglodytes. Each Jewish village has its own synagogue and rabbi. There are probably more than 10,000 of these Jews living in the desert mountains, many underground or in high rock forts. They have lived here without interruption for 2,000 years.

1500–1800 Haven for Jews fleeing persecution from Spain, Italy, Germany, Ukraine, Poland, Rumania and Russia.

Under Turkish rule 1518–1830. Jews had to wear a black skullcap and grey cloak and hood.

Tunis
TUNISIA
Algiers
ALGERIA

1574 Turks drive out Spaniards and Jewish community of 4000 flourishes as vineyard cultivators and wine merchants.

50

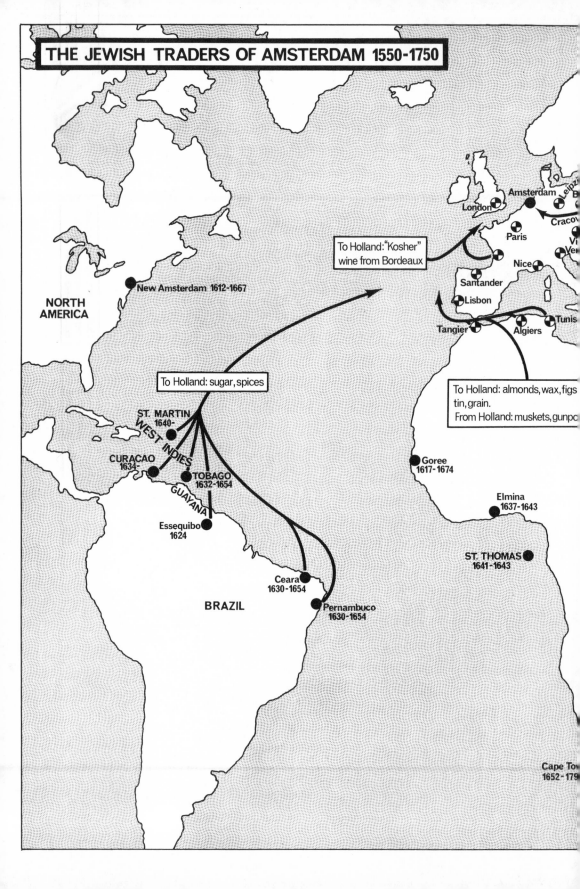

THE JEWISH TRADERS OF AMSTERDAM 1550-1750

Amsterdam

Leipzi

London

Cracov

Paris

Vi
Ve

Nice

Santander

Lisbon

Tunis

Tangier   Algiers

To Holland: "Kosher"
wine from Bordeaux

New Amsterdam 1612-1667

NORTH
AMERICA

To Holland: sugar, spices

To Holland: almonds, wax, figs
tin, grain.
From Holland: muskets, gunpo

Goree
1617-1674

ST. MARTIN
1640-

WEST INDIES

CURACAO
1634-

TOBAGO
1632-1654

GUAYANA

Essequibo
1624

Elmina
1637-1643

ST. THOMAS
1641-1643

Ceara
1630-1654

BRAZIL

Pernambuco
1630-1654

Cape To
1652-179

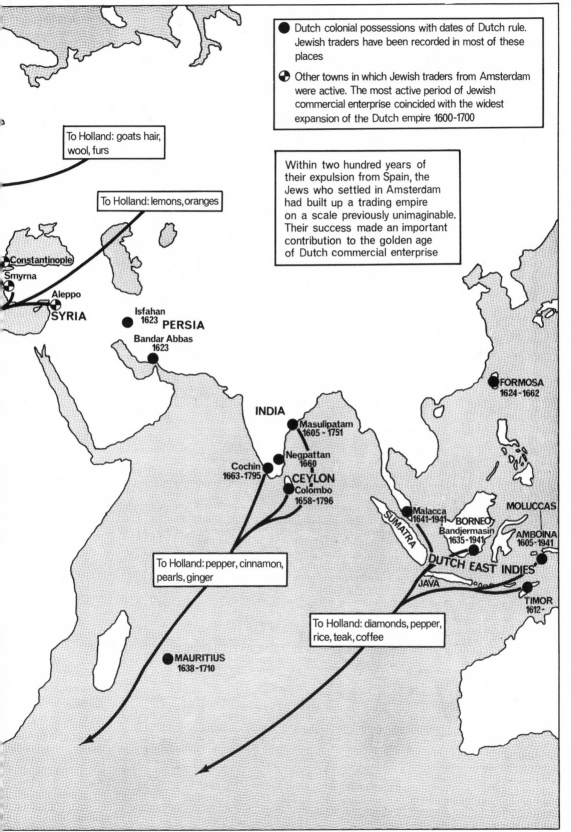

Dutch colonial possessions with dates of Dutch rule. Jewish traders have been recorded in most of these places

Other towns in which Jewish traders from Amsterdam were active. The most active period of Jewish commercial enterprise coincided with the widest expansion of the Dutch empire 1600-1700

Within two hundred years of their expulsion from Spain, the Jews who settled in Amsterdam had built up a trading empire on a scale previously unimaginable. Their success made an important contribution to the golden age of Dutch commercial enterprise

To Holland: goats hair, wool, furs

To Holland: lemons, oranges

Constantinople
Smyrna
Aleppo
SYRIA

Isfahan
1623
PERSIA
Bandar Abbas
1623

INDIA

FORMOSA
1624-1662

Masulipatam
1605 - 1751
Cochin
1663-1795
Negpattan
1660
CEYLON
Colombo
1658-1796

Malacca
1641-1941
SUMATRA
BORNEO
Bandjermasin
1635-1941
MOLUCCAS
AMBOINA
1605-1941
DUTCH EAST INDIES
JAVA
TIMOR
1612-

To Holland: pepper, cinnamon, pearls, ginger

To Holland: diamonds, pepper, rice, teak, coffee

MAURITIUS
1638-1710

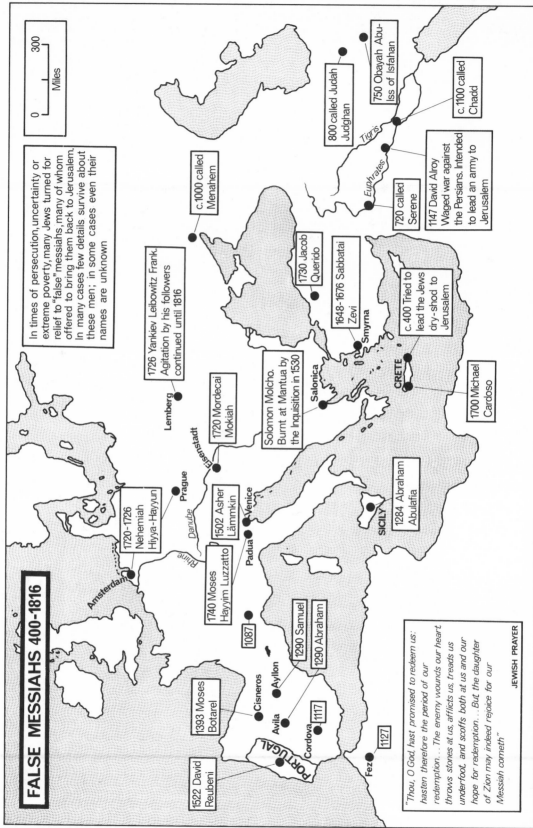

FALSE MESSIAHS 400-1816

0   300
Miles

In times of persecution, uncertainty or extreme poverty, many Jews turned for relief to "false" messiahs, many of whom offered to bring them back to Jerusalem. In many cases few details survive about these men; in some cases even their names are unknown

750 Obayah Abu-lss of Isfahan

800 called Judah Judghan

c.1100 called Chadd

1147 David Alroy Waged war against the Persians. Intended to lead an army to Jerusalem

720 called Serene

c.1000 called Menahem

1726 Yankiev Leibowitz Frank. Agitation by his followers continued until 1816

1730 Jacob Querido

1648-1676 Sabbatai Zevi

c.400 Tried to lead the Jews dry-shod to Jerusalem

1720 Mordecai Mokiah

Solomon Molcho. Burnt at Mantua by the Inquisition in 1530

1700 Michael Cardoso

1720-1726 Nehemiah Hiyya-Hayyun

1502 Asher Lämmkin

1740 Moses Hayyim Luzzatto

1284 Abraham Abulafia

1087

1290 Samuel

1290 Abraham

1393 Moses Botarel

1117

1522 David Reubeni

1127

"Thou, O God hast promised to redeem us: hasten therefore the period of our redemption... The enemy wounds our heart, throws stones at us, afflicts us, treads us underfoot, and scoffs both at us and our hope for redemption... But the daughter of Zion may indeed rejoice for our Messiah cometh"

JEWISH PRAYER

Tigris

Euphrates

Danube

Rhine

Lemberg

Eisenstadt

Prague

Amsterdam

Venice

Padua

Salonica

Smyrna

CRETE

SICILY

Cisneros

Avila

Ayllon

Cordova

PORTUGAL

Fez

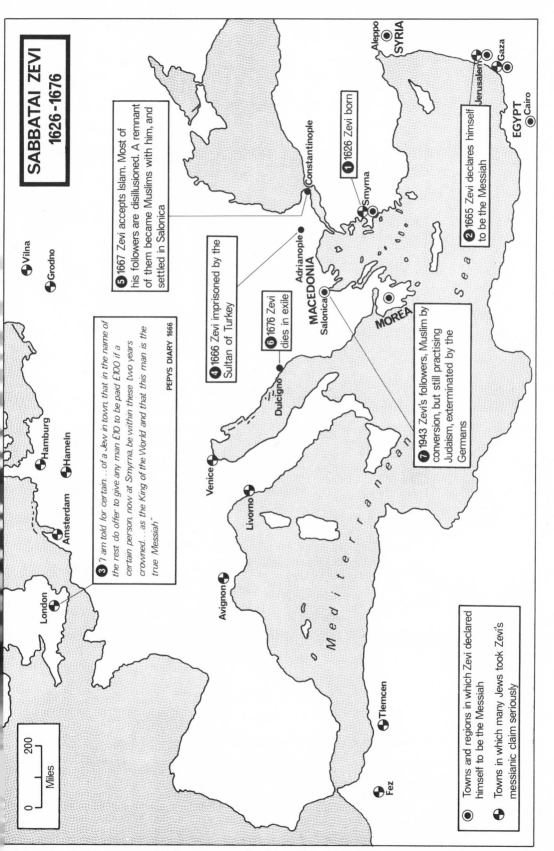

SABBATAI ZEVI
1626-1676

0 [scale] 200 Miles

Vilna
Grodno

Hamburg
Hameln

Amsterdam

London

3 "I am told for certain... of a Jew in town, that in the name of the rest do offer to give any man £10 to be paid £100 if a certain person, now at Smyrna, be within these two years crowned... as the King of the World and that this man is the true Messiah"

PEPYS DIARY 1666

5 1667 Zevi accepts Islam. Most of his followers are disillusioned. A remnant of them became Muslims with him, and settled in Salonica

Constantinople

Adrianople

4 1666 Zevi imprisoned by the Sultan of Turkey

6 1676 Zevi dies in exile

MACEDONIA
Salonica
MOREA

Dulcigno

Venice

Livorno

Avignon

7 1943 Zevi's followers, Muslim by conversion, but still practising Judaism, exterminated by the Germans

Aleppo **SYRIA**

Jerusalem **Gaza**

Cairo

EGYPT

2 1665 Zevi declares himself to be the Messiah

1 1626 Zevi born
Smyrna

Mediterranean Sea

Tiemcen

Fez

⊙ Towns and regions in which Zevi declared himself to be the Messiah

⊕ Towns in which many Jews took Zevi's messianic claim seriously

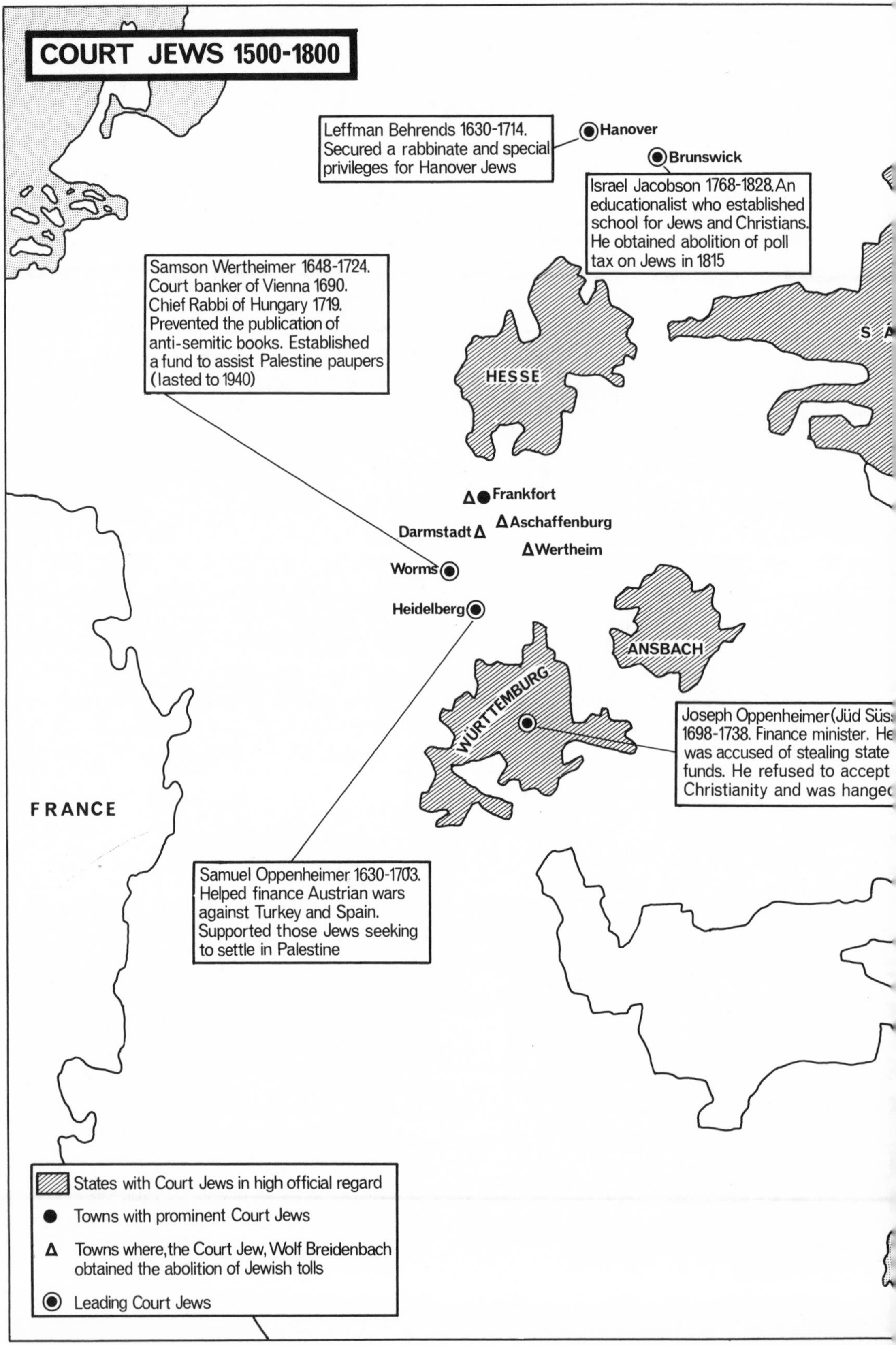

COURT JEWS 1500-1800

Leffman Behrends 1630-1714. Secured a rabbinate and special privileges for Hanover Jews

Israel Jacobson 1768-1828. An educationalist who established school for Jews and Christians. He obtained abolition of poll tax on Jews in 1815

Samson Wertheimer 1648-1724. Court banker of Vienna 1690. Chief Rabbi of Hungary 1719. Prevented the publication of anti-semitic books. Established a fund to assist Palestine paupers (lasted to 1940)

⊙Hanover

⊙Brunswick

HESSE

S·A

△●Frankfort

Darmstadt △   △Aschaffenburg
                △Wertheim

Worms⊙

Heidelberg⊙

ANSBACH

WÜRTTEMBURG

Joseph Oppenheimer(Jüd Süss 1698-1738. Finance minister. He was accused of stealing state funds. He refused to accept Christianity and was hanged

FRANCE

Samuel Oppenheimer 1630-1703. Helped finance Austrian wars against Turkey and Spain. Supported those Jews seeking to settle in Palestine

▨ States with Court Jews in high official regard

● Towns with prominent Court Jews

△ Towns where, the Court Jew, Wolf Breidenbach obtained the abolition of Jewish tolls

⊙ Leading Court Jews

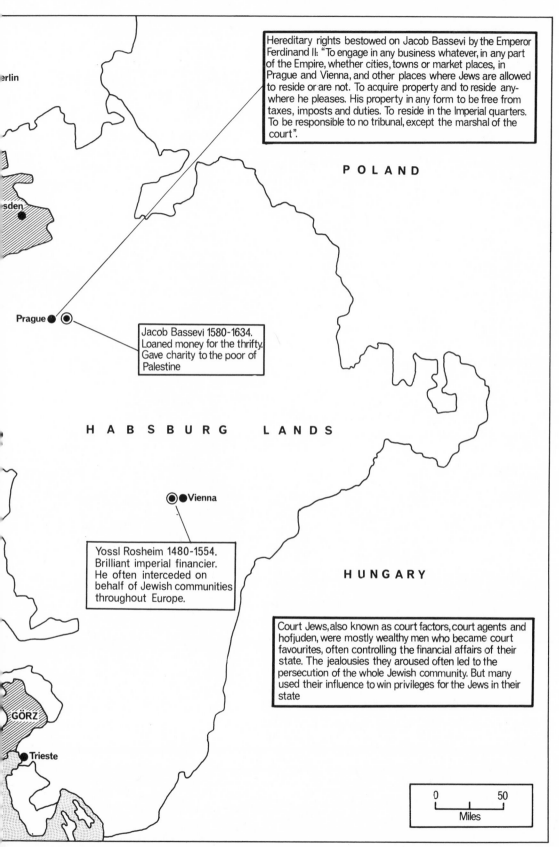

Hereditary rights bestowed on Jacob Bassevi by the Emperor Ferdinand II: "To engage in any business whatever, in any part of the Empire, whether cities, towns or market places, in Prague and Vienna, and other places where Jews are allowed to reside or are not. To acquire property and to reside anywhere he pleases. His property in any form to be free from taxes, imposts and duties. To reside in the Imperial quarters. To be responsible to no tribunal, except the marshal of the court".

P O L A N D

Berlin

Dresden

Prague ● ◉

Jacob Bassevi 1580-1634. Loaned money for the thrifty. Gave charity to the poor of Palestine

H A B S B U R G   L A N D S

◉ ● Vienna

Yossl Rosheim 1480-1554. Brilliant imperial financier. He often interceded on behalf of Jewish communities throughout Europe.

H U N G A R Y

Court Jews, also known as court factors, court agents and hofjuden, were mostly wealthy men who became court favourites, often controlling the financial affairs of their state. The jealousies they aroused often led to the persecution of the whole Jewish community. But many used their influence to win privileges for the Jews in their state

GÖRZ

● Trieste

0   50
Miles

54

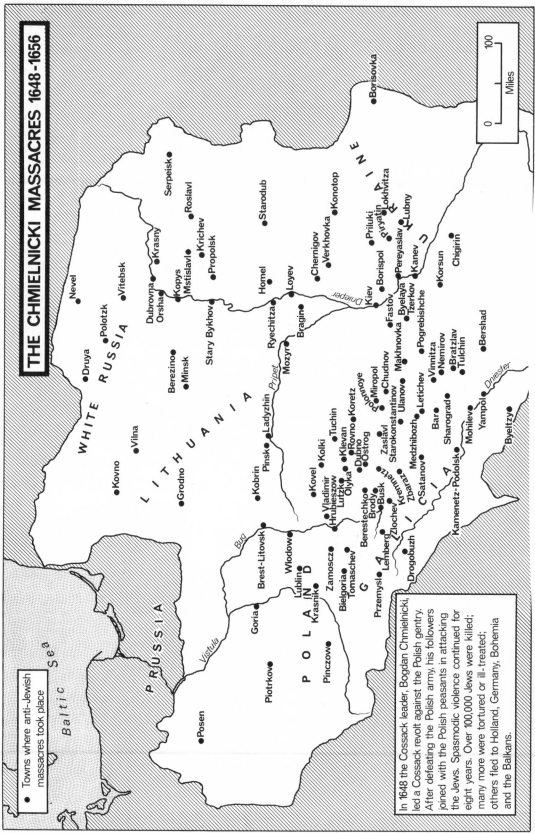

THE CHMIELNICKI MASSACRES 1648-1656

Towns where anti-Jewish massacres took place

Baltic Sea

WHITE RUSSIA

LITHUANIA

PRUSSIA

POLAND

UKRAINE

Borisovka

Serpeisk

Roslavl
Krichev
Krasny
Propolsk
Starodub
Verkhovka
Konotop

Nevel

Druya

Polotzk
Vitebsk

Dubrovna
Orsha
Kopys
Mstislavl

Homel
Loyev

Chernigov
Borispol
Kiev
Fastov
Byelaya

Priluki
Pyryatin Lokhvitza
Pereyaslav Lubny
Tzerkov Kanev

Korsun

Chigirin

Berezino
Minsk

Stary Bykhov

Ryechitza
Mozyr
Bragin

Dnieper

Bershad

Vilna

Pripet

Ladyzhin

Chudnov
Makhnovka
Pogrebishche

Polonnoye
Miropol
Ulanov
Letichev
Vinnitza
Nemirov
Bratzlav
Tulchin

Kovno

Grodno

Kobrin
Pinsk

Kolki
Tuchin
Klevan
Rovno Koretz
Olyka Ostrog
Dubno

Zaslavl
Starokonstantinov
Medzhibozh
Bar
Sharograd

Mohilev
Yampol

Byeltzy

Dniester

Kovel
Vladimir
Lutzk
Hrubieszow

Berestechko
Busk
Brody
Zlochev
Lemberg
Krzemen Zbaraz
Satanov
Drogobuzh
Przemysl

Kamenetz-Podolsk

Wlodow

Brest-Litovsk

Bug

Vistula

Zamoscz
Bielgoria
Tomaschev
Lublin
Krasnik

Goria

Piotrkov

Pinczow

Posen

| 0 | 100 |
Miles

In 1648 the Cossack leader, Bogdan Chmielnicki, led a Cossack revolt against the Polish gentry. After defeating the Polish army, his followers joined with the Polish peasants in attacking the Jews. Spasmodic violence continued for eight years. Over 100,000 Jews were killed; many more were tortured or ill-treated; others fled to Holland, Germany, Bohemia and the Balkans.

55

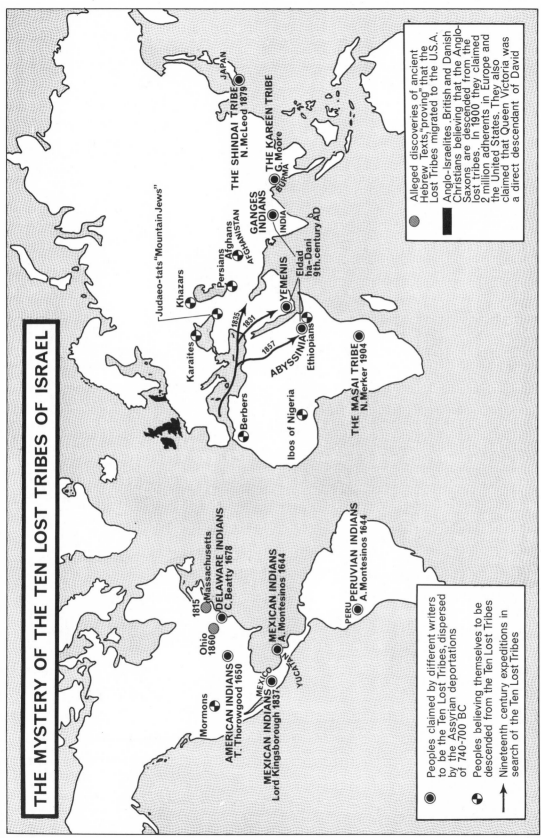

THE MYSTERY OF THE TEN LOST TRIBES OF ISRAEL

JAPAN
THE SHINDAI TRIBE
N.McLeod 1879

THE KAREEN TRIBE
B.G.Moore
BURMA

GANGES
INDIANS
INDIA

Judaeo-tats "Mountain Jews"

Khazars
Persians
Afghans
AFGHANISTAN

Karaites
YEMENIS
Eldad
ha-Dani
9th.century AD

1835
1831

1857

ABYSSINIA
Ethiopians

Berbers

Ibos of Nigeria

THE MASAI TRIBE
N.Merker 1904

Mormons

Ohio
1860

Massachusetts
1815
DELAWARE INDIANS
C.Beatty 1678

MEXICO
MEXICAN INDIANS
A.Montesinos 1644

YUCATAN

AMERICAN INDIANS
T.Thorowgood 1650

MEXICAN INDIANS
Lord Kingsborough 1837

PERU
PERUVIAN INDIANS
A.Montesinos 1644

Alleged discoveries of ancient Hebrew Texts,"proving" that the Lost Tribes migrated to the U.S.A.

Anglo-Israelites. British and Danish Christians believing that the Anglo-Saxons are descended from the lost tribes. In 1900 they claimed 2 million adherents in Europe and the United States. They also claimed that Queen Victoria was a direct descendant of David

Peoples claimed by different writers to be the Ten Lost Tribes, dispersed by the Assyrian deportations of 740-700 BC

Peoples believing themselves to be descended from the Ten Lost Tribes

Nineteenth century expeditions in search of the Ten Lost Tribes

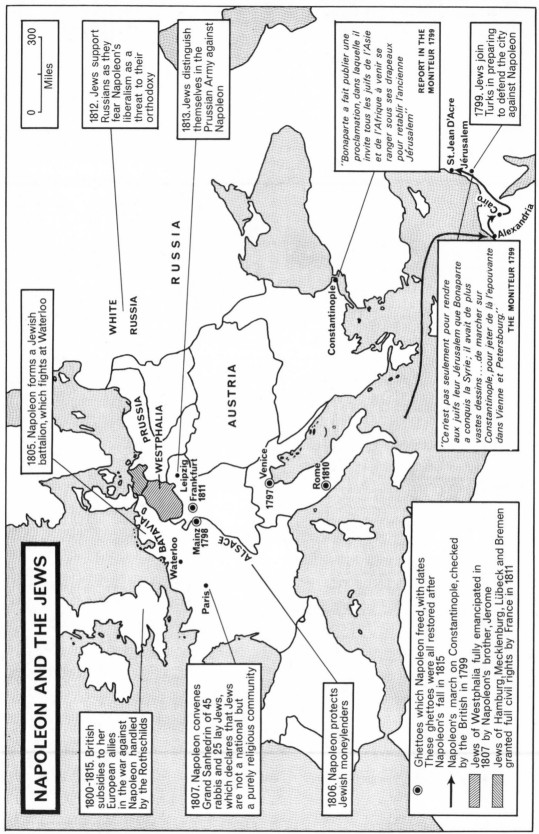

NAPOLEON AND THE JEWS

0 ___ 300
Miles

1800-1815. British subsidies to her European allies in the war against Napoleon handled by the Rothschilds

1805. Napoleon forms a Jewish battalion, which fights at Waterloo

1807. Napoleon convenes Grand Sanhedrin of 45 rabbis and 25 lay Jews, which declares that Jews are not a national but a purely religious community

1806. Napoleon protects Jewish moneylenders

1812. Jews support Russians as they fear Napoleon's liberalism as a threat to their orthodoxy

1813. Jews distinguish themselves in the Prussian Army against Napoleon

"Bonaparte a fait publier une proclamation, dans laquelle il invite tous les juifs de l'Asie et de l'Afrique à venir se ranger sous ses drapeaux pour rétablir l'ancienne Jérusalem"

REPORT IN THE MONITEUR 1799

1799. Jews join Turks in preparing to defend the city against Napoleon

"Ce n'est pas seulement pour rendre aux juifs leur Jérusalem que Bonaparte a conquis la Syrie; il avait de plus vastes desseins....de marcher sur Constantinople, pour jeter de là l'épouvante dans Vienne et Petersbourg."

THE MONITEUR 1799

WHITE RUSSIA

RUSSIA

PRUSSIA

WESTPHALIA

BATAVIA

AUSTRIA

ALSACE

Waterloo

Paris

Mainz 1798

Frankfurt 1811

Leipzig

Venice 1797

Rome 1810

Constantinople

Cairo

Alexandria

St. Jean D'Acre

Jérusalem

⊙   Ghettoes which Napoleon freed, with dates
These ghettoes were all restored after Napoleon's fall in 1815

→   Napoleon's march on Constantinople, checked by the British in 1799

▨   Jews of Westphalia fully emancipated in 1807 by Napoleon's brother, Jerome

▨   Jews of Hamburg, Mecklenburg, Lübeck and Bremen granted full civil rights by France in 1811

57

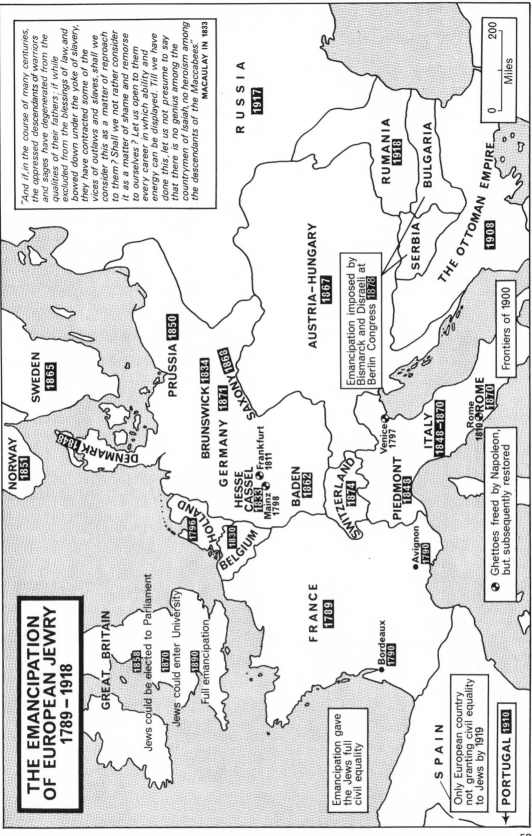

THE EMANCIPATION OF EUROPEAN JEWRY 1789–1918

"And if, in the course of many centuries, the oppressed descendants of warriors and sages have degenerated from the qualities of their fathers; if, while excluded from the blessings of law, and bowed down under the yoke of slavery, they have contracted some of the vices of outlaws and slaves, shall we consider this as a matter of reproach to them? Shall we not rather consider it as a matter of shame and remorse to ourselves? Let us open to them every career in which ability and energy can be displayed. Till we have done this, let us not presume to say that there is no genius among the countrymen of Isaiah, no heroism among the descendants of the Maccabees."

MACAULAY IN 1833

RUSSIA 1917

RUMANIA 1918

BULGARIA

SERBIA

THE OTTOMAN EMPIRE 1908

AUSTRIA–HUNGARY 1867

Emancipation imposed by Bismarck and Disraeli at Berlin Congress 1878

Frontiers of 1900

NORWAY 1851

SWEDEN 1865

DENMARK 1848

PRUSSIA 1850

BRUNSWICK 1834

SAXONY 1868

GERMANY 1871

HESSE CASSEL 1833

Frankfurt 1811

Mainz 1798

BADEN 1862

HOLLAND 1796

BELGIUM 1830

SWITZERLAND 1874

Venice 1797

PIEDMONT 1848

ITALY 1848–1870

Rome 1810 ROME 1870

GREAT BRITAIN

1858 Jews could be elected to Parliament

1870 Jews could enter University

1890 Full emancipation

FRANCE 1789

Avignon 1790

Bordeaux 1790

Ghettoes freed by Napoleon, but subsequently restored

Emancipation gave the Jews full civil equality

SPAIN

Only European country not granting civil equality to Jews by 1919

PORTUGAL 1910

0   200
Miles

58

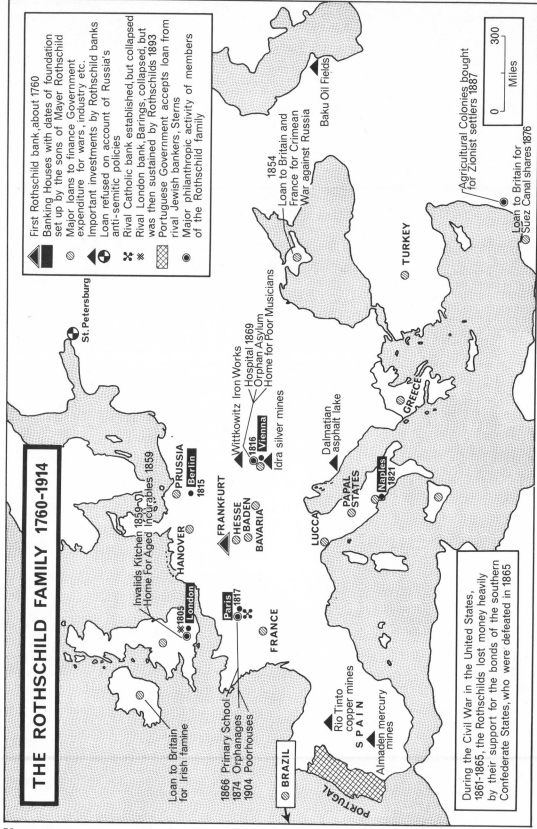

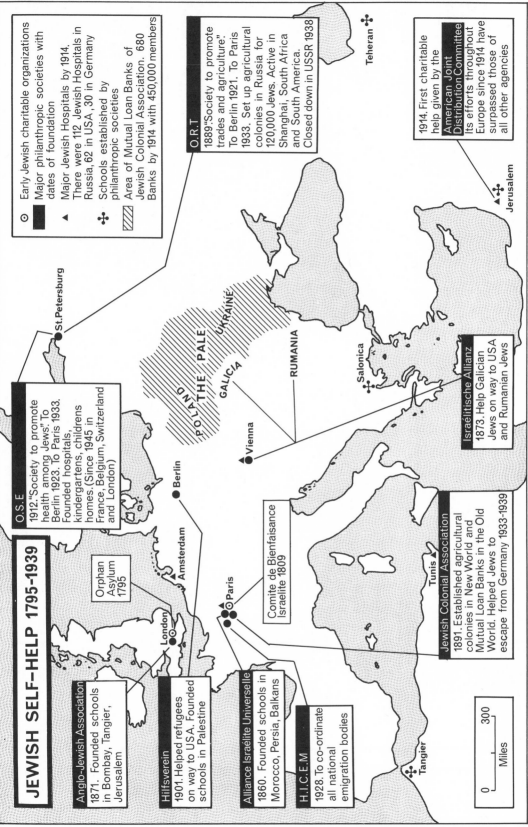

JEWISH SELF-HELP 1795-1939

Legend:

⊙ Early Jewish charitable organizations

■ Major philanthropic societies with dates of foundation

▲ Major Jewish Hospitals by 1914. There were 112 Jewish Hospitals in Russia, 62 in USA, 30 in Germany

✢ Schools established by philanthropic societies

▨ Area of Mutual Loan Banks of Jewish Colonial Association. 680 Banks by 1914 with 450,000 members

O.R.T
1889 "Society to promote trades and agriculture". To Paris 1921. To Berlin 1933. Set up agricultural colonies in Russia for 120,000 Jews. Active in Shanghai, South Africa and South America. Closed down in USSR 1938

1914. First charitable help given by the American Joint Distribution Committee. Its efforts throughout Europe since 1914 have surpassed those of all other agencies

O.S.E
1912. "Society to promote health among Jews". To Berlin 1923. To Paris 1933. Founded hospitals, kindergartens, childrens homes. (Since 1945 in France, Belgium, Switzerland and London)

Anglo-Jewish Association
1871. Founded schools in Bombay, Tangier, Jerusalem

Orphan Asylum 1795

Hilfsverein
1901. Helped refugees on way to USA. Founded schools in Palestine

Alliance Israélite Universelle
1860. Founded schools in Morocco, Persia, Balkans

H.I.C.E.M.
1928. To co-ordinate all national emigration bodies

Comite de Bienfaisance Israelite 1809

Israélitische Allianz
1873. Help Galician Jews on way to USA and Rumanian Jews

Jewish Colonial Association
1891. Established agricultural colonies in New World and Mutual Loan Banks in the Old World. Helped Jews to escape from Germany 1933-1939

Place labels: Teheran, Jerusalem, St. Petersburg, Vienna, Berlin, Amsterdam, London, Paris, Salonica, Tunis, Tangier, POLAND, UKRAINE, GALICIA, THE PALE, RUMANIA

0   300
Miles

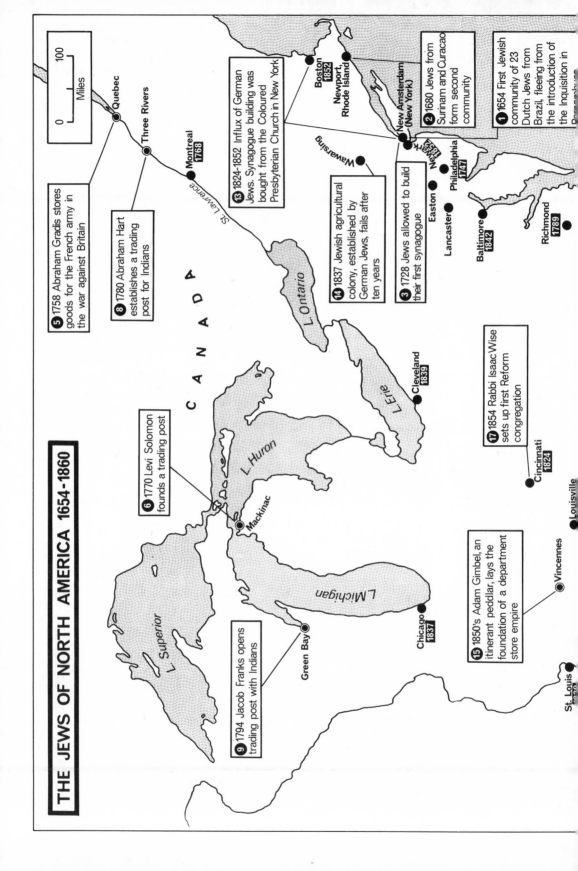

THE JEWS OF NORTH AMERICA 1654-1860

Miles
0   100

5 1758 Abraham Gradis stores goods for the French army in the war against Britain

8 1780 Abraham Hart establishes a trading post for Indians

6 1770 Levi Solomon founds a trading post

9 1794 Jacob Franks opens trading post with Indians

15 1850's Adam Gimbel, an itinerant peddlar, lays the foundation of a department store empire

17 1854 Rabbi Isaac Wise sets up first Reform congregation

13 1824-1852 Influx of German Jews. Synagogue building was bought from the Coloured Presbyterian Church in New York

14 1837 Jewish agricultural colony, established by German Jews, fails after ten years

3 1728 Jews allowed to build their first synagogue

2 1680 Jews from Surinam and Curacao form second community

1 1654 First Jewish community of 23 Dutch Jews, fleeing from the introduction of the Inquisition in

Quebec

Three Rivers

Montreal
1768

St. Lawrence

CANADA

L. Superior

L. Huron

L. Michigan

L. Erie

L. Ontario

Mackinac

Green Bay

Chicago
1837

Vincennes

St. Louis

Louisville

Cincinnati
1824

Cleveland
1839

Boston
1852

Newport,
Rhode Island

New Amsterdam
(New York)

Newark
1852

Wawarsing

Philadelphia
1747

Easton

Lancaster

Baltimore
1842

Richmond
1789

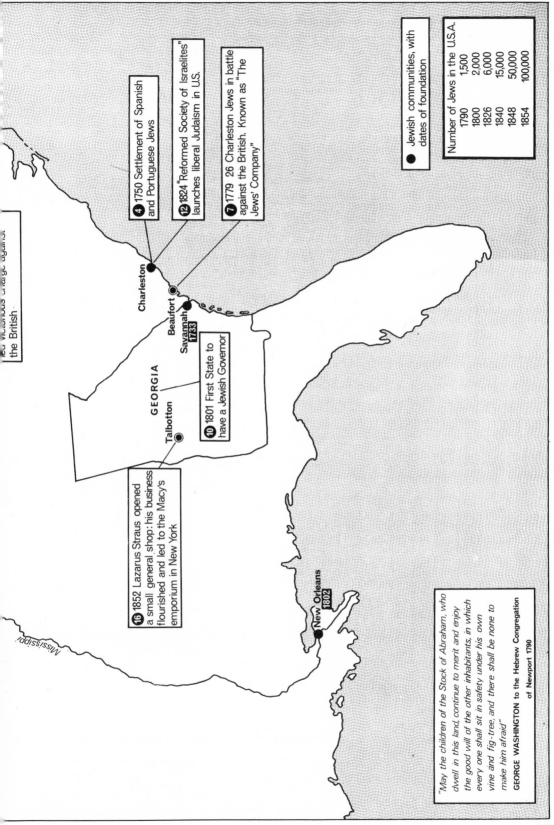

4 1750 Settlement of Spanish and Portuguese Jews

12 1824 "Reformed Society of Israelites" launches liberal Judaism in U.S.

7 1779 26 Charleston Jews in battle against the British. Known as "The Jews' Company"

● Jewish communities, with dates of foundation

Number of Jews in the U.S.A.
1790	1,500
1800	2,000
1826	6,000
1840	15,000
1848	50,000
1854	100,000

Charleston

Beaufort
Savannah 1733

GEORGIA

Talbotton

10 1801 First State to have a Jewish Governor

16 1852 Lazarus Straus opened a small general shop: his business flourished and led to the Macy's emporium in New York

Mississippi

New Orleans 1802

the British.

"May the children of the Stock of Abraham, who dwell in this land, continue to merit and enjoy the good will of the other inhabitants, in which every one shall sit in safety under his own vine and fig-tree, and there shall be none to make him afraid"

GEORGE WASHINGTON to the Hebrew Congregation of Newport 1790

61

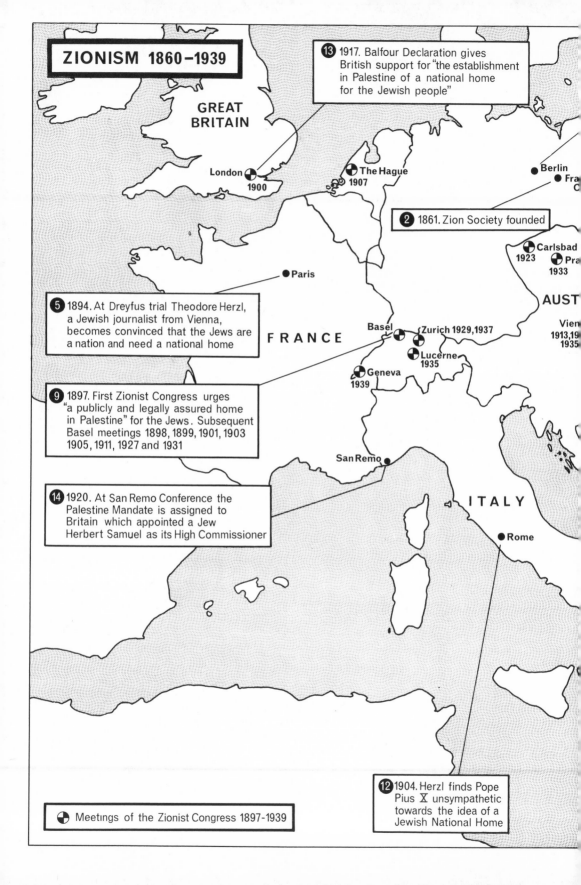

ZIONISM 1860-1939

GREAT BRITAIN

13 1917. Balfour Declaration gives British support for "the establishment in Palestine of a national home for the Jewish people"

● Berlin
● Fra

London ⊕
1900

⊕ The Hague
1907

2 1861. Zion Society founded

⊕ Carlsbad
1923   ⊕ Pra
1933

● Paris

5 1894. At Dreyfus trial Theodore Herzl, a Jewish journalist from Vienna, becomes convinced that the Jews are a nation and need a national home

FRANCE

Basel ⊕   ⊕ Zurich 1929, 1937
      ⊕ Lucerne
      1935

AUST

Vien
1913, 19
1935

⊕ Geneva
1939

9 1897. First Zionist Congress urges "a publicly and legally assured home in Palestine" for the Jews. Subsequent Basel meetings 1898, 1899, 1901, 1903 1905, 1911, 1927 and 1931

San Remo ●

14 1920. At San Remo Conference the Palestine Mandate is assigned to Britain which appointed a Jew Herbert Samuel as its High Commissioner

ITALY

● Rome

⊕ Meetings of the Zionist Congress 1897-1939

12 1904. Herzl finds Pope Pius X unsympathetic towards the idea of a Jewish National Home

1882. Leo Pinsker in "Auto-Emancipation" urged Jews to seek a national retreat, preferably on the banks of the Jordan

● Vilna

S I A

Thorn

11 1903. Herzl acclaimed "Herzl the King" during visit to Russia

1 1860. Conference discusses possibility of a Jewish home in Palestine

●Kattowitz

R U S S I A

4 1884. "Lovers of Zion" movement holds conference

IGARY

Odessa ●

1896. Herzl publishes his "Jews' State" urging the Jews to seek their national home in Palestine. Its immediate impact was on Russian Jewry

8 1897. "Lovers of Zion" revitalized by Herzl, and by its new President, Ussishkin, a disciple of Ahad Ha-am, the spiritual prophet of Zionism

B U L G A R I A

Constantinople ●

T U R K E Y

7 1896. Herzl acclaimed as the Messiah

10 1901 Herzl has audience with Sultan. Asks in vain for Palestine as a Jewish national home

0   200
Miles

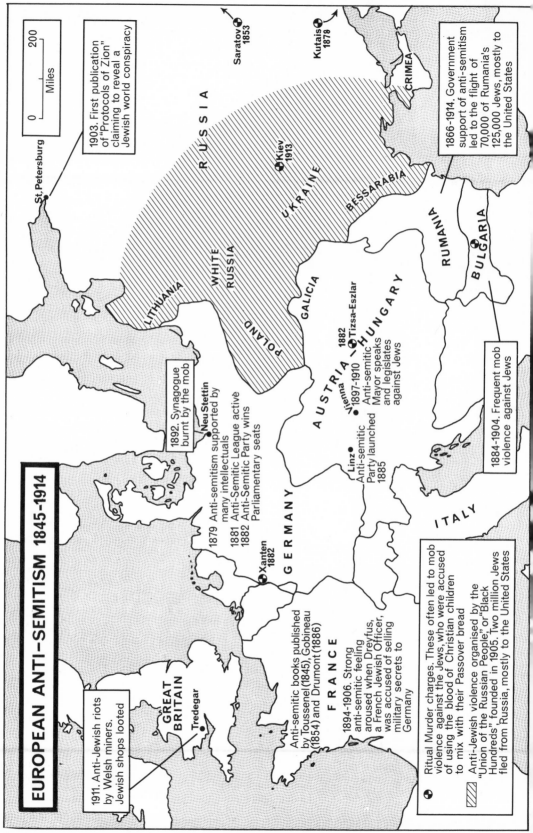

EUROPEAN ANTI-SEMITISM 1845–1914

0 ... 200
Miles

1903. First publication of "Protocols of Zion" claiming to reveal a Jewish world conspiracy

Saratov ⊕ 1853

Kutais ⊕ 1878

1866-1914. Government support of anti-semitism led to the flight of 70,000 of Rumania's 125,000 Jews, mostly to the United States

St.Petersburg

R U S S I A

CRIMEA

● Kiev 1913

U K R A I N E

BESSARABIA

WHITE RUSSIA

LITHUANIA

P O L A N D

G A L I C I A

RUMANIA

B U L G A R I A

1892. Synagogue burnt by the mob

NeuStettin ●

1879 Anti-semitism supported by many intellectuals
1881 Anti-Semitic League active
1882 Anti-Semitic Party wins Parliamentary seats

● Xanten 1882

G E R M A N Y

● Tizsa-Eszlar 1882

Vienna ● 1882
1897-1910 Anti-semitic Mayor speaks and legislates against Jews

A U S T R I A

H U N G A R Y

Linz ●
Anti-semitic Party launched 1885

1884-1904. Frequent mob violence against Jews

I T A L Y

1911. Anti-Jewish riots by Welsh miners. Jewish shops looted

GREAT BRITAIN

● Tredegar

F R A N C E

Anti-semitic books published by Toussenel(1845), Gobineau (1854) and Drumont(1886)

1894-1906. Strong anti-semitic feeling aroused when Dreyfus, a French Jewish Officer, was accused of selling military secrets to Germany

⊕ Ritual Murder charges. These often led to mob violence against the Jews, who were accused of using the blood of Christian children to mix with their Passover bread

▨ Anti-Jewish violence organised by the "Union of the Russian People", or "Black Hundreds" founded in 1905. Two million Jews fled from Russia, mostly to the United States

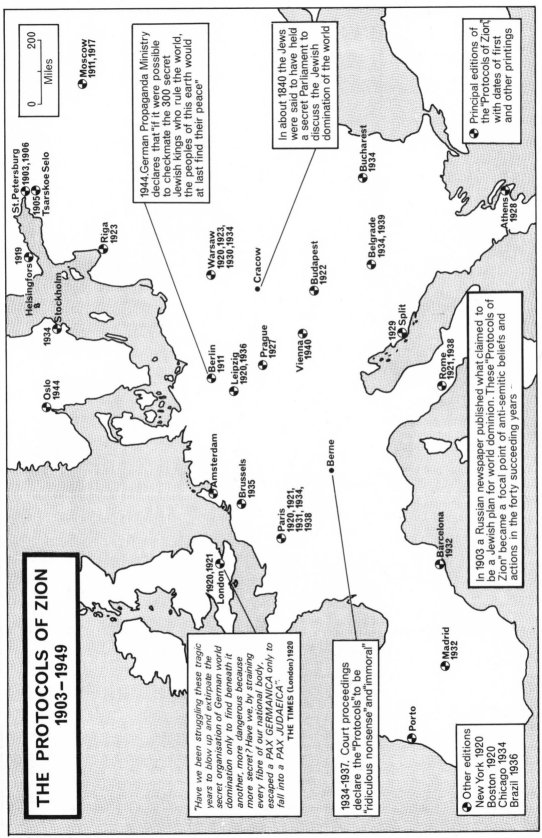

THE PROTOCOLS OF ZION
1903–1949

0 [—————] 200
Miles

"Have we been struggling these tragic years to blow up and extirpate the secret organisation of German world domination only to find beneath it another, more dangerous because more secret? Have we, by straining every fibre of our national body, escaped a PAX GERMANICA only to fall into a PAX JUDAEICA".
THE TIMES (London) 1920

1944. German Propaganda Ministry declares that "if it were possible to checkmate the 300 secret Jewish kings who rule the world, the peoples of this earth would at last find their peace"

In about 1840 the Jews were said to have held a secret Parliament to discuss the Jewish domination of the world

1934–1937. Court proceedings declare the "Protocols" to be "ridiculous nonsense" and "immoral"

In 1903 a Russian newspaper published what claimed to be a Jewish plan for world dominion. These "Protocols of Zion" became a focal point of anti-semitic beliefs and actions in the forty succeeding years –

⊕ Principal editions of the "Protocols of Zion", with dates of first and other printings

⊕ Other editions
New York 1920
Boston 1920
Chicago 1934
Brazil 1936

⊕ Moscow 1911,1917

St.Petersburg
⊕ 1903,1906
⊕ 1905
Tsarskoe Selo

⊕ Riga 1923

1919
⊕ Helsingfors

⊕ Stockholm
1934

⊕ Oslo 1944

⊕ Warsaw 1920,1923, 1930,1934

• Cracow

⊕ Budapest 1922

⊕ Bucharest 1934

⊕ Belgrade 1934,1939

⊕ Athens 1928

⊕ Berlin 1911
⊕ Leipzig 1920,1936
⊕ Prague 1927
⊕ Vienna 1940

⊕ Split
1929

⊕ Rome 1921,1938

⊕ Amsterdam
⊕ Brussels 1935
• Berne

⊕ Paris 1920,1921, 1931,1934, 1938

1920,1921
⊕ London

⊕ Barcelona 1932

⊕ Madrid 1932

⊕ Porto

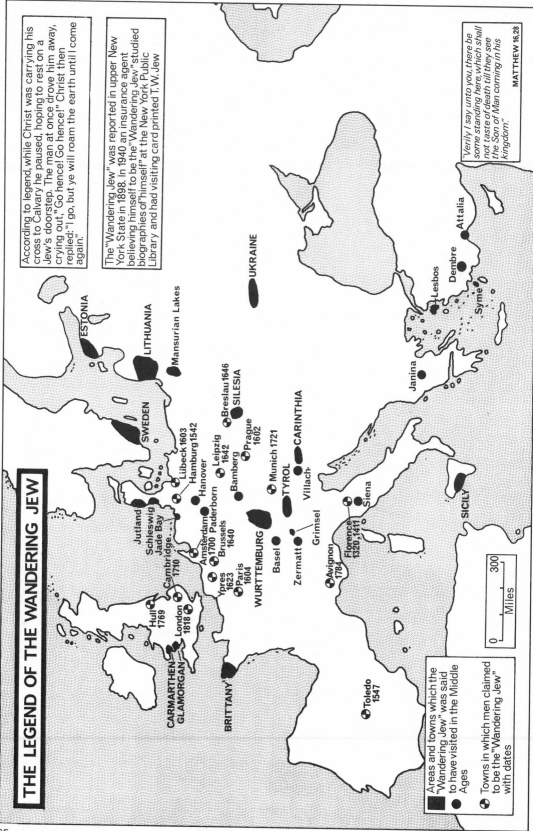

THE LEGEND OF THE WANDERING JEW

According to legend, while Christ was carrying his cross to Calvary he paused, hoping to rest on a Jew's doorstep. The man at once drove him away, crying out, "Go hence! Go hence!" Christ then replied: "I go, but ye will roam the earth until I come again."

The "Wandering Jew" was reported in upper New York State in 1898. In 1940 an insurance agent believing himself to be the "Wandering Jew" studied biographies of "himself" at the New York Public Library and had visiting card printed T.W. Jew.

Verily I say unto you, there be some standing here, which shall not taste of death till they see the Son of Man coming in his kingdom.

MATTHEW 16,28

ESTONIA

LITHUANIA

Mansurian Lakes

UKRAINE

SWEDEN

SILESIA
Breslau 1646

Lübeck 1603
Hamburg 1542
Hanover
Leipzig 1642
Bamberg
Prague 1602

Munich 1721
CARINTHIA
TYROL
Villach

Jutland
Schleswig
Jade Bay

Cambridge 1710

Amsterdam
1700 Paderborn
Brussels 1640
Ypres 1623
Paris 1604

WURTTEMBURG
Basel
Grimsel
Zermatt

Avignon 1784
Florence 1320,1411
Siena

Hull 1769
London 1818

CARMARTHEN
GLAMORGAN

BRITTANY

Toledo 1547

SICILY

Janina

Lesbos
Dembre
Attalia
Syme

	Areas and towns which the "Wandering Jew" was said to have visited in the Middle Ages
●	Towns in which men claimed to be the "Wandering Jew" with dates

0   300
Miles

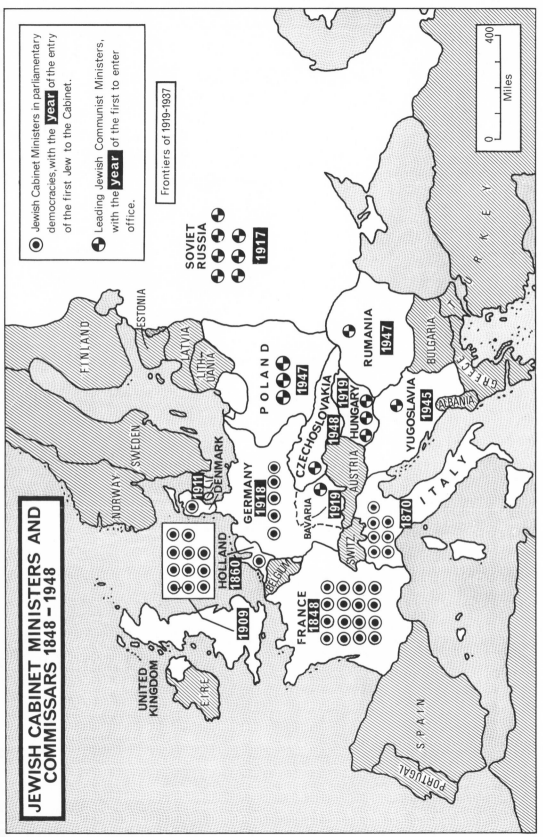

JEWISH CABINET MINISTERS AND COMMISSARS 1848–1948

Jewish Cabinet Ministers in parliamentary democracies, with the **year** of the entry of the first Jew to the Cabinet.

Leading Jewish Communist Ministers, with the **year** of the first to enter office.

Frontiers of 1919–1937

400

Miles

0

SOVIET RUSSIA
1917

FINLAND

ESTONIA

LATVIA

LITH-UANIA

POLAND
1947

RUMANIA
1947

BULGARIA

T U R K E Y

NORWAY

SWEDEN

DENMARK
1911

GERMANY
1918

CZECHOSLOVAKIA
1948

AUSTRIA
1919

HUNGARY
1919

YUGOSLAVIA
1945

ALBANIA

GREECE

UNITED KINGDOM
1909

EIRE

HOLLAND
1860

BELGIUM

BAVARIA
1919

SWITZ.

I T A L Y

1870

FRANCE
1848

S P A I N

PORTUGAL

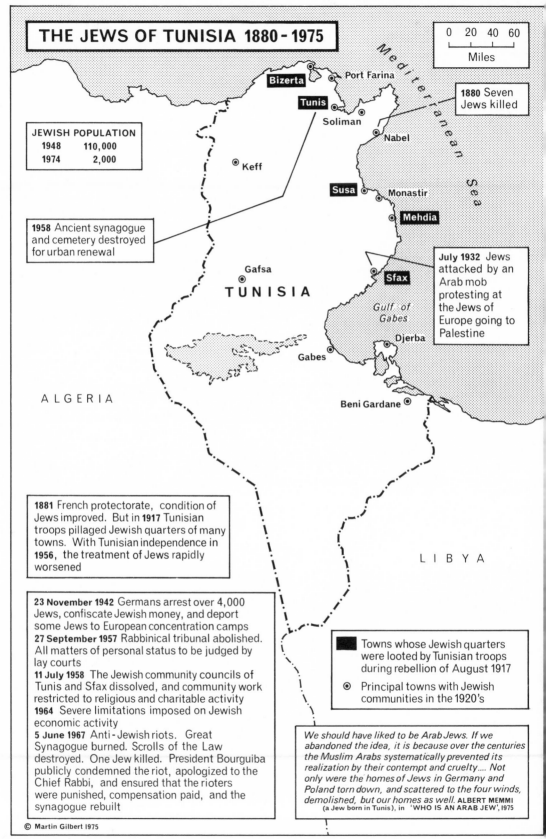

THE JEWS OF TUNISIA 1880-1975

0 20 40 60
Miles

Mediterranean Sea

Bizerta
Port Farina

1880 Seven Jews killed

Tunis
Soliman

Nabel

JEWISH POPULATION
1948	110,000
1974	2,000

◉ Keff

Susa ◉   Monastir ◉

Mehdia

1958 Ancient synagogue and cemetery destroyed for urban renewal

Gafsa ◉

T U N I S I A

Sfax

Gulf of Gabes

July 1932 Jews attacked by an Arab mob protesting at the Jews of Europe going to Palestine

Djerba

Gabes ◉

A L G E R I A

Beni Gardane ◉

1881 French protectorate, condition of Jews improved. But in **1917** Tunisian troops pillaged Jewish quarters of many towns. With Tunisian independence in **1956**, the treatment of Jews rapidly worsened

L I B Y A

23 November 1942 Germans arrest over 4,000 Jews, confiscate Jewish money, and deport some Jews to European concentration camps
27 September 1957 Rabbinical tribunal abolished. All matters of personal status to be judged by lay courts
11 July 1958 The Jewish community councils of Tunis and Sfax dissolved, and community work restricted to religious and charitable activity
1964 Severe limitations imposed on Jewish economic activity
5 June 1967 Anti-Jewish riots. Great Synagogue burned. Scrolls of the Law destroyed. One Jew killed. President Bourguiba publicly condemned the riot, apologized to the Chief Rabbi, and ensured that the rioters were punished, compensation paid, and the synagogue rebuilt

■ Towns whose Jewish quarters were looted by Tunisian troops during rebellion of August 1917

◉ Principal towns with Jewish communities in the 1920's

We should have liked to be Arab Jews. If we abandoned the idea, it is because over the centuries the Muslim Arabs systematically prevented its realization by their contempt and cruelty.... Not only were the homes of Jews in Germany and Poland torn down, and scattered to the four winds, demolished, but our homes as well. ALBERT MEMMI
(a Jew born in Tunis), in 'WHO IS AN ARAB JEW', 1975

© Martin Gilbert 1975

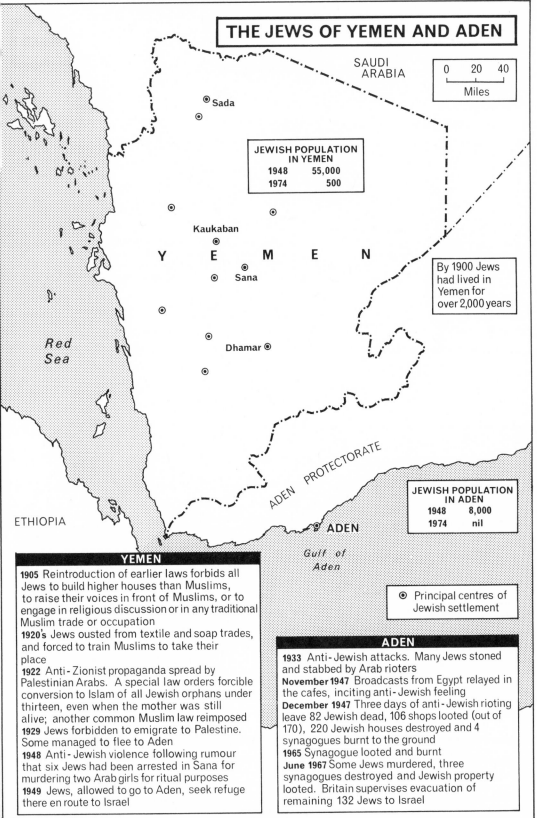

THE JEWS OF YEMEN AND ADEN

SAUDI ARABIA

0   20   40
Miles

⊙ Sada
⊙

JEWISH POPULATION IN YEMEN

1948	55,000
1974	500

⊙

Y   E   M   E   N

Kaukaban
⊙
⊙ Sana
⊙

By 1900 Jews had lived in Yemen for over 2,000 years

⊙

⊙ Dhamar ⊙
⊙

Red Sea

ADEN PROTECTORATE

JEWISH POPULATION IN ADEN

1948	8,000
1974	nil

ETHIOPIA

⊙ ADEN

Gulf of Aden

⊙ Principal centres of Jewish settlement

YEMEN

1905 Reintroduction of earlier laws forbids all Jews to build higher houses than Muslims, to raise their voices in front of Muslims, or to engage in religious discussion or in any traditional Muslim trade or occupation
1920's Jews ousted from textile and soap trades, and forced to train Muslims to take their place
1922 Anti-Zionist propaganda spread by Palestinian Arabs. A special law orders forcible conversion to Islam of all Jewish orphans under thirteen, even when the mother was still alive; another common Muslim law reimposed
1929 Jews forbidden to emigrate to Palestine. Some managed to flee to Aden
1948 Anti-Jewish violence following rumour that six Jews had been arrested in Sana for murdering two Arab girls for ritual purposes
1949 Jews, allowed to go to Aden, seek refuge there en route to Israel

ADEN

1933 Anti-Jewish attacks. Many Jews stoned and stabbed by Arab rioters
November 1947 Broadcasts from Egypt relayed in the cafes, inciting anti-Jewish feeling
December 1947 Three days of anti-Jewish rioting leave 82 Jewish dead, 106 shops looted (out of 170), 220 Jewish houses destroyed and 4 synagogues burnt to the ground
1965 Synagogue looted and burnt
June 1967 Some Jews murdered, three synagogues destroyed and Jewish property looted. Britain supervises evacuation of remaining 132 Jews to Israel

© Martin Gilbert 1975

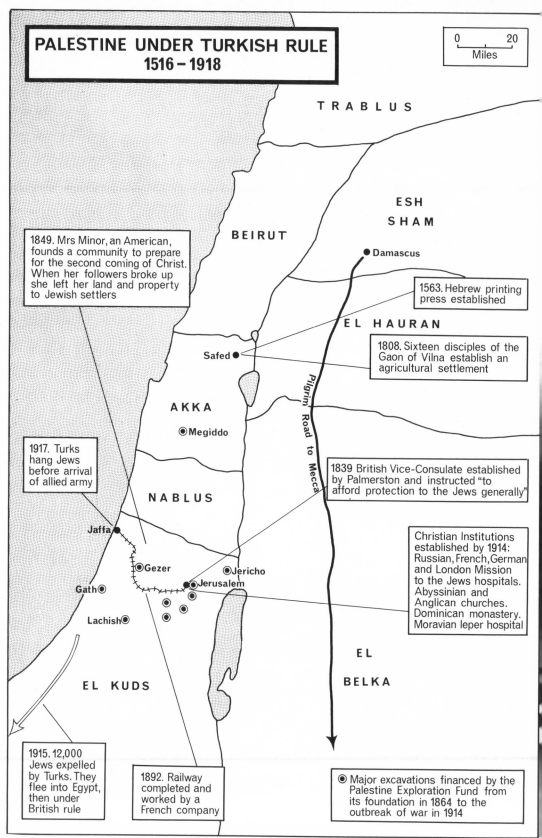

PALESTINE UNDER TURKISH RULE
1516 – 1918

0   20
Miles

TRABLUS

ESH

SHAM

● Damascus

BEIRUT

1849. Mrs Minor, an American, founds a community to prepare for the second coming of Christ. When her followers broke up she left her land and property to Jewish settlers

1563. Hebrew printing press established

EL HAURAN

1808. Sixteen disciples of the Gaon of Vilna establish an agricultural settlement

Safed ●

AKKA

◉ Megiddo

1917. Turks hang Jews before arrival of allied army

NABLUS

1839 British Vice-Consulate established by Palmerston and instructed "to afford protection to the Jews generally"

Jaffa ●

◉ Gezer

◉ Jericho

Gath ◉

◉ Jerusalem

Christian Institutions established by 1914: Russian, French, German and London Mission to the Jews hospitals. Abyssinian and Anglican churches. Dominican monastery. Moravian leper hospital

Lachish ◉

◉

◉   ◉

◉

Pilgrim Road to Mecca

EL

EL KUDS

BELKA

1915. 12,000 Jews expelled by Turks. They flee into Egypt, then under British rule

1892. Railway completed and worked by a French company

◉ Major excavations financed by the Palestine Exploration Fund from its foundation in 1864 to the outbreak of war in 1914

THE JEWS AND THE WESTWARD EXPANSION OF RUSSIA   1772–1815

0   100
Miles

1727, 1747. Jews expelled from Russia emigrated to Poland

LITHUANIA

Polotzk

Vitebsk

EAST PRUSSIA

Kovno

Troki ● Vilna

Grodno

Minsk

Mogilev

Bialystok

Slutzk

Gomel

P O L A N D

Warsaw

Brest-Litovsk

Pinsk

Kalisz

Piotrkow ● Radom

Lublin

Lutzk

Kielce

Zhitomir

SILESIA

G A L I C I A

BESSARABIA

Balta

BUKOVINA

Russian westward expansion led to the transfer of over 1,200,000 Jews from Polish to Russian sovereignty and created a "Jewish problem" for Tsarist Russia. The Russians prevented the spread of Jews from this area by turning it into a "Pale of Jewish Settlement"

●   Towns with large Jewish communities

—·—·—   Western frontier of Russia in 1772 following first partition of Poland

··········   Western frontier of Russia in 1793 following second partition of Poland

▬ ▬ ▬   Western frontier of Russia in 1795 following third partition of Poland

▬▬▬▬   Western frontier of Russia in 1815 following the defeat of Napoleon

THE PALE 1835–1917

0   200
Miles

Baltic Sea

●St.Petersburg

1891. 2,000 Jews deported, many of them in chains

1865. Open to Jews

●Moscow

1891. 20,000 Jews expelled

GERMANY

KOVNO

VITEBSK

SUWALKI

VILNA

PLOCK

LOMZA

MOGILEV

WARSAW

KALISZ

GRODNO

MINSK

PIOTRKOW

SYEDLITZ

RADOM

LUBLIN

KIELCE

VOLHYNIA

CHERNIGOV

Brody●

Kiev●

POLTAVA

AUSTRIA-HUNGARY

KIEV

PODOLIA

EKATERINOSLAV

RUMANIA

BESSARABIA

KHERSON

Nikolaev●

TAURIDA

Sebastopol● ●Yalta

Black Sea

Principal town from which in 1880 began the exodus of over two million Jews from the Pale to the United States, Britain, Europe, South America, and Palestine

In 1882 500,000 Jews living in rural areas of the Pale were forced to leave their homes and live in towns or townlets (shtetls) in the Pale. 250,000 Jews living along the western frontier of Russia were also moved into the Pale. 700,000 Jews living east of the Pale were driven into the Pale by 1891

⬛ The Pale of Settlement. Russian Jews confined to this area by laws of 1795 and 1835. By 1885 there were over 4 million Jews living in the Pale

● Towns within the Pale barred to Jews without special residence permits

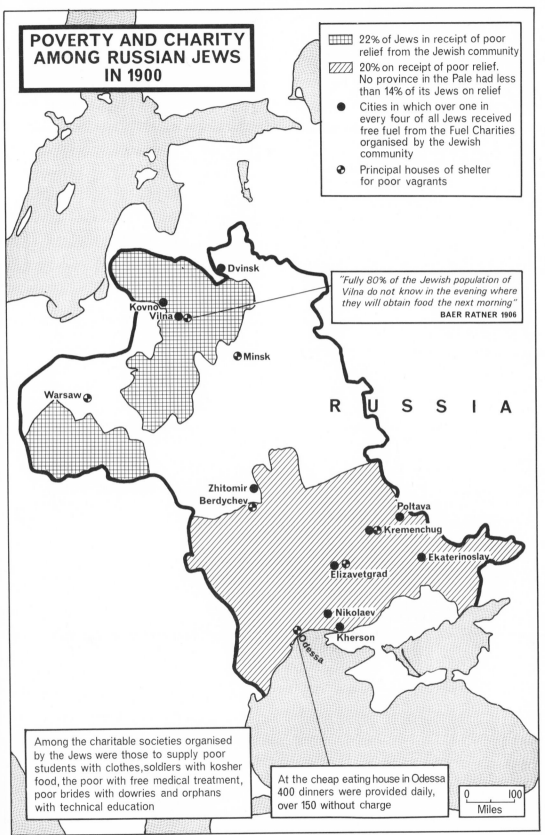

POVERTY AND CHARITY AMONG RUSSIAN JEWS IN 1900

22% of Jews in receipt of poor relief from the Jewish community

20% on receipt of poor relief. No province in the Pale had less than 14% of its Jews on relief

● Cities in which over one in every four of all Jews received free fuel from the Fuel Charities organised by the Jewish community

⊕ Principal houses of shelter for poor vagrants

Dvinsk

Kovno
Vilna

"Fully 80% of the Jewish population of Vilna do not know in the evening where they will obtain food the next morning"
BAER RATNER 1906

⊕ Minsk

Warsaw ⊕

R U S S I A

Zhitomir
Berdychev

Poltava
Kremenchug

Ekaterinoslav

Elizavetgrad

Nikolaev

Kherson

Odessa

Among the charitable societies organised by the Jews were those to supply poor students with clothes, soldiers with kosher food, the poor with free medical treatment, poor brides with dowries and orphans with technical education

At the cheap eating house in Odessa 400 dinners were provided daily, over 150 without charge

0   100
Miles

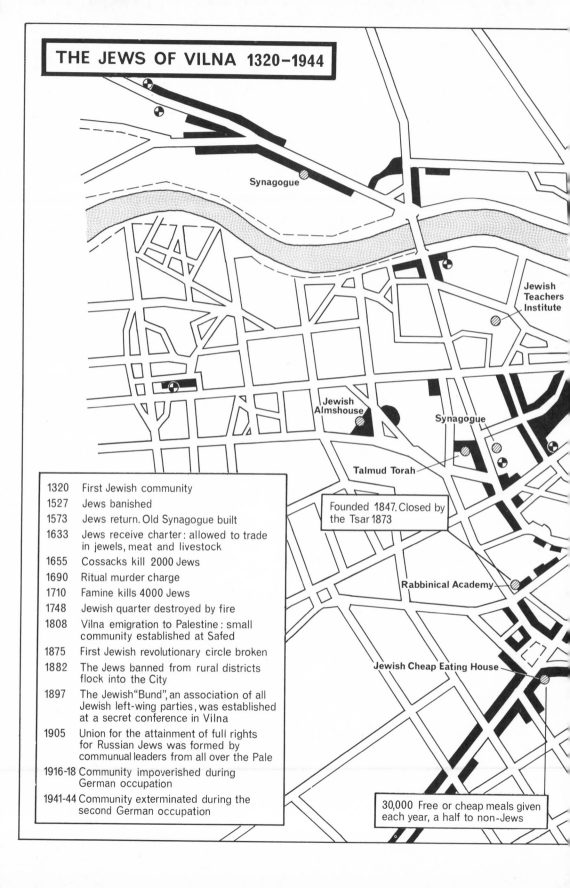

THE JEWS OF VILNA 1320–1944

Synagogue

Jewish Teachers Institute

Synagogue

Jewish Almshouse

Talmud Torah

Founded 1847. Closed by the Tsar 1873

Rabbinical Academy

Jewish Cheap Eating House

1320	First Jewish community
1527	Jews banished
1573	Jews return. Old Synagogue built
1633	Jews receive charter: allowed to trade in jewels, meat and livestock
1655	Cossacks kill 2000 Jews
1690	Ritual murder charge
1710	Famine kills 4000 Jews
1748	Jewish quarter destroyed by fire
1808	Vilna emigration to Palestine: small community established at Safed
1875	First Jewish revolutionary circle broken
1882	The Jews banned from rural districts flock into the City
1897	The Jewish "Bund", an association of all Jewish left-wing parties, was established at a secret conference in Vilna
1905	Union for the attainment of full rights for Russian Jews was formed by communual leaders from all over the Pale
1916-18	Community impoverished during German occupation
1941-44	Community exterminated during the second German occupation

30,000 Free or cheap meals given each year, a half to non-Jews

From the time of the Vilna Gaon (1720-1797) Vilna was a centre of Jewish intellectual, cultural and political life. It was known as "The Citadel of Culture". In 1900 it had 150,000 Jewish inhabitants.

New
Jewish Cemetery

Old
Jewish
Cemetery

anical Gardens

hedral

Public Library

Old
Synagogue

Jewish
Hospital

to St.Petersburg→

New Synagogue

to Warsaw

Station

Jewish quarter by 1655
Jewish quarters by 1914
Schools of adult religious instruction in 1914

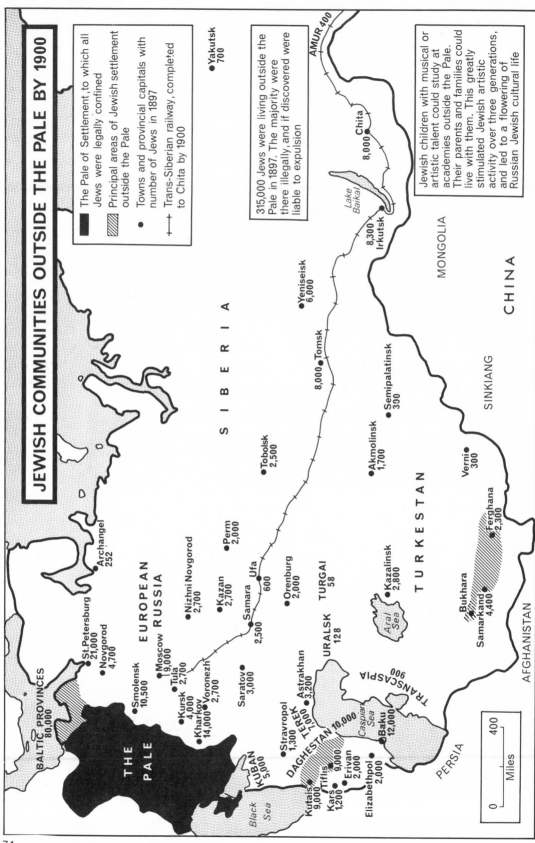

JEWISH COMMUNITIES OUTSIDE THE PALE BY 1900

The Pale of Settlement, to which all Jews were legally confined

Principal areas of Jewish settlement outside the Pale

● Towns and provincial capitals with number of Jews in 1897

┼┼┼ Trans-Siberian railway, completed to Chita by 1900

315,000 Jews were living outside the Pale in 1897. The majority were there illegally, and if discovered were liable to expulsion

Jewish children with musical or artistic talent could study at academies outside the Pale. Their parents and families could live with them. This greatly stimulated Jewish artistic activity over three generations, and led to a flowering of Russian Jewish cultural life

AMUR 400

● Yakutsk 700

● Chita 8,000

Lake Baikal

8,300 Irkutsk●

MONGOLIA

CHINA

● Yeniseisk 6,000

SIBERIA

8,000 ● Tomsk

● Semipalatinsk 300

● Akmolinsk 1,700

● Tobolsk 2,500

SINKIANG

● Verni 300

● Ferghana 2,300

TURKESTAN

● Kazalinsk 2,800

TURGAI 58

Aral Sea

● Bukhara

● Samarkand 4,400

Archangel 252 ●

EUROPEAN RUSSIA

● Perm 2,000

● Nizhni Novgorod 2,700

● Kazan 2,700

Ufa ● 600

Samara ● 2,500

● Orenburg 2,000

● St.Petersburg 21,000

● Novgorod 4,700

● Smolensk 10,500

● Moscow 19,000

Tula ● 4,000

● Kursk 4,000

● Voronezh 2,700

● Kharkov 14,000

● Saratov 3,000

● Astrakhan 3,200

URALSK 128

TRANSCASPIA 900

AFGHANISTAN

BALTIC PROVINCES 80,000

THE PALE

KUBAN 5,000

● Stravropol 1,300

TEREK 7,000

DAGHESTAN 10,000

Caspian Sea

● Baku 12,000

Black Sea

● Kutais 9,000

Tiflis 9,000 ●

Kars ● 1,200

Erivan ● 2,000

● Elizabethpol 2,000

PERSIA

0   400
|___|___|___|___|
        Miles

74

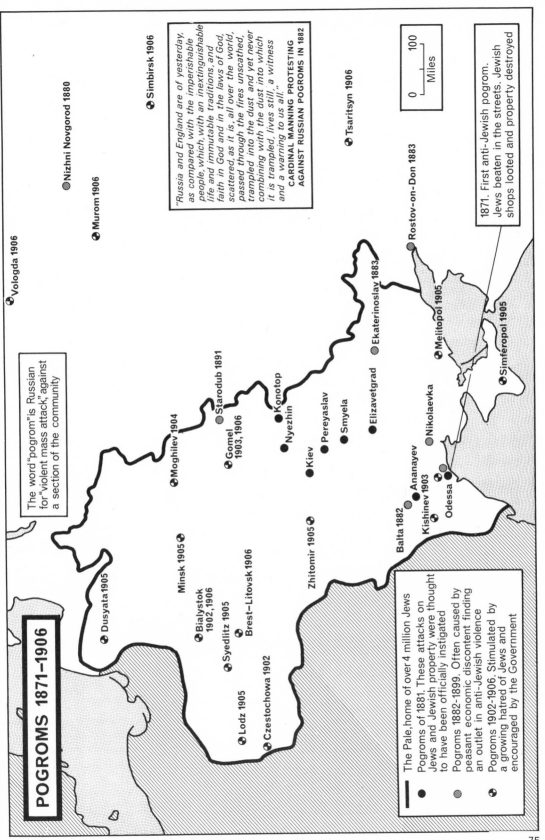

POGROMS 1871–1906

The word "pogrom" is Russian for "violent mass attack", against a section of the community

"Russia and England are of yesterday, as compared with the imperishable people, which, with an inextinguishable life and immutable traditions, and faith in God and in the laws of God, scattered, as it is, all over the world, passed through the fires unscathed, trampled into the dust and yet never combining with the dust into which it is trampled, lives still; a witness and a warning to us all."
CARDINAL MANNING PROTESTING AGAINST RUSSIAN POGROMS IN 1882

1871. First anti-Jewish pogrom. Jews beaten in the streets. Jewish shops looted and property destroyed

The Pale, home of over 4 million Jews

Pogroms of 1881. These attacks on Jews and Jewish property were thought to have been officially instigated

Pogroms 1882-1899. Often caused by peasant economic discontent finding an outlet in anti-Jewish violence

Pogroms 1902-1906. Stimulated by a growing hatred of Jews and encouraged by the Government

0   100
Miles

⊕ Vologda 1906

⊕ Nizhni Novgorod 1880

⊕ Murom 1906

⊕ Simbirsk 1906

⊕ Tsaritsyn 1906

⊕ Dusyata 1905

Minsk 1905 ⊕

⊕ Moghilev 1904

⊕ Bialystok 1902, 1906

⊕ Syedlitz 1905

⊕ Lodz 1905

Brest–Litovsk 1906 ⊕

⊕ Czestochowa 1902

Zhitomir 1905 ⊕

⊕ Gomel 1903, 1906

⊕ Starodub 1891

● Konotop

● Nyezhin

● Kiev

● Pereyaslav

● Smyela

● Elizavetgrad

⊕ Ekaterinoslav 1883

⊕ Melitopol 1905

⊕ Simferopol 1905

⊕ Rostov-on-Don 1883

Balta 1882 ⊕

⊕ Ananayev

Kishinev 1903 ⊕

● Nikolaevka

Odessa

75

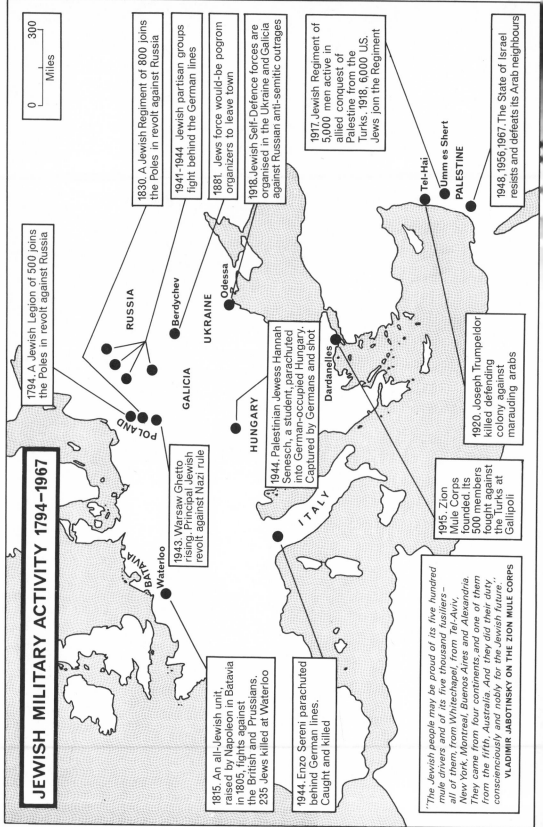

JEWISH MILITARY ACTIVITY 1794–1967

0   300
Miles

1794. A Jewish Legion of 500 joins the Poles in revolt against Russia

1830. A Jewish Regiment of 800 joins the Poles in revolt against Russia

1941-1944 Jewish partisan groups fight behind the German lines

1881. Jews force would-be pogrom organizers to leave town

1918. Jewish Self-Defence forces are organised in the Ukraine and Galicia against Russian anti-semitic outrages

1917. Jewish Regiment of 5,000 men active in allied conquest of Palestine from the Turks. 1918, 6,000 U.S. Jews join the Regiment

1948, 1956, 1967. The State of Israel resists and defeats its Arab neighbours

Tel-Hai
Umm es Shert
PALESTINE

1920. Joseph Trumpeldor killed defending colony against marauding arabs

1944. Palestinian Jewess Hannah Senesch, a student, parachuted into German-occupied Hungary. Captured by Germans and shot

Dardanelles

1915. Zion Mule Corps founded. Its 500 members fought against the Turks at Gallipoli

Odessa

Berdychev

RUSSIA

UKRAINE

GALICIA

POLAND

HUNGARY

ITALY

Waterloo

BATAVIA

1943. Warsaw Ghetto rising. Principal Jewish revolt against Nazi rule

1815. An all-Jewish unit, raised by Napoleon in Batavia in 1805, fights against the British and Prussians. 235 Jews killed at Waterloo

1944. Enzo Sereni parachuted behind German lines. Caught and killed

"The Jewish people may be proud of its five hundred mule drivers and of its five thousand fusiliers – all of them, from Whitechapel, from Tel-Aviv, New York, Montreal, Buenos Aires and Alexandria. They came from four continents, and one of them from the fifth, Australia. And they did their duty, conscienciously and nobly for the Jewish future."
VLADIMIR JABOTINSKY ON THE ZION MULE CORPS

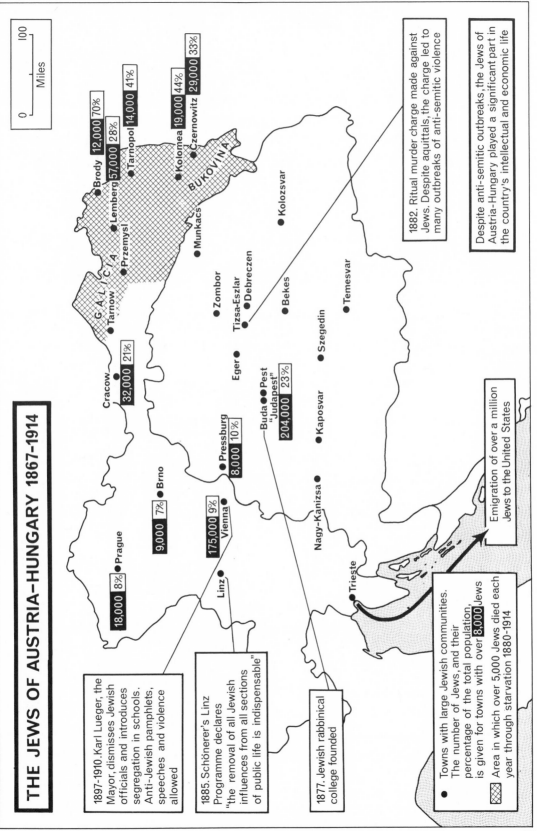

THE JEWS OF AUSTRIA–HUNGARY 1867–1914

Brody 12,000 70%
Lemberg 57,000 28%
Tarnopol 14,000 41%
Kolomea 19,000 44%
Czernowitz 29,000 33%

GALICIA

BUKOVINA

Munkacs ●
Kolozsvar ●

Tarnow ●
Przemysl ●

Cracow ● 32,000 21%

Zombor ●
Tizsa-Eszlar ●
Debreczen ●
Bekes ●
Temesvar ●

Brno ● 9,000 7%

Eger ●
Pressburg ● 8,000 10%
Buda ●● Pest
"Judapest"
204,000 23%
Kaposvar ●
Szegedin ●

Prague ● 18,000 8%

Vienna 175,000 9%

Linz ●

Nagy-Kanizsa ●

Trieste ●

0   100
Miles

1882. Ritual murder charge made against Jews. Despite aquittals, the charge led to many outbreaks of anti-semitic violence

Despite anti-semitic outbreaks, the Jews of Austria-Hungary played a significant part in the country's intellectual and economic life

Emigration of over a million Jews to the United States

1897-1910. Karl Lueger, the Mayor, dismisses Jewish officials and introduces segregation in schools. Anti-Jewish pamphlets, speeches and violence allowed

1885. Schönerer's Linz Programme declares "the removal of all Jewish influences from all sections of public life is indispensable"

1877. Jewish rabbinical college founded

● Towns with large Jewish communities. The number of Jews, and their percentage of the total population, is given for towns with over 8,000 Jews

▨ Area in which over 5,000 Jews died each year through starvation 1880-1914

77

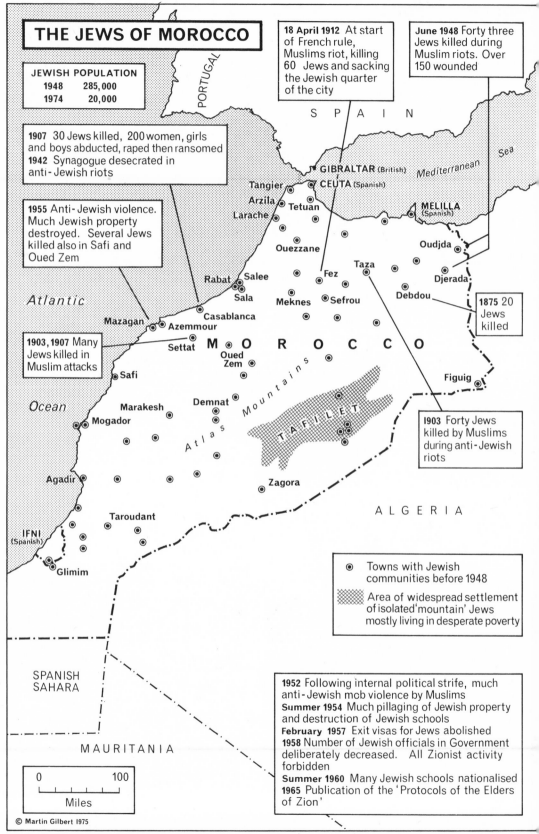

THE JEWS OF MOROCCO

JEWISH POPULATION
1948   285,000
1974   20,000

1907 30 Jews killed, 200 women, girls and boys abducted, raped then ransomed
1942 Synagogue desecrated in anti-Jewish riots

1955 Anti-Jewish violence. Much Jewish property destroyed. Several Jews killed also in Safi and Oued Zem

1903, 1907 Many Jews killed in Muslim attacks

18 April 1912 At start of French rule, Muslims riot, killing 60 Jews and sacking the Jewish quarter of the city

June 1948 Forty three Jews killed during Muslim riots. Over 150 wounded

1875 20 Jews killed

1903 Forty Jews killed by Muslims during anti-Jewish riots

PORTUGAL

S P A I N

Mediterranean Sea

GIBRALTAR (British)
CEUTA (Spanish)
Tangier
Arzila
Tetuan
Larache
MELILLA (Spanish)

Oudjda
Djerada

Rabat
Salee
Sala
Casablanca
Azemmour
Mazagan
Settat
Oued Zem
Safi

Fez
Taza
Meknes
Sefrou
Debdou

Atlantic

Ocean

M O R O C C O

Demnat
Atlas Mountains
T A F I L E L T
Figuig

Marakesh
Mogador

Zagora

A L G E R I A

Agadir

Taroudant

IFNI (Spanish)
Glimim

⊙ Towns with Jewish communities before 1948

▦ Area of widespread settlement of isolated 'mountain' Jews mostly living in desperate poverty

SPANISH SAHARA

MAURITANIA

1952 Following internal political strife, much anti-Jewish mob violence by Muslims
Summer 1954 Much pillaging of Jewish property and destruction of Jewish schools
February 1957 Exit visas for Jews abolished
1958 Number of Jewish officials in Government deliberately decreased. All Zionist activity forbidden
Summer 1960 Many Jewish schools nationalised
1965 Publication of the 'Protocols of the Elders of Zion'

0   100
Miles

© Martin Gilbert 1975

THE JEWS OF BRITAIN
1660 – 1914

⊕ Principal Jewish communities by 1914
● Other towns with Jewish communities

1905. Aliens Act gives immigration officers the right to deport any "undesirable immigrant". Flow of Jews reduced by 40%

⊕ Glasgow 6,500
⊕ Edinburgh 1,500

2,000 Newcastle ⊕
● North Shields
● South Shields
Gateshead ● Sunderland
West Hartlepool ●
Stockton ● ● Middlesborough

THE JEWS IN BRITAIN	
1660	150
1690	400
1734	6,000
1790	26,000
1850	30,000
1882	46,000
1914	300,000

Hull 1,500 ⊕

Bradford ● ⊕ Leeds 15,000

0 ——— 50
Miles

Liverpool ⊕ 5,000
⊕ Manchester 25,000
● Sheffield

● King's Lynn
Norwich ● ● Yarmouth

● Wolverhampton
Birmingham ⊕ 5,500
● Coventry

1911. Anti-Jewish riots by miners

● Cambridge
● Bedford
Ipswich ●

● Cheltenham
Merthyr ● Tredegar
Aberdare ●
● Stroud
● Oxford
London 180,000 ⊕
Swansea ● Newport
Pontypridd Cardiff ● Bristol ● Bath
● Reading
Chatham ●
Canterbury ●
Ramsgate ●
Dover ●

1882–1914. 4 ships a week from Hamburg, 3 from Rotterdam, 3 from Breslau and 1 from Libau bring nearly 300,000 Russian, Galician and Rumanian Jews

Southampton ● ● Portsmouth Brighton ●

Exeter ●

Plymouth ●

Falmouth ●

MAIN JEWISH TRADES
Tailoring 40%
Boot & Slipper Trade 12%
Furniture Trade 10%

JEWISH TRADE UNIONS IN 1900:
Tailors, Capmakers, Boot & Shoe Operatives, Cabinet Makers, Cigarette & Tobacco Cutters, Iron & Tin Plate Makers, Brush Makers, Cardboard Box Makers, House Painters & Decorators, Butchers, Poulterers, Bakers.

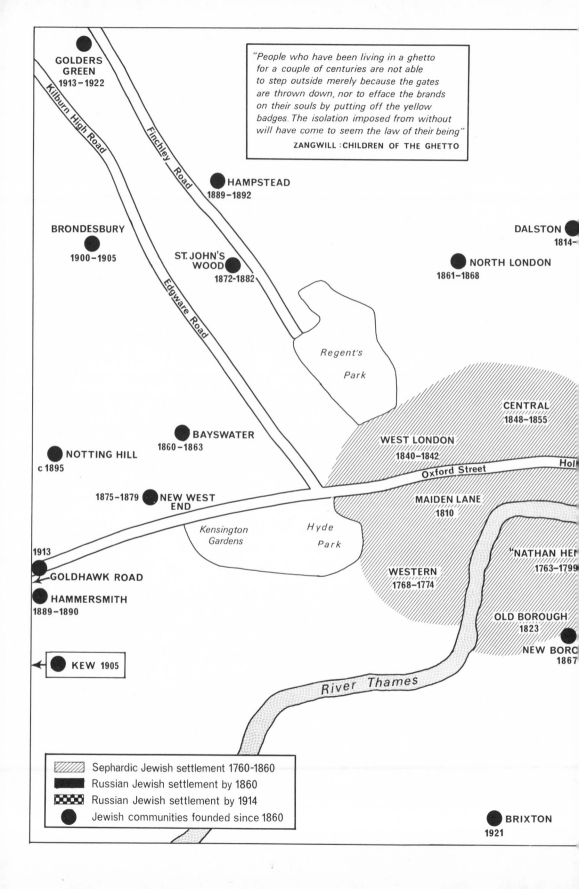

GOLDERS
GREEN
1913–1922

Kilburn High Road

Finchley Road

"People who have been living in a ghetto
for a couple of centuries are not able
to step outside merely because the gates
are thrown down, nor to efface the brands
on their souls by putting off the yellow
badges. The isolation imposed from without
will have come to seem the law of their being"
ZANGWILL : CHILDREN OF THE GHETTO

HAMPSTEAD
1889–1892

DALSTON
1814–

BRONDESBURY

1900–1905

ST. JOHN'S
WOOD
1872–1882

Edgware Road

NORTH LONDON
1861–1868

Regent's

Park

CENTRAL
1848–1855

BAYSWATER
1860–1863

WEST LONDON
1840–1842

NOTTING HILL
c 1895

Oxford Street

Hol

MAIDEN LANE
1810

1875–1879 NEW WEST
END

Kensington
Gardens

Hyde

Park

"NATHAN HE
1763–1799

1913

GOLDHAWK ROAD

WESTERN
1768–1774

OLD BOROUGH
1823

HAMMERSMITH
1889–1890

NEW BORO
1867

KEW 1905

River Thames

	Sephardic Jewish settlement 1760-1860
	Russian Jewish settlement by 1860
	Russian Jewish settlement by 1914
	Jewish communities founded since 1860

BRIXTON
1921

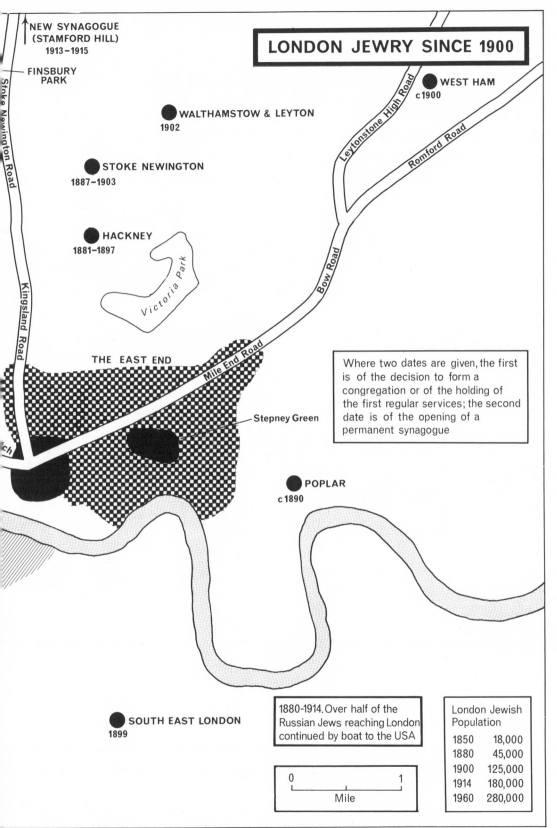

LONDON JEWRY SINCE 1900

NEW SYNAGOGUE
(STAMFORD HILL)
1913–1915

FINSBURY PARK

WEST HAM
c 1900

WALTHAMSTOW & LEYTON
1902

STOKE NEWINGTON
1887–1903

HACKNEY
1881–1897

Victoria Park

Stoke Newington Road

Kingsland Road

Leytonstone High Road

Romford Road

Bow Road

THE EAST END

Mile End Road

Stepney Green

Where two dates are given, the first is of the decision to form a congregation or of the holding of the first regular services; the second date is of the opening of a permanent synagogue

POPLAR
c 1890

SOUTH EAST LONDON
1899

1880–1914. Over half of the Russian Jews reaching London continued by boat to the USA

London Jewish Population	
1850	18,000
1880	45,000
1900	125,000
1914	180,000
1960	280,000

0 ———————— 1
Mile

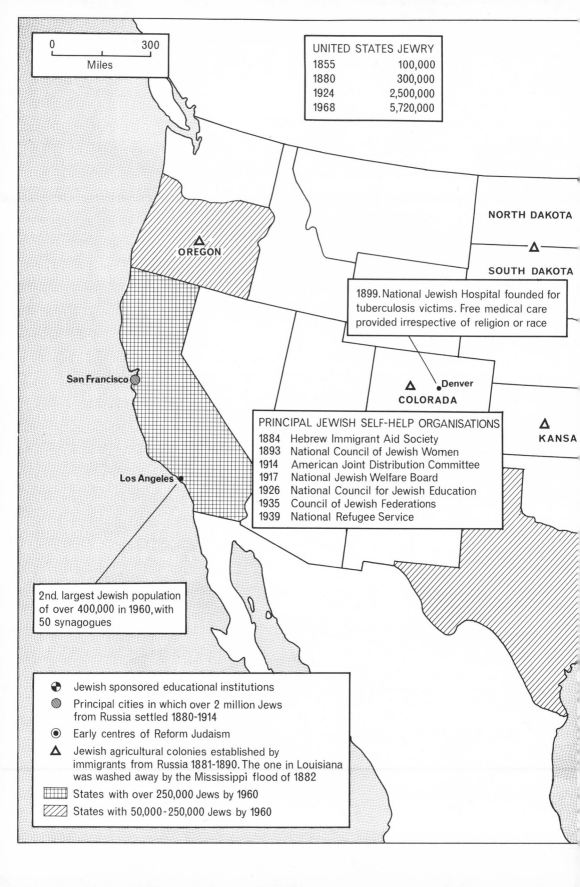

0	**300**

Miles

UNITED STATES JEWRY
1855	100,000
1880	300,000
1924	2,500,000
1968	5,720,000

NORTH DAKOTA

SOUTH DAKOTA

1899. National Jewish Hospital founded for
tuberculosis victims. Free medical care
provided irrespective of religion or race

OREGON

San Francisco

•Denver
COLORADA

KANSA

PRINCIPAL JEWISH SELF-HELP ORGANISATIONS
1884	Hebrew Immigrant Aid Society
1893	National Council of Jewish Women
1914	American Joint Distribution Committee
1917	National Jewish Welfare Board
1926	National Council for Jewish Education
1935	Council of Jewish Federations
1939	National Refugee Service

Los Angeles •

2nd. largest Jewish population
of over 400,000 in 1960, with
50 synagogues

⊕ Jewish sponsored educational institutions

◍ Principal cities in which over 2 million Jews
from Russia settled 1880-1914

◉ Early centres of Reform Judaism

▲ Jewish agricultural colonies established by
immigrants from Russia 1881-1890. The one in Louisiana
was washed away by the Mississippi flood of 1882

▦ States with over 250,000 Jews by 1960

▨ States with 50,000-250,000 Jews by 1960

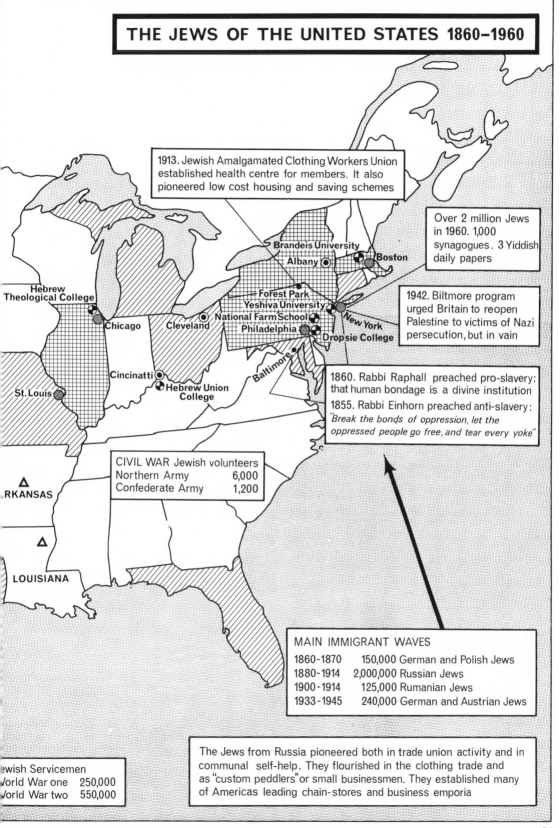

THE JEWS OF THE UNITED STATES 1860–1960

1913. Jewish Amalgamated Clothing Workers Union established health centre for members. It also pioneered low cost housing and saving schemes

Over 2 million Jews in 1960. 1,000 synagogues. 3 Yiddish daily papers

Brandeis University
Albany
Boston

Hebrew Theological College

Forest Park
Yeshiva University
National Farm School
Chicago
Cleveland
Philadelphia
New York
Dropsie College

1942. Biltmore program urged Britain to reopen Palestine to victims of Nazi persecution, but in vain

Cincinatti
St. Louis
Hebrew Union College

Baltimore

1860. Rabbi Raphall preached pro-slavery: that human bondage is a divine institution

1855. Rabbi Einhorn preached anti-slavery:
"Break the bonds of oppression, let the oppressed people go free, and tear every yoke"

△
RKANSAS

CIVIL WAR Jewish volunteers
Northern Army   6,000
Confederate Army   1,200

△

LOUISIANA

MAIN IMMIGRANT WAVES

1860-1870	150,000 German and Polish Jews
1880-1914	2,000,000 Russian Jews
1900-1914	125,000 Rumanian Jews
1933-1945	240,000 German and Austrian Jews

ewish Servicemen
Vorld War one   250,000
Vorld War two   550,000

The Jews from Russia pioneered both in trade union activity and in communal self-help. They flourished in the clothing trade and as "custom peddlers" or small businessmen. They established many of Americas leading chain-stores and business emporia

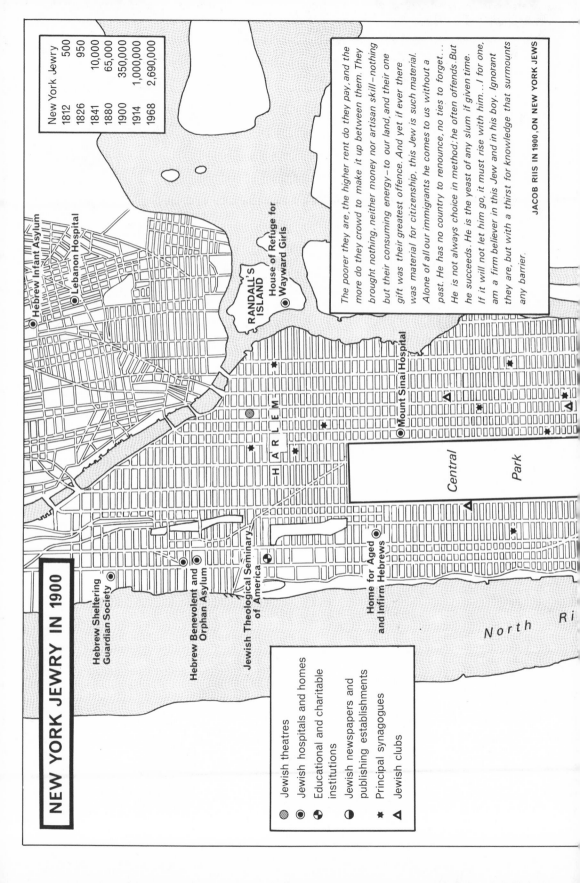

NEW YORK JEWRY IN 1900

New York Jewry	
1812	500
1826	950
1841	10,000
1880	65,000
1900	350,000
1914	1,000,000
1968	2,690,000

The poorer they are, the higher rent do they pay, and the more do they crowd to make it up between them. They brought nothing, neither money nor artisan skill–nothing but their consuming energy–to our land, and their one gift was their greatest offence. And yet if ever there was material for citizenship, this Jew is such material. Alone of all our immigrants he comes to us without a past. He has no country to renounce, no ties to forget... He is not always choice in method; he often offends. But he succeeds. He is the yeast of any slum if given time. If it will not let him go, it must rise with him... I for one, am a firm believer in this Jew and in his boy. Ignorant they are, but with a thirst for knowledge that surmounts any barrier.

JACOB RIIS IN 1900, ON NEW YORK JEWS

Hebrew Infant Asylum

Lebanon Hospital

RANDALL'S ISLAND

House of Refuge for Wayward Girls

Hebrew Sheltering Guardian Society

Hebrew Benevolent and Orphan Asylum

Jewish Theological Seminary of America

HARLEM

Mount Sinai Hospital

Home for Aged and Infirm Hebrews

Central

Park

North Ri...

◉ Jewish theatres

◉ Jewish hospitals and homes

◑ Educational and charitable institutions

◐ Jewish newspapers and publishing establishments

✱ Principal synagogues

△ Jewish clubs

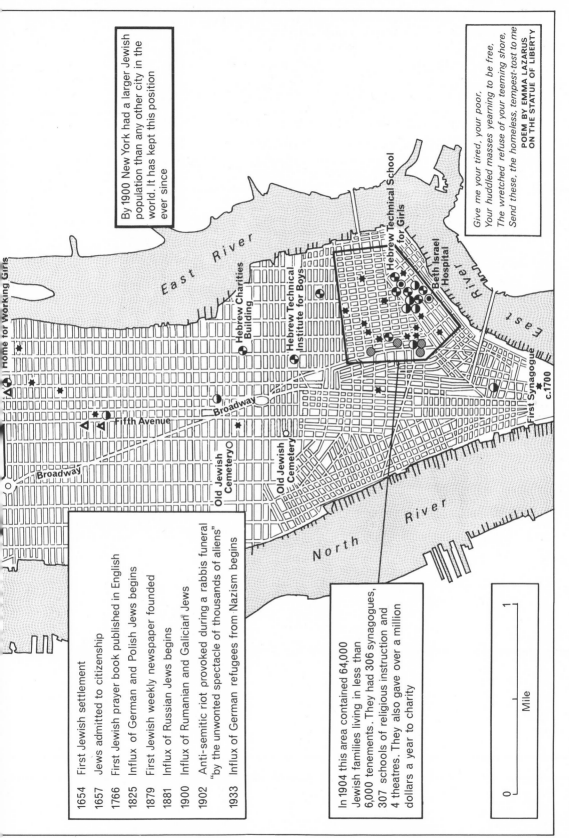

By 1900 New York had a larger Jewish population than any other city in the world. It has kept this position ever since

Give me your tired, your poor,
Your huddled masses yearning to be free,
The wretched refuse of your teeming shore.
Send these, the homeless, tempest-tost to me

POEM BY EMMA LAZARUS
ON THE STATUE OF LIBERTY

Home for Working Girls

East River

Hebrew Charities Building

Hebrew Technical School for Girls

Beth Israel Hospital

Hebrew Technical Institute for Boys

Fifth Avenue

Broadway

Broadway

Old Jewish Cemetery

Old Jewish Cemetery

First Synagogue
c.1700

East River

North River

1654   First Jewish settlement
1657   Jews admitted to citizenship
1766   First Jewish prayer book published in English
1825   Influx of German and Polish Jews begins
1879   First Jewish weekly newspaper founded
1881   Influx of Russian Jews begins
1900   Influx of Rumanian and Galician Jews
1902   Anti-semitic riot provoked during a rabbis funeral "by the unwonted spectacle of thousands of aliens"
1933   Influx of German refugees from Nazism begins

In 1904 this area contained 64,000 Jewish families living in less than 6,000 tenements. They had 306 synagogues, 307 schools of religious instruction and 4 theatres. They also gave over a million dollars a year to charity

0   1
Mile

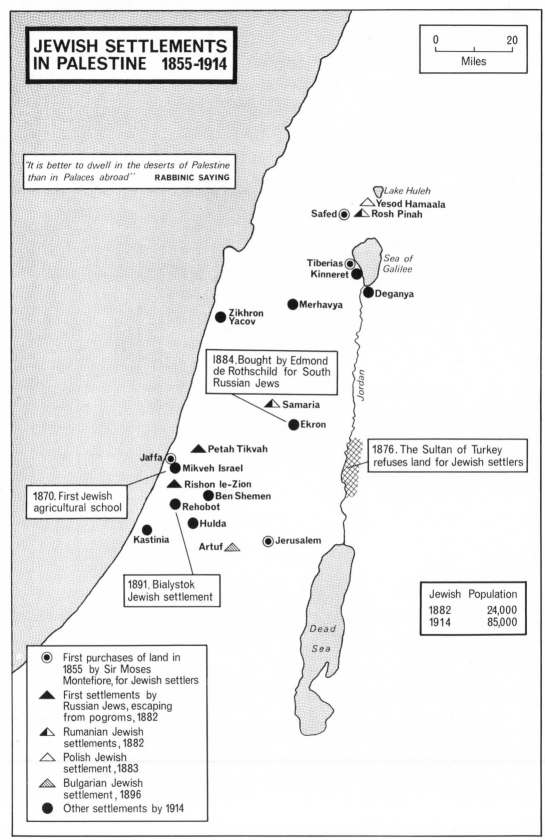

JEWISH SETTLEMENTS IN PALESTINE 1855-1914

0   20
Miles

"It is better to dwell in the deserts of Palestine than in Palaces abroad"   RABBINIC SAYING

Lake Huleh

△ **Yesod Hamaala**

Safed ◉   △ **Rosh Pinah**

Tiberias ◉   *Sea of Galilee*
Kinneret ●

● **Deganya**

● **Merhavya**

● **Zikhron Yacov**

1884. Bought by Edmond de Rothschild for South Russian Jews

△ **Samaria**

● **Ekron**

1876. The Sultan of Turkey refuses land for Jewish settlers

▲ **Petah Tikvah**

Jaffa ◉
● **Mikveh Israel**

▲ **Rishon le-Zion**
● **Ben Shemen**

1870. First Jewish agricultural school

● **Rehobot**

● **Hulda**

● **Kastinia**

Artuf ◿   ◉ **Jerusalem**

1891. Bialystok Jewish settlement

Jordan

Dead Sea

Jewish Population
1882	24,000
1914	85,000

◉   First purchases of land in 1855 by Sir Moses Montefiore, for Jewish settlers

▲   First settlements by Russian Jews, escaping from pogroms, 1882

◿   Rumanian Jewish settlements, 1882

△   Polish Jewish settlement, 1883

◿   Bulgarian Jewish settlement, 1896

●   Other settlements by 1914

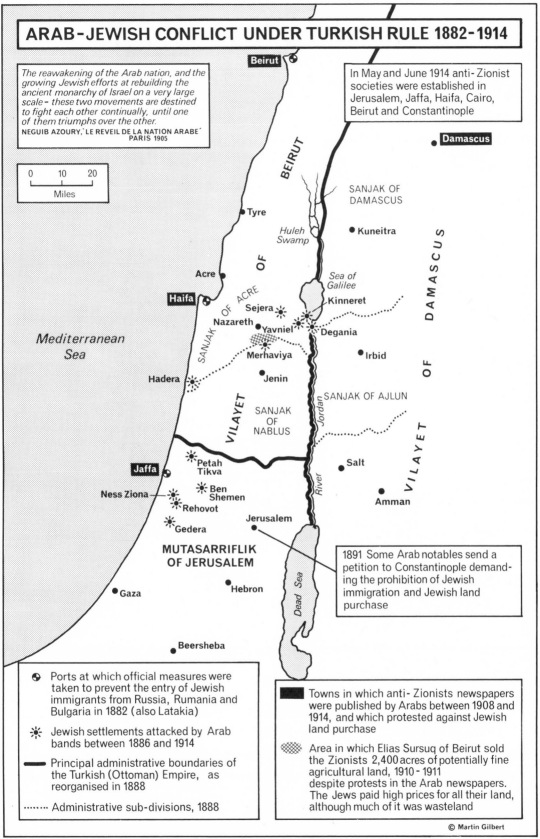

ARAB-JEWISH CONFLICT UNDER TURKISH RULE 1882-1914

The reawakening of the Arab nation, and the growing Jewish efforts at rebuilding the ancient monarchy of Israel on a very large scale – these two movements are destined to fight each other continually, until one of them triumphs over the other.
NEGUIB AZOURY, `LE REVEIL DE LA NATION ARABE´ PARIS 1905

0   10   20
Miles

In May and June 1914 anti-Zionist societies were established in Jerusalem, Jaffa, Haifa, Cairo, Beirut and Constantinople

Beirut

Damascus

BEIRUT

SANJAK OF DAMASCUS

Tyre

Huleh Swamp

Kuneitra

Acre

VILAYET OF ACRE

Haifa

Sejera

Nazareth

Yavniel

Sea of Galilee

Kinneret

Degania

Irbid

Mediterranean Sea

Merhaviya

Hadera

Jenin

SANJAK OF AJLUN

Jordan River

VILAYET OF DAMASCUS

VILAYET OF NABLUS

Petah Tikva

Salt

Ness Ziona

Ben Shemen

Rehovot

Amman

Gedera

Jerusalem

MUTASARRIFLIK OF JERUSALEM

Gaza

Hebron

Dead Sea

1891 Some Arab notables send a petition to Constantinople demanding the prohibition of Jewish immigration and Jewish land purchase

Beersheba

⊕ Ports at which official measures were taken to prevent the entry of Jewish immigrants from Russia, Rumania and Bulgaria in 1882 (also Latakia)

☀ Jewish settlements attacked by Arab bands between 1886 and 1914

— Principal administrative boundaries of the Turkish (Ottoman) Empire, as reorganised in 1888

······· Administrative sub-divisions, 1888

■ Towns in which anti-Zionists newspapers were published by Arabs between 1908 and 1914, and which protested against Jewish land purchase

▨ Area in which Elias Sursuq of Beirut sold the Zionists 2,400 acres of potentially fine agricultural land, 1910-1911 despite protests in the Arab newspapers. The Jews paid high prices for all their land, although much of it was wasteland

© Martin Gilbert

84

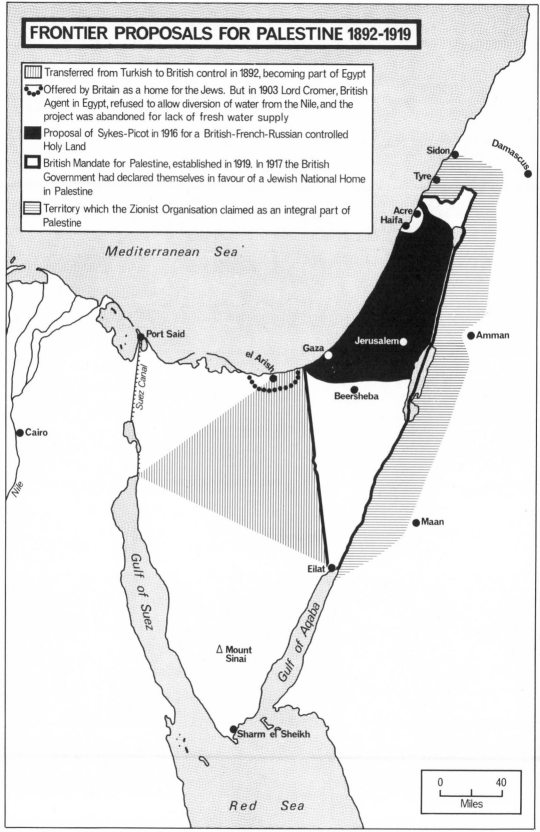

FRONTIER PROPOSALS FOR PALESTINE 1892-1919

Transferred from Turkish to British control in 1892, becoming part of Egypt

Offered by Britain as a home for the Jews. But in 1903 Lord Cromer, British Agent in Egypt, refused to allow diversion of water from the Nile, and the project was abandoned for lack of fresh water supply

Proposal of Sykes-Picot in 1916 for a British-French-Russian controlled Holy Land

British Mandate for Palestine, established in 1919. In 1917 the British Government had declared themselves in favour of a Jewish National Home in Palestine

Territory which the Zionist Organisation claimed as an integral part of Palestine

Mediterranean Sea

Damascus

Sidon

Tyre

Acre
Haifa

Port Said

Suez Canal

el Arish

Gaza

Jerusalem

Amman

Beersheba

Cairo

Nile

Maan

Eilat

Gulf of Suez

Gulf of Aqaba

△ Mount Sinai

Sharm el Sheikh

Red Sea

0   40

Miles

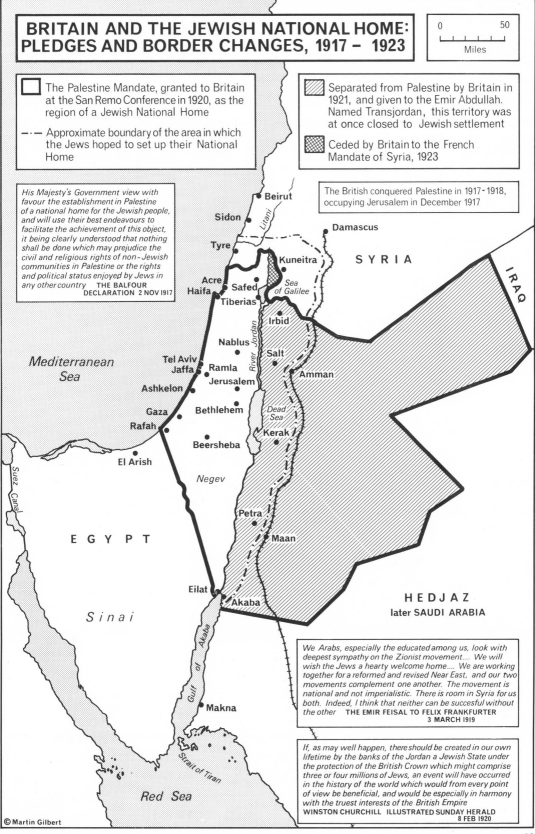

BRITAIN AND THE JEWISH NATIONAL HOME: PLEDGES AND BORDER CHANGES, 1917 – 1923

0   50
Miles

☐ The Palestine Mandate, granted to Britain at the San Remo Conference in 1920, as the region of a Jewish National Home

–·– Approximate boundary of the area in which the Jews hoped to set up their National Home

Separated from Palestine by Britain in 1921, and given to the Emir Abdullah. Named Transjordan, this territory was at once closed to Jewish settlement

Ceded by Britain to the French Mandate of Syria, 1923

His Majesty's Government view with favour the establishment in Palestine of a national home for the Jewish people, and will use their best endeavours to facilitate the achievement of this object, it being clearly understood that nothing shall be done which may prejudice the civil and religious rights of non-Jewish communities in Palestine or the rights and political status enjoyed by Jews in any other country **THE BALFOUR DECLARATION 2 NOV 1917**

The British conquered Palestine in 1917-1918, occupying Jerusalem in December 1917

Mediterranean Sea

Beirut
Sidon
Tyre
Damascus
Kuneitra
S Y R I A
Litani
Acre
Haifa
Safed
Sea of Galilee
Tiberias
Irbid
Nablus
River Jordan
Salt
Tel Aviv
Jaffa
Ramla
Amman
Ashkelon
Jerusalem
Gaza
Bethlehem
Dead Sea
Rafah
Kerak
Beersheba
El Arish
Negev
Petra
Maan
I R A Q

E G Y P T

Suez Canal

Eilat
Akaba
Gulf of Akaba

H E D J A Z
later SAUDI ARABIA

S i n a i

Makna

Strait of Tiran

Red Sea

We Arabs, especially the educated among us, look with deepest sympathy on the Zionist movement.... We will wish the Jews a hearty welcome home.... We are working together for a reformed and revised Near East, and our two movements complement one another. The movement is national and not imperialistic. There is room in Syria for us both. Indeed, I think that neither can be succesful without the other **THE EMIR FEISAL TO FELIX FRANKFURTER 3 MARCH 1919**

If, as may well happen, there should be created in our own lifetime by the banks of the Jordan a Jewish State under the protection of the British Crown which might comprise three or four millions of Jews, an event will have occurred in the history of the world which would from every point of view be beneficial, and would be especially in harmony with the truest interests of the British Empire **WINSTON CHURCHILL ILLUSTRATED SUNDAY HERALD 8 FEB 1920**

© Martin Gilbert

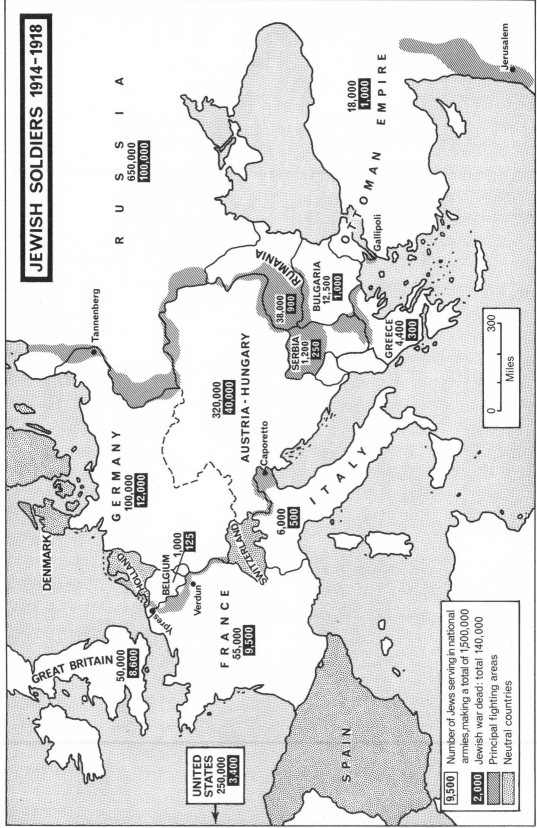

JEWISH SOLDIERS 1914-1918

RUSSIA
650,000
100,000

OTTOMAN EMPIRE
18,000
1,000

Jerusalem

Gallipoli

RUMANIA
38,000
800

BULGARIA
12,500
1,000

SERBIA
1,200
250

GREECE
4,400
300

GERMANY
100,000
12,000

AUSTRIA-HUNGARY
320,000
40,000

Tannenberg

Caporetto

ITALY
6,000
500

DENMARK

HOLLAND

BELGIUM
1,000
125

Ypres

Verdun

SWITZERLAND

FRANCE
55,000
9,500

GREAT BRITAIN
50,000
8,600

SPAIN

UNITED STATES
250,000
3,400

0 — 300
Miles

9,500   Number of Jews serving in national
armies, making a total of 1,500,000
2,000   Jewish war dead: total 140,000
▨   Principal fighting areas
▧   Neutral countries

87

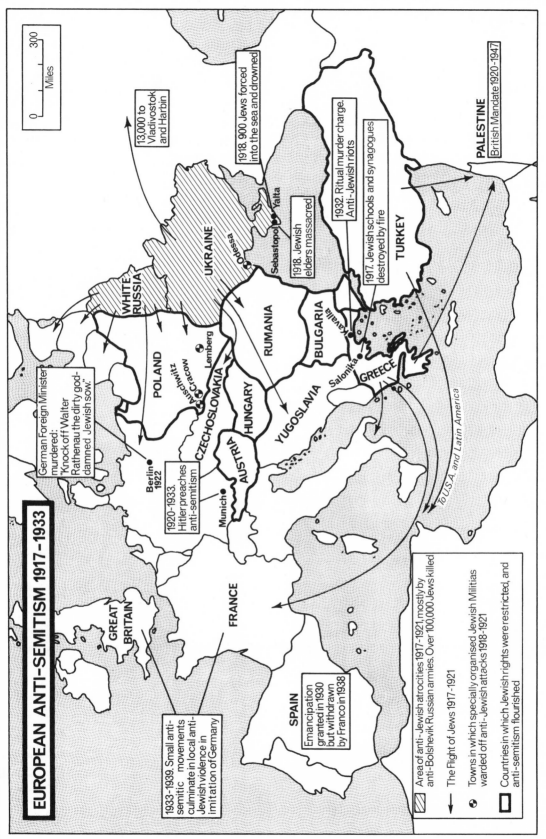

EUROPEAN ANTI-SEMITISM 1917-1933

300

0
Miles

13,000 to
Vladivostok
and Harbin

1918. 900 Jews forced
into the sea and drowned

PALESTINE
British Mandate 1920-1947

1932. Ritual murder charge.
Anti-Jewish riots

1917. Jewish schools and synagogues
destroyed by fire

UKRAINE

Yalta

Odessa

Sebastopol

1918. Jewish
elders massacred

WHITE
RUSSIA

TURKEY

RUMANIA

BULGARIA

Kavalla

German Foreign Minister
murdered:
"Knock off Walter
Rathenau the dirty god-
damned Jewish sow."

POLAND

Lemberg

Cracow
Auschwitz

Salonika

GREECE

YUGOSLAVIA

CZECHOSLOVAKIA

Berlin
1922

1920-1933.
Hitler preaches
anti-semitism

AUSTRIA
HUNGARY

Munich

To U.S.A. and Latin America

GREAT
BRITAIN

FRANCE

1933-1939. Small anti-
semitic movements
culminate in local anti-
Jewish violence in
imitation of Germany

SPAIN

Emancipation
granted in 1930
but withdrawn
by Franco in 1938

Area of anti-Jewish atrocities 1917-1921, mostly by
anti-Bolshevik Russian armies. Over 100,000 Jews killed

The Flight of Jews 1917-1921

Towns in which specially organised Jewish Militias
warded off anti-Jewish attacks 1918-1921

Countries in which Jewish rights were restricted, and
anti-semitism flourished

88

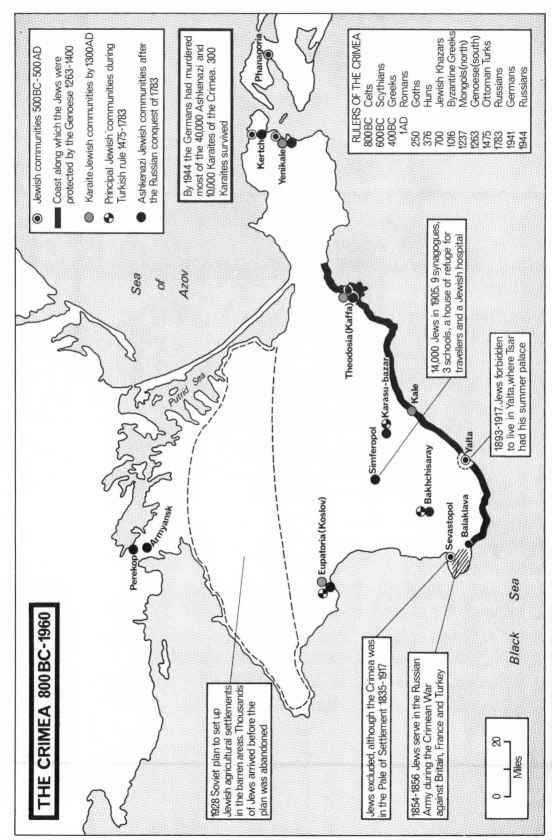

THE CRIMEA 800 BC–1960

Jewish communities 500BC–500AD

Coast along which the Jews were protected by the Genoese 1263–1400

Karaite Jewish communities by 1300AD

Principal Jewish communities during Turkish rule 1475–1783

Ashkenazi Jewish communities after the Russian conquest of 1783

By 1944 the Germans had murdered most of the 40,000 Ashkenazi and 10,000 Karaites of the Crimea. 300 Karaites survived

RULERS OF THE CRIMEA

800BC	Celts
600BC	Scythians
400BC	Greeks
1AD	Romans
250	Goths
376	Huns
700	Jewish Khazars
1016	Byzantine Greeks
1237	Mongols(north)
1263	Genoese(south)
1475	Ottoman Turks
1783	Russians
1941	Germans
1944	Russians

14,000 Jews in 1905. 9 synagogues, 3 schools, a house of refuge for travellers and a Jewish hospital

1893–1917. Jews forbidden to live in Yalta, where Tsar had his summer palace

1928 Soviet plan to set up Jewish agricultural settlements in the barren areas. Thousands of Jews arrived before the plan was abandoned

Jews excluded, although the Crimea was in the Pale of Settlement 1835–1917

1854–1856 Jews serve in the Russian Army during the Crimean War against Britain, France and Turkey

Sea of Azov

Putrid Sea

Phanagoria

Kertch

Yenikale

Theodosia (Kaffa)

Karasu-bazar

Kale

Simferopol

Yalta

Bakhchisaray

Sevastopol

Balaklava

Eupatoria (Koslov)

Perekop

Armyansk

Black Sea

0   20
Miles

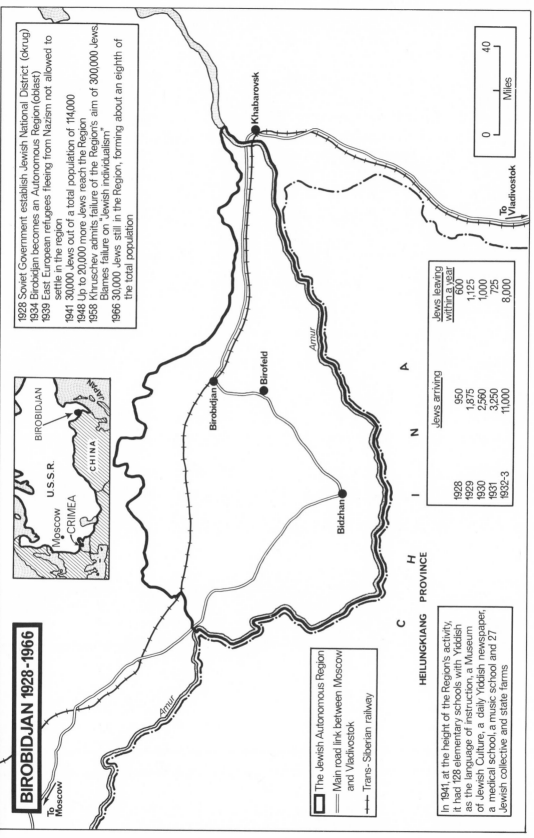

BIROBIDJAN 1928-1966

To Moscow

1928 Soviet Government establish Jewish National District (okrug)
1934 Birobidjan becomes an Autonomous Region (oblast)
1939 East European refugees fleeing from Nazism not allowed to settle in the region
1941 30,000 Jews out of a total population of 114,000
1948 Up to 20,000 more Jews reach the Region
1958 Khruschev admits failure of the Region's aim of 300,000 Jews. Blames failure on "Jewish individualism"
1966 30,000 Jews still in the Region, forming about an eighth of the total population

Moscow • CRIMEA
U.S.S.R.
BIROBIDJAN
CHINA
JAPAN

Khabarovsk

Birobidjan
Birofeld
Bidzhan

Amur

C H I N A

HEILUNGKIANG PROVINCE

To Vladivostok

	Jews arriving	Jews leaving within a year
1928	950	600
1929	1,875	1,125
1930	2,560	1,000
1931	3,250	725
1932-3	11,000	8,000

☐ The Jewish Autonomous Region
═══ Main road link between Moscow and Vladivostok
┼┼┼ Trans-Siberian railway

In 1941, at the height of the Region's activity, it had 128 elementary schools with Yiddish as the language of instruction, a Museum of Jewish Culture, a daily Yiddish newspaper, a medical school, a music school and 27 Jewish collective and state farms

0   40
Miles

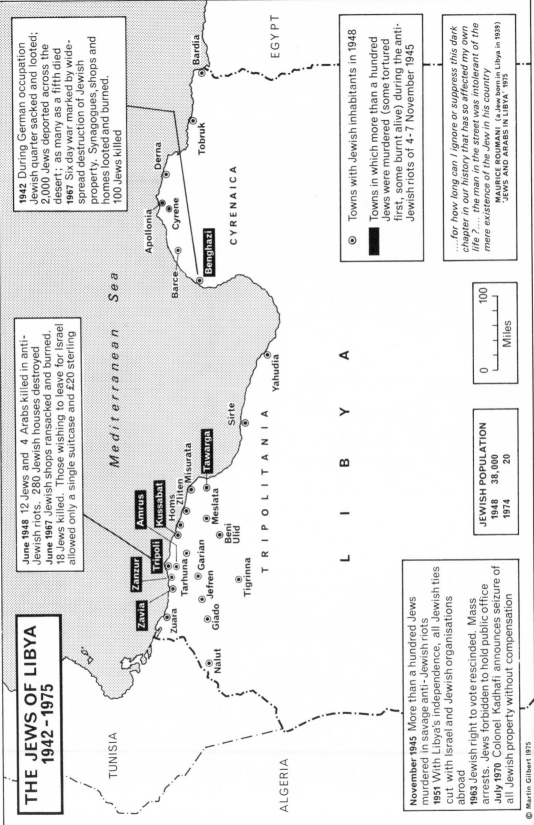

THE JEWS OF LIBYA 1942–1975

1942 During German occupation Jewish quarter sacked and looted; 2,000 Jews deported across the desert; as many as a fifth died **1967** Six day war marked by widespread destruction of Jewish property. Synagogues, shops and homes looted and burned. 100 Jews killed.

June 1948 12 Jews and 4 Arabs killed in anti-Jewish riots. 280 Jewish houses destroyed **June 1967** Jewish shops ransacked and burned. 18 Jews killed. Those wishing to leave for Israel allowed only a single suitcase and £20 sterling

- ◉ Towns with Jewish inhabitants in 1948
- ▮ Towns in which more than a hundred Jews were murdered (some tortured first, some burnt alive) during the anti-Jewish riots of 4–7 November 1945

...for how long can I ignore or suppress this dark chapter in our history that has so affected my own life ?.... the man in the street was intolerant of the mere existence of the Jew in his country
MAURICE ROUMANI (a Jew born in Libya in 1939) **'JEWS AND ARABS IN LIBYA' 1975**

EGYPT

CYRENAICA

Bardia
Tobruk
Derna
Apollonia
Cyrene
Benghazi
Barce

Mediterranean Sea

Zavia **Zanzur** **Tripoli** **Amrus** **Kussabat**
Zuara Homs Zliten
Tarhuna Misurata
Nalut Garian Meslata **Tawarga**
Giado Jefren Beni Ulid
Tigrinna Sirte

Yahudia

L I B Y A

T R I P O L I T A N I A

TUNISIA

ALGERIA

0		100
	Miles	

JEWISH POPULATION	
1948	38,000
1974	20

November 1945 More than a hundred Jews murdered in savage anti-Jewish riots **1951** With Libya's independence, all Jewish ties cut with Israel and Jewish organisations abroad **1963** Jewish right to vote rescinded. Mass arrests. Jews forbidden to hold public office **July 1970** Colonel Kadhafi announces seizure of all Jewish property without compensation

© Martin Gilbert 1975

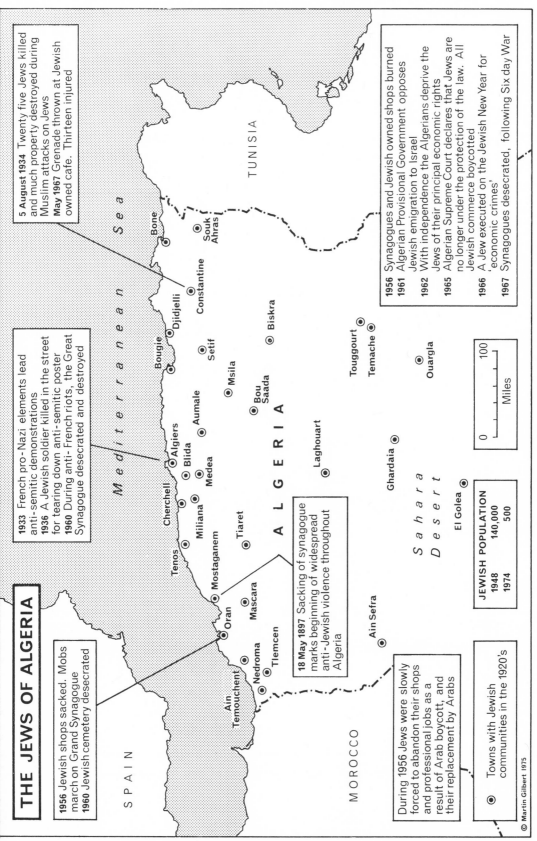

THE JEWS OF ALGERIA

1956 Jewish shops sacked. Mobs march on Grand Synagogue
1960 Jewish cemetery desecrated

5 August 1934 Twenty five Jews killed and much property destroyed during Muslim attacks on Jews
May 1967 Grenade thrown at Jewish owned cafe. Thirteen injured

1933 French pro-Nazi elements lead anti-semitic demonstrations
1936 A Jewish soldier killed in the street for tearing down anti-semitic poster
1960 During anti-French riots, the Great Synagogue desecrated and destroyed

1956 Synagogues and Jewish owned shops burned
1961 Algerian Provisional Government opposes Jewish emigration to Israel
1962 With independence the Algerians deprive the Jews of their principal economic rights
1965 Algerian Supreme Court declares that Jews are no longer under the protection of the law. All Jewish commerce boycotted
1966 A Jew executed on the Jewish New Year for 'economic crimes'
1967 Synagogues desecrated, following Six day War

18 May 1897 Sacking of synagogue marks beginning of widespread anti-Jewish violence throughout Algeria

During 1956 Jews were slowly forced to abandon their shops and professional jobs as a result of Arab boycott, and their replacement by Arabs

JEWISH POPULATION
1948   140,000
1974   500

⊙ Towns with Jewish communities in the 1920's

© Martin Gilbert 1975

TUNISIA

Mediterranean Sea

SPAIN

MOROCCO

A L G E R I A

S a h a r a   D e s e r t

Bone
Souk Ahras
Constantine
Djidjelli
Bougie
Setif
Biskra
Msila
Bou Saada
Aumale
Algiers
Blida
Medea
Cherchell
Miliana
Tiaret
Tenos
Mostaganem
Mascara
Oran
Nedroma
Tlemcen
Ain Temouchent
Ain Sefra
Laghouart
Ghardaia
El Golea
Ouargla
Touggourt
Temache

0   100
Miles

92

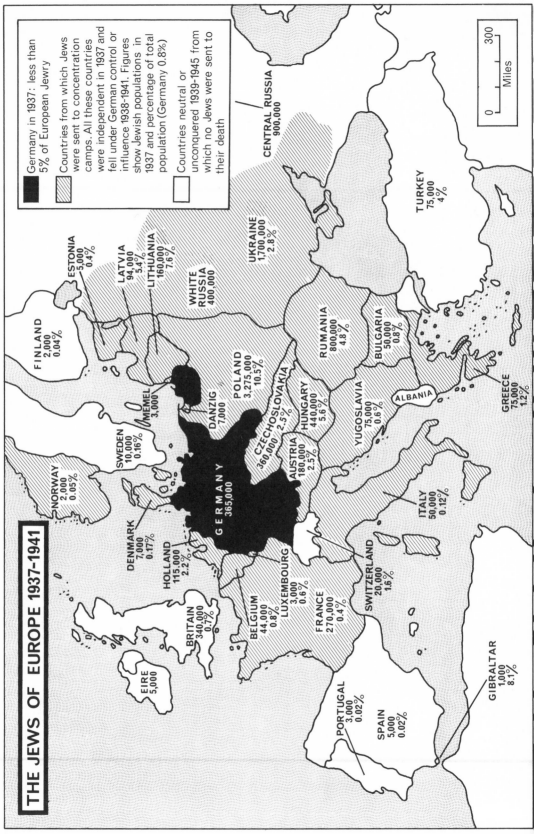

THE JEWS OF EUROPE 1937-1941

Germany in 1937: less than 5% of European Jewry

Countries from which Jews were sent to concentration camps. All these countries were independent in 1937 and fell under German control or influence 1938-1941. Figures show Jewish populations in 1937 and percentage of total population (Germany 0.8%)

Countries neutral or unconquered 1939-1945 from which no Jews were sent to their death

0   300
Miles

CENTRAL RUSSIA
900,000

TURKEY
75,000
4%

ESTONIA
5,000
0.4%

LATVIA
94,000
5.4%

LITHUANIA
160,000
7.6%

UKRAINE
1,700,000
2.8%

FINLAND
2,000
0.04%

WHITE
RUSSIA
400,000

RUMANIA
800,000
4.8%

BULGARIA
50,000
0.8%

POLAND
3,275,000
10.5%

MEMEL
3,000

SWEDEN
10,000
0.16%

DANZIG
7,000

CZECHOSLOVAKIA
360,000 2.5%

HUNGARY
440,000
5.6%

YUGOSLAVIA
75,000
0.6%

ALBANIA

GREECE
75,000
1.2%

NORWAY
2,000
0.05%

AUSTRIA
180,000
2.5%

G E R M A N Y
365,000

DENMARK
7,000
0.17%

HOLLAND
115,000
2.2%

LUXEMBOURG
3,000
0.6%

SWITZERLAND
20,000
1.6%

ITALY
50,000
0.12%

BELGIUM
44,000
0.8%

FRANCE
270,000
0.4%

BRITAIN
340,000
0.7%

EIRE
5,000

GIBRALTAR
1,000
8.1%

PORTUGAL
3,000
0.02%

SPAIN
5,000
0.02%

93

THE VOYAGE OF THE "ST. LOUIS" MAY-JUNE 1939

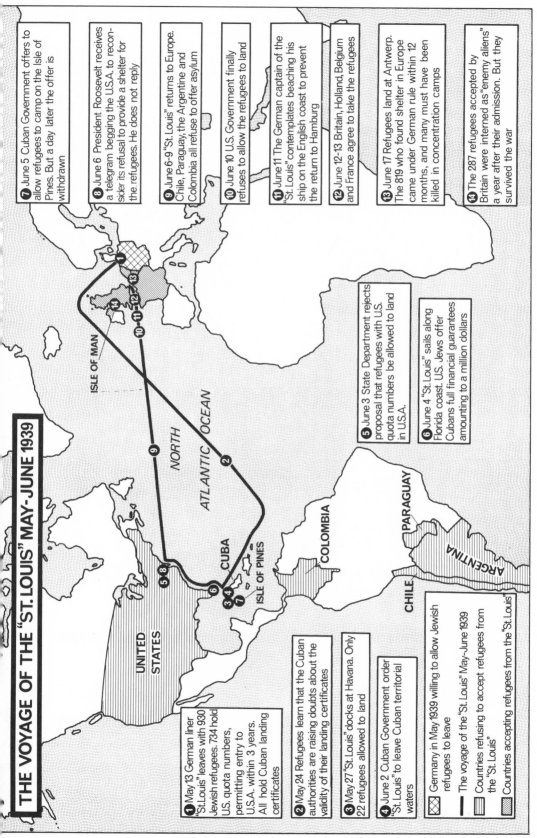

1 May 13 German liner "St. Louis" leaves with 930 Jewish refugees. 734 hold U.S. quota numbers, permitting entry to U.S.A. within 3 years. All hold Cuban landing certificates

2 May 24 Refugees learn that the Cuban authorities are raising doubts about the validity of their landing certificates

3 May 27 "St. Louis" docks at Havana. Only 22 refugees allowed to land

4 June 2 Cuban Government order "St. Louis" to leave Cuban territorial waters

5 June 3 State Department rejects proposal that refugees with U.S. quota numbers be allowed to land in U.S.A.

6 June 4 "St. Louis" sails along Florida coast. U.S. Jews offer Cubans full financial guarantees amounting to a million dollars

7 June 5 Cuban Government offers to allow refugees to camp on the Isle of Pines. But a day later the offer is withdrawn

8 June 6 President Roosevelt receives a telegram begging the U.S.A. to reconsider its refusal to provide a shelter for the refugees. He does not reply

9 June 6-9 "St. Louis" returns to Europe. Chile, Paraguay, the Argentine and Colombia all refuse to offer asylum

10 June 10 U.S. Government finally refuses to allow the refugees to land

11 June 11 The German captain of the "St. Louis" contemplates beaching his ship on the English coast to prevent the return to Hamburg

12 June 12-13 Britain, Holland, Belgium and France agree to take the refugees

13 June 17 Refugees land at Antwerp. The 819 who found shelter in Europe came under German rule within 12 months, and many must have been killed in concentration camps

14 The 287 refugees accepted by Britain were interned as "enemy aliens" a year after their admission. But they survived the war

⊠ Germany in May 1939 willing to allow Jewish refugees to leave

— The voyage of the "St. Louis" May-June 1939

▨ Countries refusing to accept refugees from the "St. Louis"

▨ Countries accepting refugees from the "St. Louis"

ISLE OF MAN

NORTH ATLANTIC OCEAN

UNITED STATES

CUBA

ISLE OF PINES

COLOMBIA

CHILE

PARAGUAY

ARGENTINA

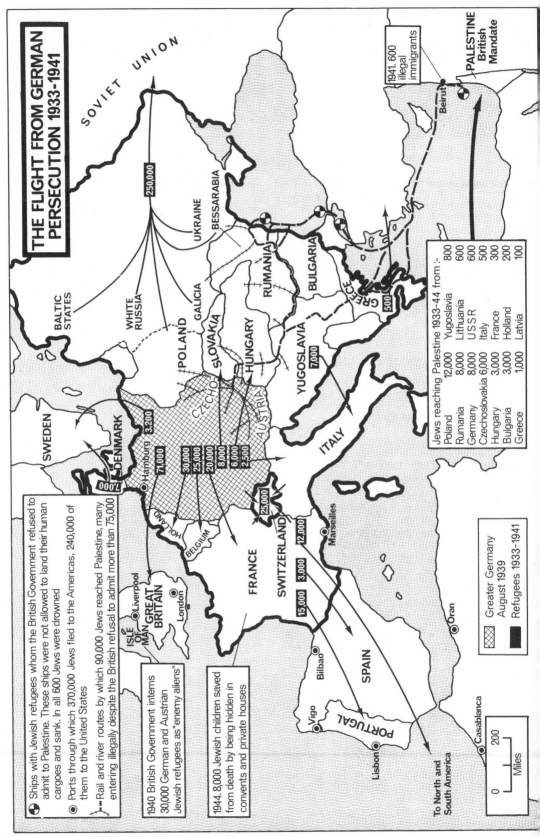

THE FLIGHT FROM GERMAN PERSECUTION 1933-1941

SOVIET UNION

250,000

UKRAINE

BESSARABIA

BALTIC STATES

WHITE RUSSIA

GALICIA

POLAND

SLOVAKIA

CZECHO-

AUSTRIA

HUNGARY

RUMANIA

BULGARIA

GREECE

500

YUGOSLAVIA

7,000

ITALY

1941. 600 illegal immigrants

PALESTINE British Mandate

Beirut

Jews reaching Palestine 1933-44 from :-

Poland	12,000	Yugoslavia	800
Rumania	8,000	Lithuania	600
Germany	8,000	USSR	600
Czechoslovakia	6,000	Italy	500
Hungary	3,000	France	300
Bulgaria	3,000	Holland	200
Greece	1,000	Latvia	100

SWEDEN

DENMARK

7,000

Hamburg 3,200

71,000

30,000

25,000

20,000

8,000

6,000

2,500

HOLLAND

BELGIUM

FRANCE

SWITZERLAND

25,000

12,000

3,000

15,000

Marseilles

GREAT BRITAIN

ISLE OF MAN

Liverpool

London

SPAIN

PORTUGAL

Bilbao

Vigo

Lisbon

Oran

Casablanca

To North and South America

Ships with Jewish refugees whom the British Government refused to admit to Palestine. These ships were not allowed to land their human cargoes and sank. In all 600 Jews were drowned

Ports through which 370,000 Jews fled to the Americas, 240,000 of them to the United States

Rail and river routes by which 90,000 Jews reached Palestine, many entering illegally despite the British refusal to admit more than 75,000

1940 British Government interns 30,000 German and Austrian Jewish refugees as "enemy aliens"

1944. 8,000 Jewish children saved from death by being hidden in convents and private houses

Greater Germany August 1939

Refugees 1933-1941

0   200

Miles

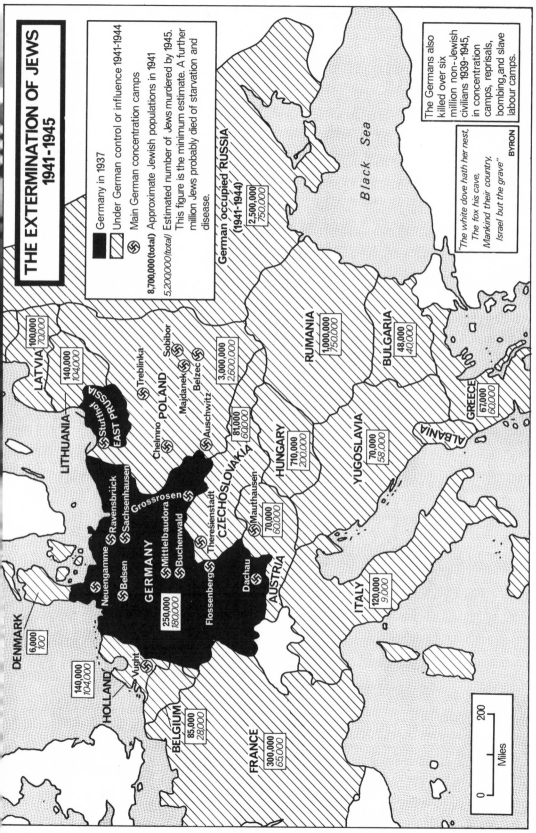

THE EXTERMINATION OF JEWS 1941-1945

■ Germany in 1937

▨ Under German control or influence 1941-1944

卐 Main German concentration camps

8,700,000(total) Approximate Jewish populations in 1941

5,200,000(total) Estimated number of Jews murdered by 1945. This figure is the minimum estimate. A further million Jews probably died of starvation and disease.

German occupied 'RUSSIA'
(1941-1944)
2,500,000
750,000

The Germans also killed over six million non-Jewish civilians 1939-1945, in concentration camps, reprisals, bombing, and slave labour camps.

"The white dove hath her nest,
The fox his cave,
Mankind their country,
Israel but the grave"
BYRON

LATVIA **100,000** *70,000*

140,000 *104,000*

卐 Treblinka

Sobibor 卐

POLAND
Chelmno 卐
Majdanek 卐
Belzec
卐 Auschwitz

3,000,000
2,600,000

EAST PRUSSIA
Stutthof 卐

LITHUANIA

RUMANIA **1,000,000** *750,000*

BULGARIA **48,000** *40,000*

GREECE **67,000** *60,000*

ALBANIA

卐 Grossrosen

Ravensbrück 卐
Sachsenhausen 卐

Neuengamme 卐
Belsen 卐

GERMANY

Mittelbaudora 卐
Buchenwald 卐

Flossenberg 卐

Dachau 卐

Theresienstadt 卐
CZECHOSLOVAKIA

Mauthausen 卐

AUSTRIA

HUNGARY **710,000** *200,000*

81,000 *60,000*

70,000 *60,000*

YUGOSLAVIA **70,000** *58,000*

DENMARK **6,000** *100*

HOLLAND **140,000** *104,000*

Vught 卐

BELGIUM **85,000** *28,000*

FRANCE **300,000** *65,000*

ITALY **120,000** *9,000*

Black Sea

0   200
Miles

96

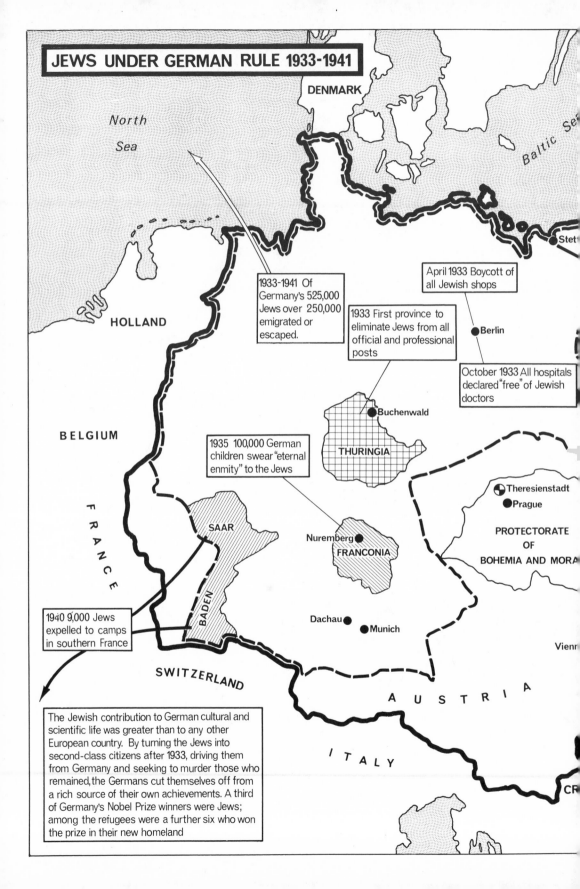

JEWS UNDER GERMAN RULE 1933-1941

DENMARK

North
Sea

Baltic Se

Stet

HOLLAND

1933-1941 Of Germany's 525,000 Jews over 250,000 emigrated or escaped.

April 1933 Boycott of all Jewish shops

1933 First province to eliminate Jews from all official and professional posts

Berlin

October 1933 All hospitals declared "free" of Jewish doctors

BELGIUM

Buchenwald

THURINGIA

1935 100,000 German children swear "eternal enmity" to the Jews

Theresienstadt
Prague

FRANCE

SAAR

Nuremberg
FRANCONIA

PROTECTORATE
OF
BOHEMIA AND MORA

1940 9,000 Jews expelled to camps in southern France

BADEN

Dachau
Munich

Vienr

SWITZERLAND

AUSTRIA

The Jewish contribution to German cultural and scientific life was greater than to any other European country. By turning the Jews into second-class citizens after 1933, driving them from Germany and seeking to murder those who remained, the Germans cut themselves off from a rich source of their own achievements. A third of Germany's Nobel Prize winners were Jews; among the refugees were a further six who won the prize in their new homeland

ITALY

CR

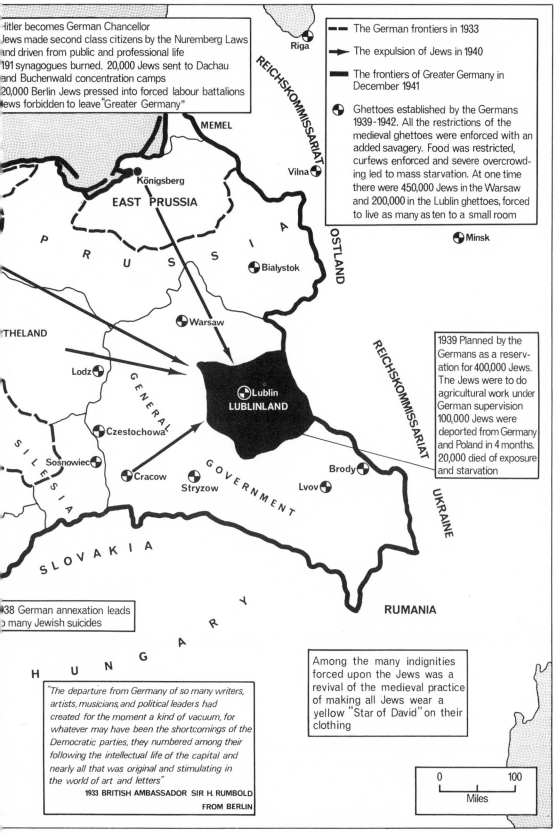

Hitler becomes German Chancellor
Jews made second class citizens by the Nuremberg Laws
and driven from public and professional life
191 synagogues burned. 20,000 Jews sent to Dachau
and Buchenwald concentration camps
20,000 Berlin Jews pressed into forced labour battalions
Jews forbidden to leave "Greater Germany"

Riga

REICHSKOMMISSARIAT

---- The German frontiers in 1933

→ The expulsion of Jews in 1940

━━ The frontiers of Greater Germany in
December 1941

✛ Ghettoes established by the Germans
1939-1942. All the restrictions of the
medieval ghettoes were enforced with an
added savagery. Food was restricted,
curfews enforced and severe overcrowd-
ing led to mass starvation. At one time
there were 450,000 Jews in the Warsaw
and 200,000 in the Lublin ghettoes, forced
to live as many as ten to a small room

MEMEL

Vilna ✛

Königsberg

EAST PRUSSIA

✛ Minsk

P R U S S I A

OSTLAND

✛ Bialystok

✛ Warsaw

RTHELAND

Lodz ✛

G E N E R A L

Lublin ✛
LUBLINLAND

REICHSKOMMISSARIAT

1939 Planned by the
Germans as a reserv-
ation for 400,000 Jews.
The Jews were to do
agricultural work under
German supervision
100,000 Jews were
deported from Germany
and Poland in 4 months.
20,000 died of exposure
and starvation

S I L E S I A

✛ Czestochowa

Sosnowiec ✛

✛ Cracow
Stryzow

G O V E R N M E N T

Brody ✛

Lvov ✛

UKRAINE

S L O V A K I A

RUMANIA

38 German annexation leads
to many Jewish suicides

H U N G A R Y

"The departure from Germany of so many writers,
artists, musicians, and political leaders had
created for the moment a kind of vacuum, for
whatever may have been the shortcomings of the
Democratic parties, they numbered among their
following the intellectual life of the capital and
nearly all that was original and stimulating in
the world of art and letters"
1933 BRITISH AMBASSADOR SIR H. RUMBOLD
FROM BERLIN

Among the many indignities
forced upon the Jews was a
revival of the medieval practice
of making all Jews wear a
yellow "Star of David" on their
clothing

0   100
Miles

THE SEARCH FOR SAFETY 1933-1945

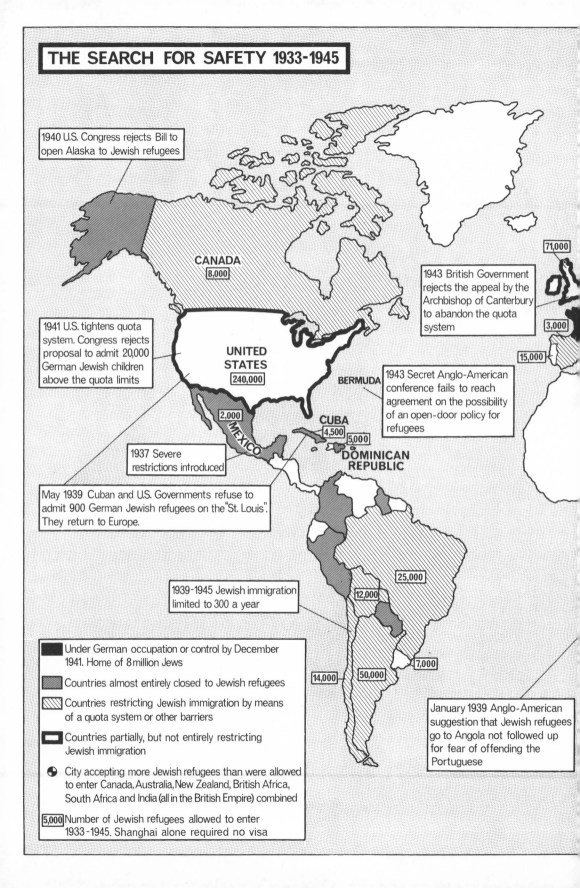

1940 U.S. Congress rejects Bill to open Alaska to Jewish refugees

CANADA
8,000

1943 British Government rejects the appeal by the Archbishop of Canterbury to abandon the quota system

71,000

3,000

1941 U.S. tightens quota system. Congress rejects proposal to admit 20,000 German Jewish children above the quota limits

UNITED STATES
240,000

15,000

BERMUDA

1943 Secret Anglo-American conference fails to reach agreement on the possibility of an open-door policy for refugees

2,000
MEXICO

CUBA
4,500 **5,000**

DOMINICAN REPUBLIC

1937 Severe restrictions introduced

May 1939 Cuban and U.S. Governments refuse to admit 900 German Jewish refugees on the "St. Louis". They return to Europe.

25,000

12,000

1939-1945 Jewish immigration limited to 300 a year

14,000 **50,000** **7,000**

Under German occupation or control by December 1941. Home of 8 million Jews

Countries almost entirely closed to Jewish refugees

Countries restricting Jewish immigration by means of a quota system or other barriers

Countries partially, but not entirely restricting Jewish immigration

✚ City accepting more Jewish refugees than were allowed to enter Canada, Australia, New Zealand, British Africa, South Africa and India (all in the British Empire) combined

5,000 Number of Jewish refugees allowed to enter 1933-1945. Shanghai alone required no visa

January 1939 Anglo-American suggestion that Jewish refugees go to Angola not followed up for fear of offending the Portuguese

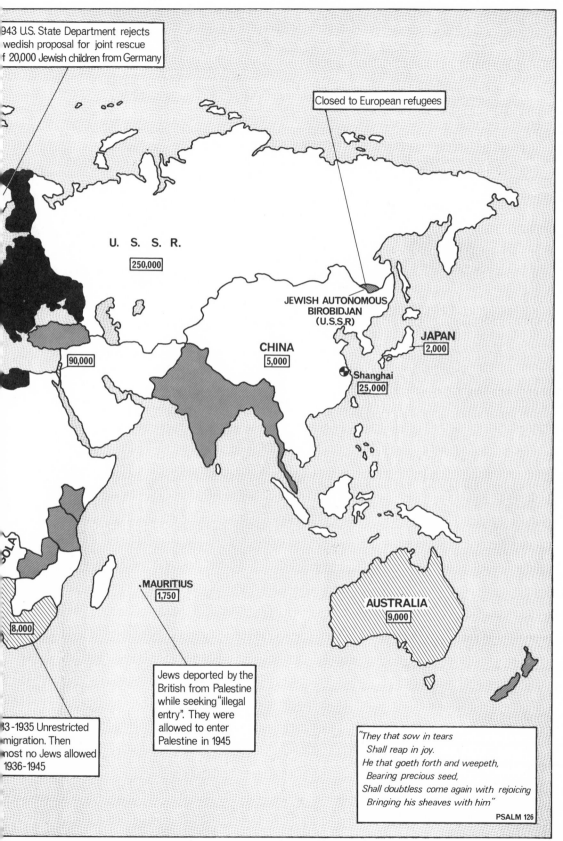

1943 U.S. State Department rejects
wedish proposal for joint rescue
f 20,000 Jewish children from Germany

Closed to European refugees

U. S. S. R.
250,000

JEWISH AUTONOMOUS
BIROBIDJAN
(U.S.S.R)

90,000

CHINA
5,000

JAPAN
2,000

Shanghai
25,000

OLA

8,000

MAURITIUS
1,750

AUSTRALIA
9,000

Jews deported by the
British from Palestine
while seeking "illegal
entry". They were
allowed to enter
Palestine in 1945

33-1935 Unrestricted
migration. Then
nost no Jews allowed
1936-1945

"They that sow in tears
  Shall reap in joy.
He that goeth forth and weepeth,
  Bearing precious seed,
Shall doubtless come again with rejoicing
  Bringing his sheaves with him"

PSALM 126

98

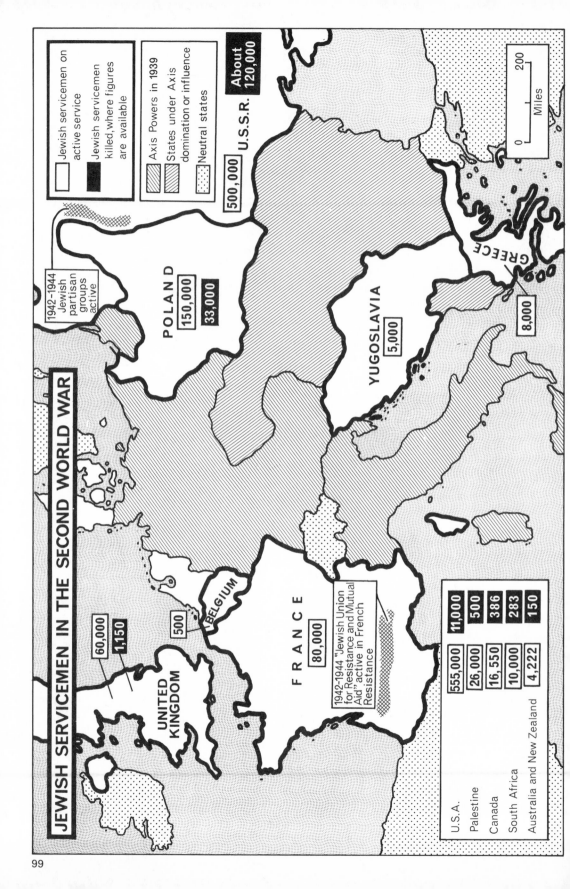

JEWISH SERVICEMEN IN THE SECOND WORLD WAR

| Jewish servicemen on active service |
| Jewish servicemen killed, where figures are available |

| Axis Powers in 1939 |
| States under Axis domination or influence |
| Neutral states |

1942–1944 Jewish partisan groups active

U.S.S.R.
500,000
About 120,000

POLAND
150,000
33,000

YUGOSLAVIA
5,000

GREECE
8,000

UNITED KINGDOM
60,000
1,150

BELGIUM
500

FRANCE
80,000

1942–1944 "Jewish Union for Resistance and Mutual Aid" active in French Resistance

U.S.A.	555,000	11,000
Palestine	26,000	500
Canada	16,550	386
South Africa	10,000	283
Australia and New Zealand	4,222	150

0   200
Miles

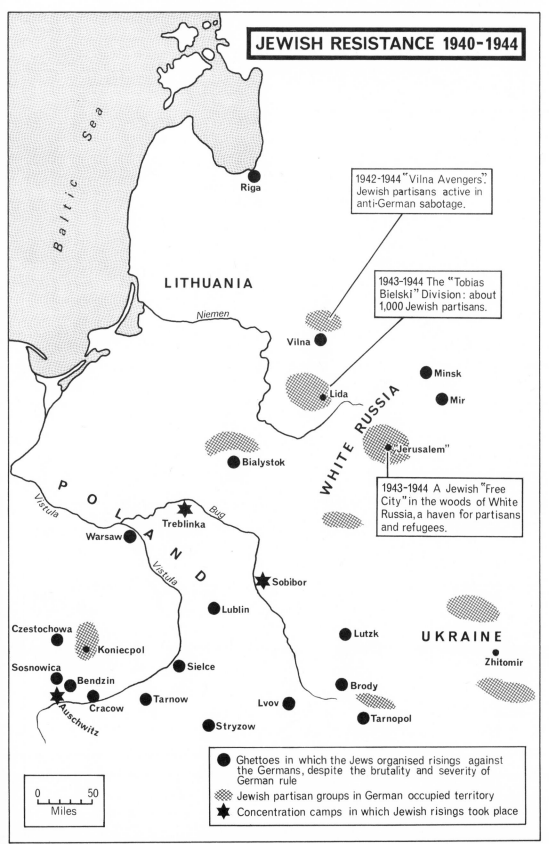

JEWISH RESISTANCE 1940-1944

Baltic Sea

Riga

1942-1944 "Vilna Avengers". Jewish partisans active in anti-German sabotage.

LITHUANIA

Niemen

1943-1944 The "Tobias Bielski" Division: about 1,000 Jewish partisans.

Vilna

Minsk

Lida

Mir

WHITE RUSSIA

"Jerusalem"

Bialystok

1943-1944 A Jewish "Free City" in the woods of White Russia, a haven for partisans and refugees.

P O L A N D

Vistula

Bug

Treblinka

Warsaw

Vistula

Sobibor

Lublin

Lutzk

UKRAINE

Czestochowa

Koniecpol

Zhitomir

Sosnowica

Bendzin

Sielce

Brody

Auschwitz

Cracow

Tarnow

Lvov

Tarnopol

Stryzow

● Ghettoes in which the Jews organised risings against the Germans, despite the brutality and severity of German rule

▓ Jewish partisan groups in German occupied territory

★ Concentration camps in which Jewish risings took place

0   50
Miles

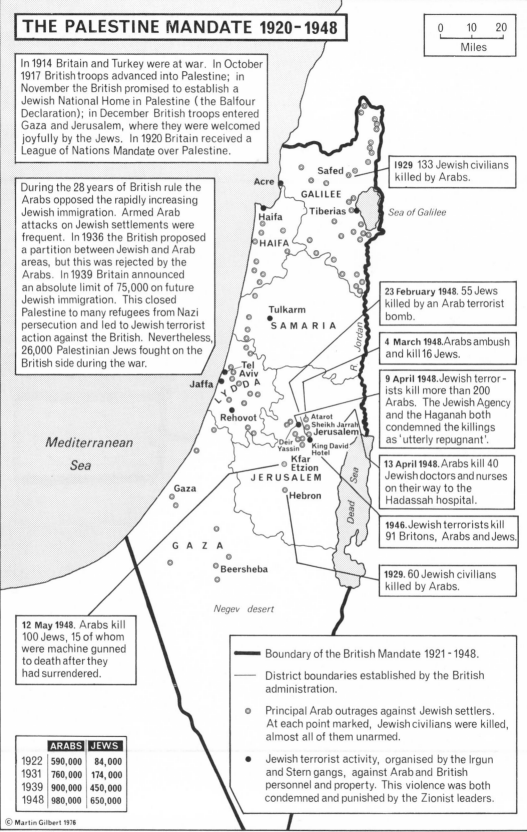

THE PALESTINE MANDATE 1920-1948

0	10	20

Miles

In 1914 Britain and Turkey were at war. In October 1917 British troops advanced into Palestine; in November the British promised to establish a Jewish National Home in Palestine (the Balfour Declaration); in December British troops entered Gaza and Jerusalem, where they were welcomed joyfully by the Jews. In 1920 Britain received a League of Nations Mandate over Palestine.

During the 28 years of British rule the Arabs opposed the rapidly increasing Jewish immigration. Armed Arab attacks on Jewish settlements were frequent. In 1936 the British proposed a partition between Jewish and Arab areas, but this was rejected by the Arabs. In 1939 Britain announced an absolute limit of 75,000 on future Jewish immigration. This closed Palestine to many refugees from Nazi persecution and led to Jewish terrorist action against the British. Nevertheless, 26,000 Palestinian Jews fought on the British side during the war.

1929 133 Jewish civilians killed by Arabs.

Safed
Acre
GALILEE
Tiberias
Haifa · Sea of Galilee
HAIFA

Tulkarm
SAMARIA

23 February 1948. 55 Jews killed by an Arab terrorist bomb.

4 March 1948. Arabs ambush and kill 16 Jews.

9 April 1948. Jewish terror-ists kill more than 200 Arabs. The Jewish Agency and the Haganah both condemned the killings as 'utterly repugnant'.

R. Jordan

Tel Aviv
Jaffa
LYDDA
Rehovot

Atarot
Sheikh Jarrah
Jerusalem
Deir Yassin · King David Hotel

13 April 1948. Arabs kill 40 Jewish doctors and nurses on their way to the Hadassah hospital.

Kfar Etzion
JERUSALEM
Hebron

Dead Sea

1946. Jewish terrorists kill 91 Britons, Arabs and Jews.

Gaza

GAZA

Beersheba

1929. 60 Jewish civilians killed by Arabs.

Mediterranean Sea

Negev desert

12 May 1948. Arabs kill 100 Jews, 15 of whom were machine gunned to death after they had surrendered.

— Boundary of the British Mandate 1921-1948.

— District boundaries established by the British administration.

◎ Principal Arab outrages against Jewish settlers. At each point marked, Jewish civilians were killed, almost all of them unarmed.

● Jewish terrorist activity, organised by the Irgun and Stern gangs, against Arab and British personnel and property. This violence was both condemned and punished by the Zionist leaders.

	ARABS	JEWS
1922	590,000	84,000
1931	760,000	174,000
1939	900,000	450,000
1948	980,000	650,000

© Martin Gilbert 1976

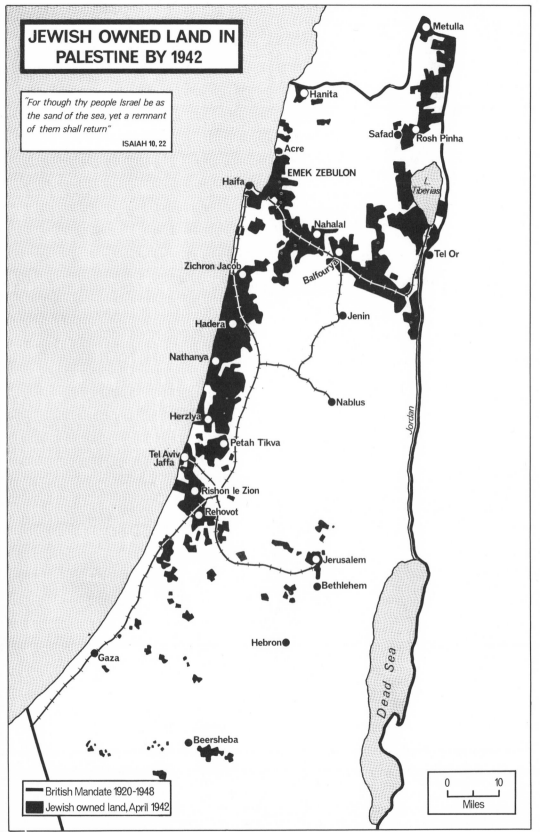

JEWISH OWNED LAND IN PALESTINE BY 1942

"For though thy people Israel be as the sand of the sea, yet a remnant of them shall return"

ISAIAH 10, 22

Metulla

Hanita

Safad

Rosh Pinha

Acre

EMEK ZEBULON

L. Tiberias

Haifa

Nahalal

Zichron Jacob

Tel Or

Balfourya

Jenin

Hadera

Nathanya

Nablus

Herzlya

Petah Tikva

Tel Aviv
Jaffa

Rishon le Zion

Rehovot

Jerusalem

Bethlehem

Hebron

Jordan

Dead Sea

Gaza

Beersheba

British Mandate 1920-1948

Jewish owned land, April 1942

0   10
Miles

102

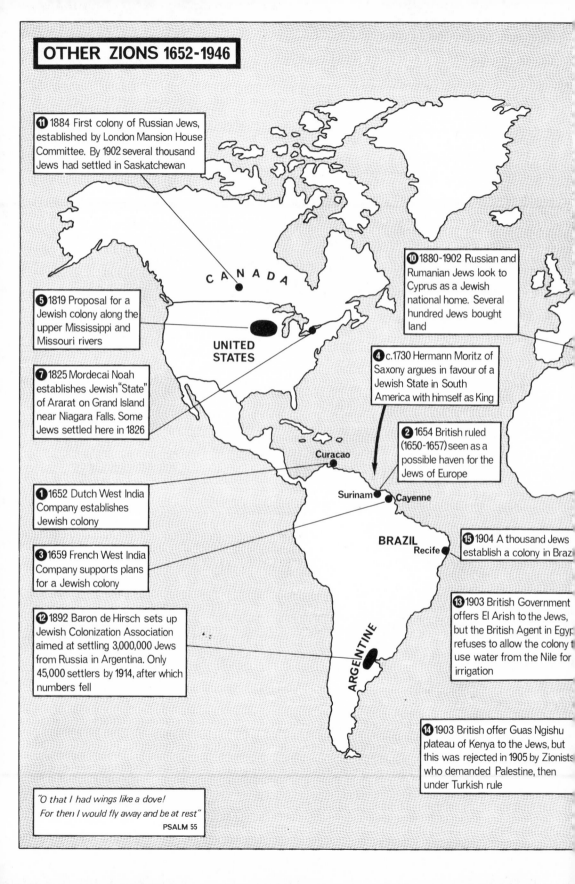

OTHER ZIONS 1652-1946

11 1884 First colony of Russian Jews, established by London Mansion House Committee. By 1902 several thousand Jews had settled in Saskatchewan

10 1880-1902 Russian and Rumanian Jews look to Cyprus as a Jewish national home. Several hundred Jews bought land

5 1819 Proposal for a Jewish colony along the upper Mississippi and Missouri rivers

7 1825 Mordecai Noah establishes Jewish "State" of Ararat on Grand Island near Niagara Falls. Some Jews settled here in 1826

4 c.1730 Hermann Moritz of Saxony argues in favour of a Jewish State in South America with himself as King

2 1654 British ruled (1650-1657) seen as a possible haven for the Jews of Europe

1 1652 Dutch West India Company establishes Jewish colony

3 1659 French West India Company supports plans for a Jewish colony

15 1904 A thousand Jews establish a colony in Brazi

12 1892 Baron de Hirsch sets up Jewish Colonization Association aimed at settling 3,000,000 Jews from Russia in Argentina. Only 45,000 settlers by 1914, after which numbers fell

13 1903 British Government offers El Arish to the Jews, but the British Agent in Egyp refuses to allow the colony t use water from the Nile for irrigation

14 1903 British offer Guas Ngishu plateau of Kenya to the Jews, but this was rejected in 1905 by Zionists who demanded Palestine, then under Turkish rule

CANADA

UNITED STATES

Curacao

Surinam   Cayenne

BRAZIL
Recife

ARGENTINE

"O that I had wings like a dove!
For then I would fly away and be at rest"
PSALM 55

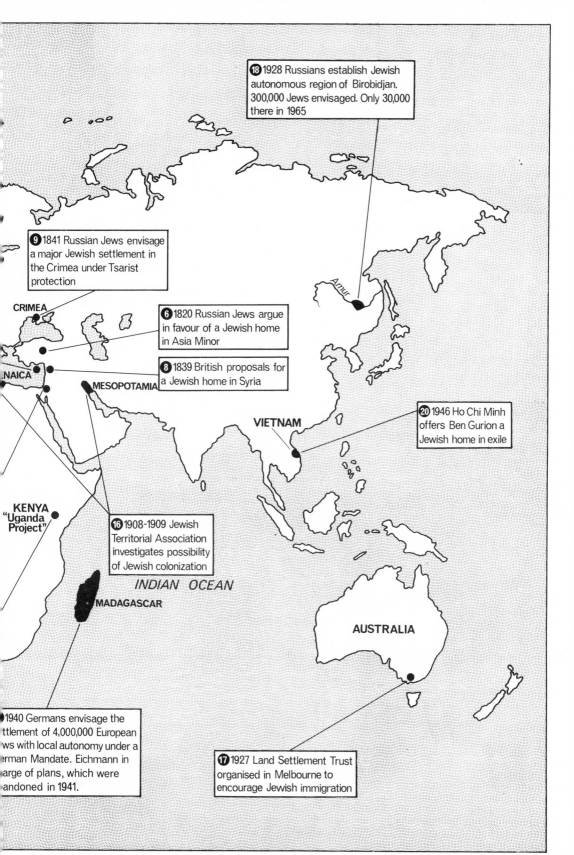

18 1928 Russians establish Jewish autonomous region of Birobidjan. 300,000 Jews envisaged. Only 30,000 there in 1965

9 1841 Russian Jews envisage a major Jewish settlement in the Crimea under Tsarist protection

CRIMEA

6 1820 Russian Jews argue in favour of a Jewish home in Asia Minor

8 1839 British proposals for a Jewish home in Syria

NAICA

MESOPOTAMIA

Amur

VIETNAM

20 1946 Ho Chi Minh offers Ben Gurion a Jewish home in exile

KENYA "Uganda Project"

16 1908-1909 Jewish Territorial Association investigates possibility of Jewish colonization

INDIAN OCEAN

MADAGASCAR

AUSTRALIA

1940 Germans envisage the ttlement of 4,000,000 European ws with local autonomy under a rman Mandate. Eichmann in arge of plans, which were andoned in 1941.

17 1927 Land Settlement Trust organised in Melbourne to encourage Jewish immigration

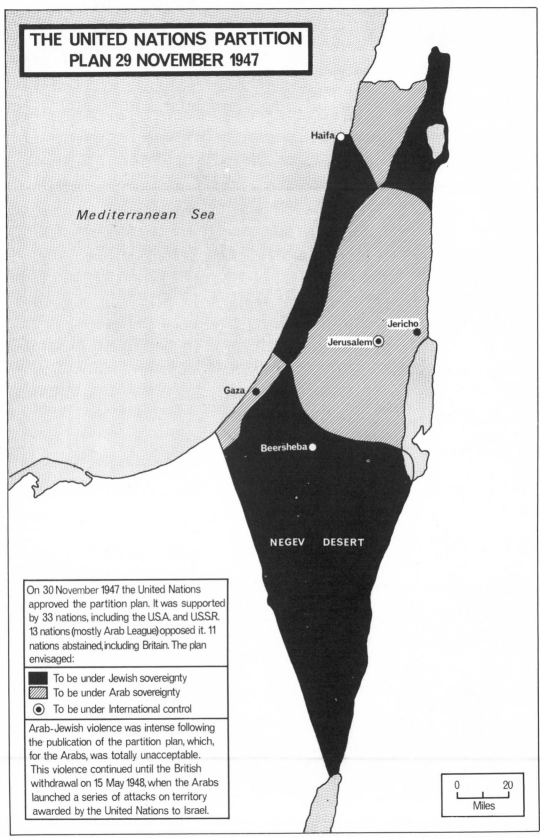

THE UNITED NATIONS PARTITION PLAN 29 NOVEMBER 1947

Mediterranean Sea

Haifa

Jericho

Jerusalem

Gaza

Beersheba

NEGEV   DESERT

On 30 November 1947 the United Nations
approved the partition plan. It was supported
by 33 nations, including the U.S.A. and U.S.S.R.
13 nations (mostly Arab League) opposed it. 11
nations abstained, including Britain. The plan
envisaged:

To be under Jewish sovereignty
To be under Arab sovereignty
To be under International control

Arab-Jewish violence was intense following
the publication of the partition plan, which,
for the Arabs, was totally unacceptable.
This violence continued until the British
withdrawal on 15 May 1948, when the Arabs
launched a series of attacks on territory
awarded by the United Nations to Israel.

0   20
Miles

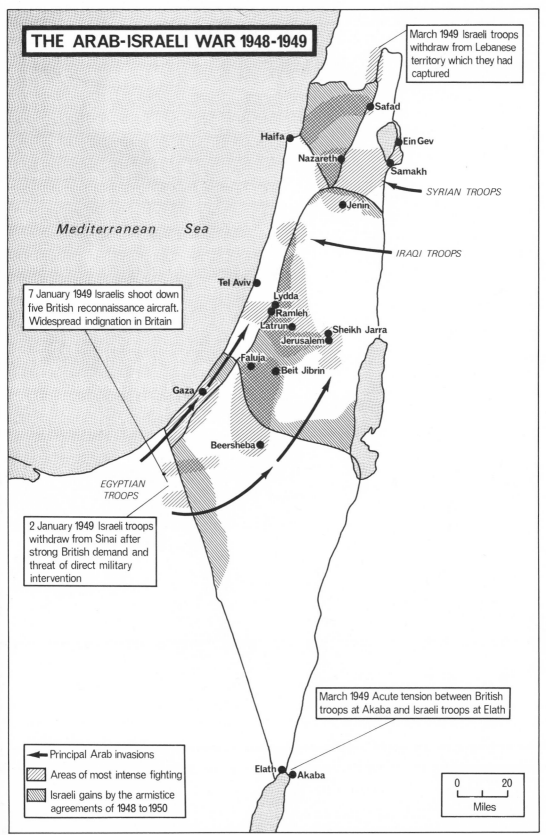

THE ARAB-ISRAELI WAR 1948-1949

March 1949 Israeli troops withdraw from Lebanese territory which they had captured

Safad

Ein Gev

Haifa

Nazareth

Samakh

SYRIAN TROOPS

Jenin

Mediterranean Sea

IRAQI TROOPS

Tel Aviv

7 January 1949 Israelis shoot down five British reconnaissance aircraft. Widespread indignation in Britain

Lydda

Ramleh

Latrun

Sheikh Jarra

Jerusalem

Faluja

Beit Jibrin

Gaza

Beersheba

EGYPTIAN TROOPS

2 January 1949 Israeli troops withdraw from Sinai after strong British demand and threat of direct military intervention

March 1949 Acute tension between British troops at Akaba and Israeli troops at Elath

Elath   Akaba

Principal Arab invasions

Areas of most intense fighting

Israeli gains by the armistice agreements of 1948 to 1950

0   20
Miles

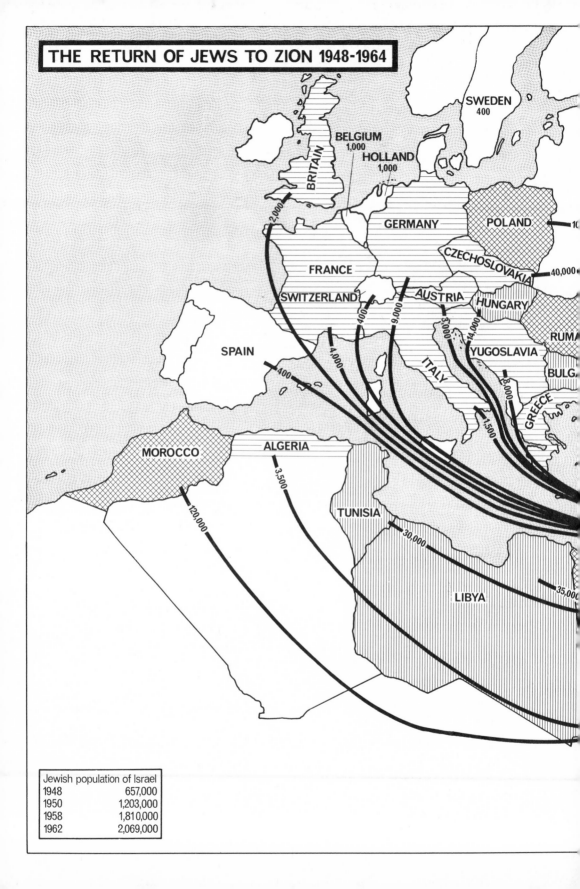

THE RETURN OF JEWS TO ZION 1948-1964

SWEDEN
400

BRITAIN

BELGIUM
1,000

HOLLAND
1,000

GERMANY

POLAND

CZECHOSLOVAKIA

FRANCE

SWITZERLAND

AUSTRIA

HUNGARY

RUMA

YUGOSLAVIA

BULG.

ITALY

GREECE

SPAIN

2,000

400

9,000

3,000

14,000

8,000

4,000

11,500

400

MOROCCO

ALGERIA

3,500

TUNISIA

30,000

35,000

120,000

LIBYA

Jewish population of Israel	
1948	657,000
1950	1,203,000
1958	1,810,000
1962	2,069,000

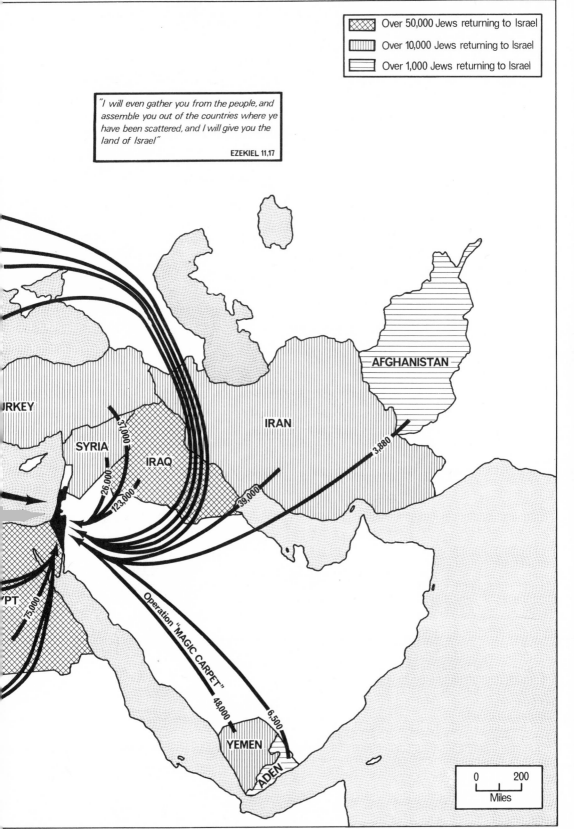

Over 50,000 Jews returning to Israel

Over 10,000 Jews returning to Israel

Over 1,000 Jews returning to Israel

"I will even gather you from the people, and assemble you out of the countries where ye have been scattered, and I will give you the land of Israel"

EZEKIEL 11,17

AFGHANISTAN

IRAN

URKEY

SYRIA

IRAQ

31,000

26,000

123,000

39,000

3,880

PT

75,000

Operation "MAGIC CARPET"

48,000

6,500

YEMEN

ADEN

0   200
Miles

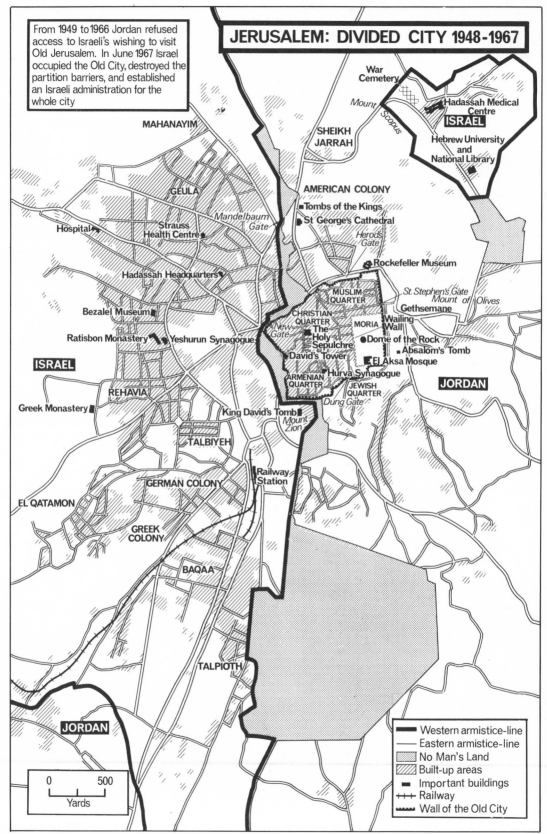

JERUSALEM: DIVIDED CITY 1948-1967

From 1949 to 1966 Jordan refused access to Israeli's wishing to visit Old Jerusalem. In June 1967 Israel occupied the Old City, destroyed the partition barriers, and established an Israeli administration for the whole city

War Cemetery

Mount Scopus

ISRAEL

Hadassah Medical Centre

Hebrew University and National Library

MAHANAYIM

SHEIKH JARRAH

AMERICAN COLONY

GEULA

Mandelbaum Gate

Tombs of the Kings

St George's Cathedral

Herods Gate

Hospital

Strauss Health Centre

Rockefeller Museum

Hadassah Headquarters

MUSLIM QUARTER

St. Stephen's Gate
Mount of Olives

Gethsemane

Bezalel Museum

CHRISTIAN QUARTER

Wailing Wall

MORIA

Ratisbon Monastery

Yeshurun Synagogue

New Gate

The Holy Sepulchre

Dome of the Rock

Absalom's Tomb

ISRAEL

David's Tower

El Aksa Mosque

REHAVIA

Hurva Synagogue

ARMENIAN QUARTER

JEWISH QUARTER

JORDAN

Greek Monastery

King David's Tomb

Dung Gate

Mount Zion

TALBIYEH

Railway Station

GERMAN COLONY

EL QATAMON

GREEK COLONY

BAQAA

TALPIOTH

JORDAN

0   500
Yards

Western armistice-line
Eastern armistice-line
No Man's Land
Built-up areas
Important buildings
Railway
Wall of the Old City

107

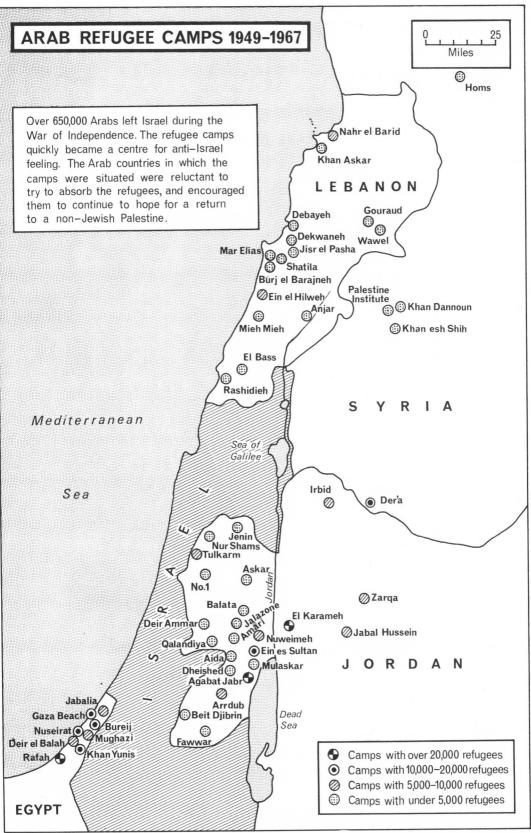

ARAB REFUGEE CAMPS 1949–1967

0   25
Miles

Over 650,000 Arabs left Israel during the War of Independence. The refugee camps quickly became a centre for anti–Israel feeling. The Arab countries in which the camps were situated were reluctant to try to absorb the refugees, and encouraged them to continue to hope for a return to a non–Jewish Palestine.

Homs

Nahr el Barid

Khan Askar

LEBANON

Debayeh

Gouraud

Dekwaneh

Wawel

Mar Elias   Jisr el Pasha

Shatila

Burj el Barajneh

Palestine
Institute   Khan Dannoun

Ein el Hilweh

Anjar   Khan esh Shih

Mieh Mieh

El Bass

Rashidieh   SYRIA

Mediterranean

Sea of
Galilee

Sea   Irbid   Der'a

Jenin

Nur Shams

Tulkarm

Askar

No.1   Zarqa

Balata   Jordan

Deir Ammar   Jalazone   El Karameh

Amari   Jabal Hussein

Qalandiya   Nuweimeh

Aida   Ein es Sultan

Dheished   Mulaskar   JORDAN

Agabat Jabr

Jabalia   Arrdub

Gaza Beach   Beit Djibrin

Nuseirat   Dead
Sea

Bureij   Mughazi

Deir el Balah   Fawwar

Rafah   Khan Yunis

ISRAEL

EGYPT

⊕ Camps with over 20,000 refugees
⊙ Camps with 10,000–20,000 refugees
⊘ Camps with 5,000–10,000 refugees
⊞ Camps with under 5,000 refugees

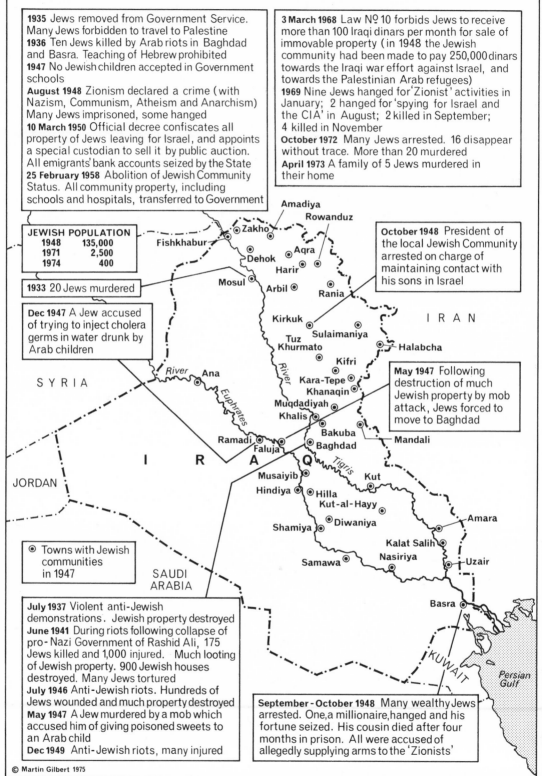

THE JEWS OF IRAQ IN THE TWENTIETH CENTURY

0   50
Miles

1935 Jews removed from Government Service. Many Jews forbidden to travel to Palestine
1936 Ten Jews killed by Arab riots in Baghdad and Basra. Teaching of Hebrew prohibited
1947 No Jewish children accepted in Government schools
August 1948 Zionism declared a crime (with Nazism, Communism, Atheism and Anarchism) Many Jews imprisoned, some hanged
10 March 1950 Official decree confiscates all property of Jews leaving for Israel, and appoints a special custodian to sell it by public auction. All emigrants' bank accounts seized by the State
25 February 1958 Abolition of Jewish Community Status. All community property, including schools and hospitals, transferred to Government

3 March 1968 Law № 10 forbids Jews to receive more than 100 Iraqi dinars per month for sale of immovable property (in 1948 the Jewish community had been made to pay 250,000 dinars towards the Iraqi war effort against Israel, and towards the Palestinian Arab refugees)
1969 Nine Jews hanged for 'Zionist' activities in January; 2 hanged for 'spying for Israel and the CIA' in August; 2 killed in September; 4 killed in November
October 1972 Many Jews arrested. 16 disappear without trace. More than 20 murdered
April 1973 A family of 5 Jews murdered in their home

JEWISH POPULATION	
1948	135,000
1971	2,500
1974	400

1933 20 Jews murdered

Dec 1947 A Jew accused of trying to inject cholera germs in water drunk by Arab children

October 1948 President of the local Jewish Community arrested on charge of maintaining contact with his sons in Israel

May 1947 Following destruction of much Jewish property by mob attack, Jews forced to move to Baghdad

⊙ Towns with Jewish communities in 1947

July 1937 Violent anti-Jewish demonstrations. Jewish property destroyed
June 1941 During riots following collapse of pro-Nazi Government of Rashid Ali, 175 Jews killed and 1,000 injured. Much looting of Jewish property. 900 Jewish houses destroyed. Many Jews tortured
July 1946 Anti-Jewish riots. Hundreds of Jews wounded and much property destroyed
May 1947 A Jew murdered by a mob which accused him of giving poisoned sweets to an Arab child
Dec 1949 Anti-Jewish riots, many injured

September - October 1948 Many wealthy Jews arrested. One, a millionaire, hanged and his fortune seized. His cousin died after four months in prison. All were accused of allegedly supplying arms to the 'Zionists'

Amadiya
Rowanduz
⊙ Zakho
Fishkhabur
⊙ Aqra
Dehok
Harir
Mosul ⊙
Arbil ⊙
Rania
Kirkuk
IRAN
Tuz Khurmato
Sulaimaniya
⊙ Halabcha
Kifri
River
Ana
Kara-Tepe
SYRIA
River
Euphrates
Khanaqin
Muqdadiyah
Khalis
Bakuba
Ramadi
Baghdad
Mandali
Faluja
I R A Q
Tigris
JORDAN
Musaiyib
Kut
Hindiya
Hilla
Kut-al-Hayy
Amara
Shamiya
Diwaniya
Kalat Salih
SAUDI ARABIA
Samawa
Nasiriya
Uzair
Basra
KUWAIT
Persian Gulf

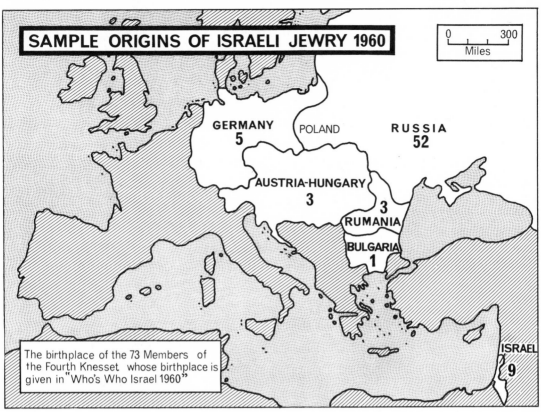

SAMPLE ORIGINS OF ISRAELI JEWRY 1960

0 ——— 300
Miles

GERMANY
5

POLAND

RUSSIA
52

AUSTRIA-HUNGARY
3

RUMANIA
3

BULGARIA
1

ISRAEL
9

The birthplace of the 73 Members of the Fourth Knesset whose birthplace is given in "Who's Who Israel 1960"

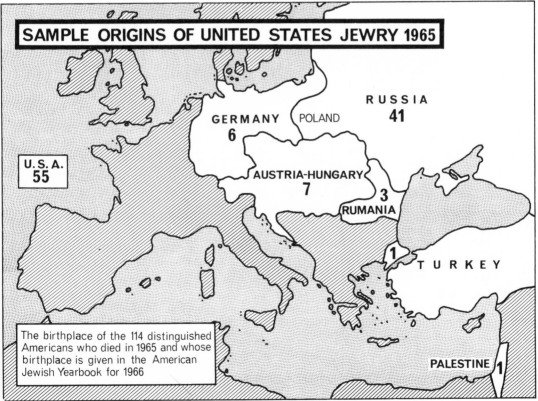

SAMPLE ORIGINS OF UNITED STATES JEWRY 1965

GERMANY
6

POLAND

RUSSIA
41

U.S.A.
55

AUSTRIA-HUNGARY
7

RUMANIA
3

1

TURKEY

The birthplace of the 114 distinguished Americans who died in 1965 and whose birthplace is given in the American Jewish Yearbook for 1966

PALESTINE 1

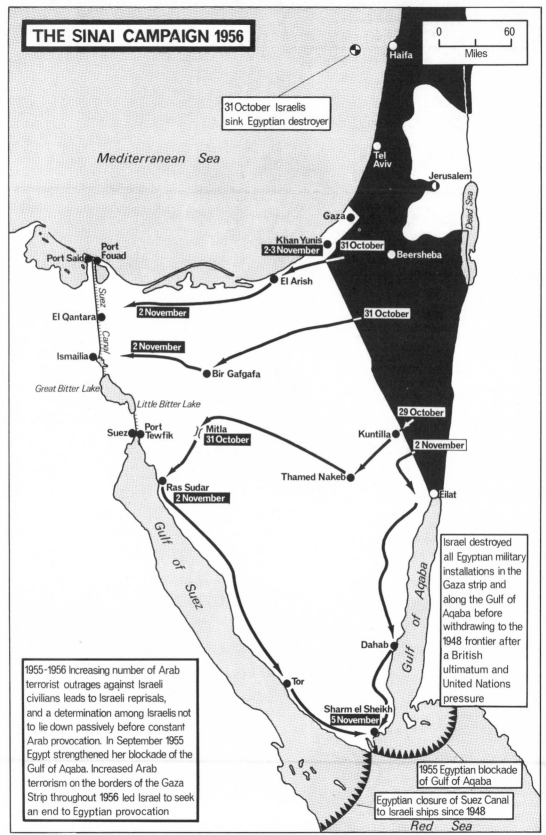

THE SINAI CAMPAIGN 1956

0   60
Miles

31 October Israelis
sink Egyptian destroyer

Mediterranean   Sea

Haifa

Tel Aviv

Jerusalem

Dead Sea

Gaza

Khan Yunis
2-3 November

31 October

Beersheba

Port Said
Port Fouad

El Arish

2 November

31 October

El Qantara

Suez Canal

2 November

Ismailia

Bir Gafgafa

Great Bitter Lake

Little Bitter Lake

29 October

Suez   Port Tewfik

Mitla
31 October

Kuntilla

2 November

Ras Sudar
2 November

Thamed Nakeb

Eilat

Gulf of Suez

Israel destroyed
all Egyptian military
installations in the
Gaza strip and
along the Gulf of
Aqaba before
withdrawing to the
1948 frontier after
a British
ultimatum and
United Nations
pressure

Gulf of Aqaba

Dahab

1955-1956 Increasing number of Arab
terrorist outrages against Israeli
civilians leads to Israeli reprisals,
and a determination among Israelis not
to lie down passively before constant
Arab provocation. In September 1955
Egypt strengthened her blockade of the
Gulf of Aqaba. Increased Arab
terrorism on the borders of the Gaza
Strip throughout 1956 led Israel to seek
an end to Egyptian provocation

Tor

Sharm el Sheikh
5 November

1955 Egyptian blockade
of Gulf of Aqaba

Egyptian closure of Suez Canal
to Israeli ships since 1948

Red   Sea

112

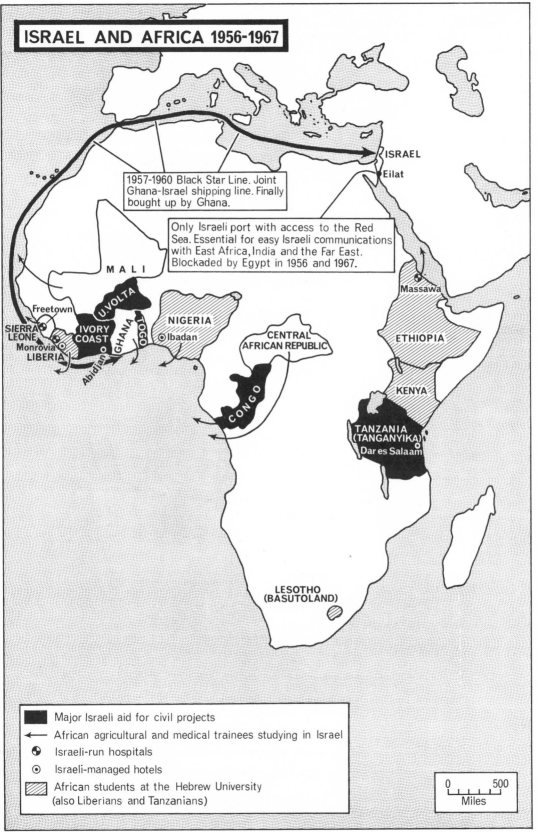

ISRAEL AND AFRICA 1956-1967

1957-1960 Black Star Line. Joint Ghana-Israel shipping line. Finally bought up by Ghana.

Only Israeli port with access to the Red Sea. Essential for easy Israeli communications with East Africa, India and the Far East. Blockaded by Egypt in 1956 and 1967.

ISRAEL

Eilat

Massawa

MALI

U.VOLTA

GHANA

TOGO

NIGERIA

Ibadan

CENTRAL AFRICAN REPUBLIC

ETHIOPIA

KENYA

Freetown

SIERRA LEONE

IVORY COAST

Monrovia

LIBERIA

Abidjan

CONGO

TANZANIA (TANGANYIKA)

Dar es Salaam

LESOTHO (BASUTOLAND)

Major Israeli aid for civil projects

African agricultural and medical trainees studying in Israel

Israeli-run hospitals

Israeli-managed hotels

African students at the Hebrew University (also Liberians and Tanzanians)

0   500
Miles

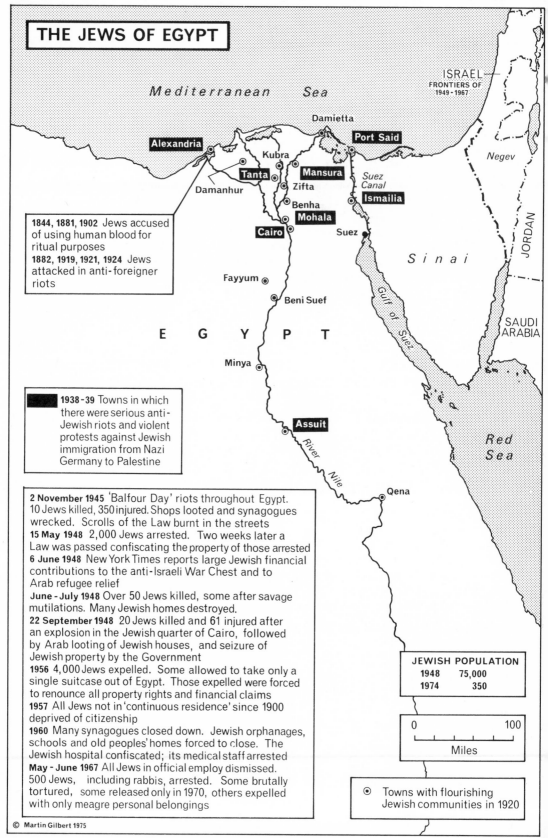

THE JEWS OF EGYPT

Mediterranean Sea

ISRAEL
FRONTIERS OF
1949-1967

Damietta

Alexandria

Kubra

Port Said

Negev

Tanta

Mansura

Damanhur

Zifta

Suez Canal

Benha

Ismailia

Mohala

Cairo

Suez

JORDAN

Sinai

1844, 1881, 1902 Jews accused of using human blood for ritual purposes
1882, 1919, 1921, 1924 Jews attacked in anti-foreigner riots

Fayyum

Beni Suef

E G Y P T

SAUDI ARABIA

Minya

■ **1938-39** Towns in which there were serious anti-Jewish riots and violent protests against Jewish immigration from Nazi Germany to Palestine

Assuit

Red Sea

River Nile

---

2 November 1945 'Balfour Day' riots throughout Egypt. 10 Jews killed, 350 injured. Shops looted and synagogues wrecked. Scrolls of the Law burnt in the streets
15 May 1948 2,000 Jews arrested. Two weeks later a Law was passed confiscating the property of those arrested
6 June 1948 New York Times reports large Jewish financial contributions to the anti-Israeli War Chest and to Arab refugee relief
June - July 1948 Over 50 Jews killed, some after savage mutilations. Many Jewish homes destroyed.
22 September 1948 20 Jews killed and 61 injured after an explosion in the Jewish quarter of Cairo, followed by Arab looting of Jewish houses, and seizure of Jewish property by the Government
1956 4,000 Jews expelled. Some allowed to take only a single suitcase out of Egypt. Those expelled were forced to renounce all property rights and financial claims
1957 All Jews not in 'continuous residence' since 1900 deprived of citizenship
1960 Many synagogues closed down. Jewish orphanages, schools and old peoples' homes forced to close. The Jewish hospital confiscated; its medical staff arrested
May - June 1967 All Jews in official employ dismissed. 500 Jews, including rabbis, arrested. Some brutally tortured, some released only in 1970, others expelled with only meagre personal belongings

Qena

JEWISH POPULATION
1948	75,000
1974	350

0 ———— 100
Miles

⊙ Towns with flourishing Jewish communities in 1920

© Martin Gilbert 1975

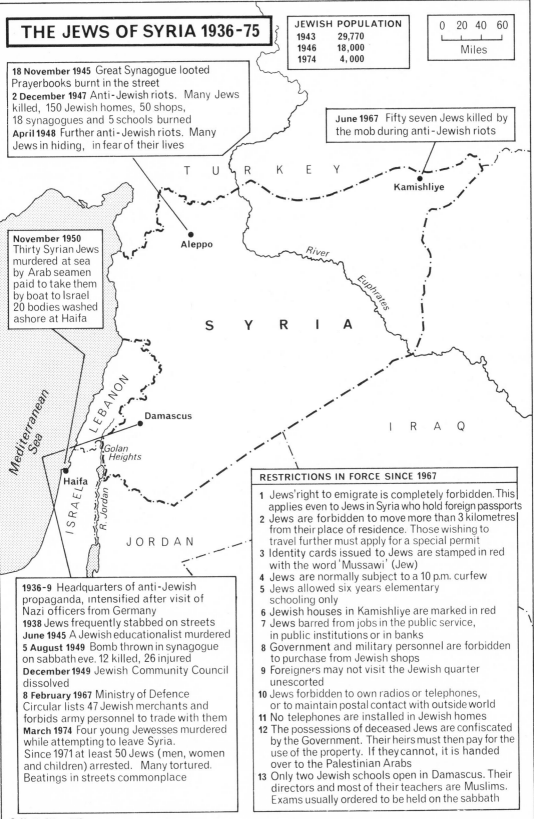

THE JEWS OF SYRIA 1936-75

JEWISH POPULATION
1943   29,770
1946   18,000
1974   4,000

0   20   40   60
Miles

18 November 1945 Great Synagogue looted
Prayerbooks burnt in the street
2 December 1947 Anti-Jewish riots. Many Jews
killed, 150 Jewish homes, 50 shops,
18 synagogues and 5 schools burned
April 1948 Further anti-Jewish riots. Many
Jews in hiding, in fear of their lives

June 1967 Fifty seven Jews killed by
the mob during anti-Jewish riots

T U R K E Y

Kamishliye

November 1950
Thirty Syrian Jews
murdered at sea
by Arab seamen
paid to take them
by boat to Israel
20 bodies washed
ashore at Haifa

Aleppo

River
Euphrates

S Y R I A

Mediterranean
Sea

LEBANON

Damascus

Golan
Heights

I R A Q

Haifa

ISRAEL

R. Jordan

JORDAN

1936-9 Headquarters of anti-Jewish
propaganda, intensified after visit of
Nazi officers from Germany
1938 Jews frequently stabbed on streets
June 1945 A Jewish educationalist murdered
5 August 1949 Bomb thrown in synagogue
on sabbath eve. 12 killed, 26 injured
December 1949 Jewish Community Council
dissolved
8 February 1967 Ministry of Defence
Circular lists 47 Jewish merchants and
forbids army personnel to trade with them
March 1974 Four young Jewesses murdered
while attempting to leave Syria.
Since 1971 at least 50 Jews (men, women
and children) arrested. Many tortured.
Beatings in streets commonplace

RESTRICTIONS IN FORCE SINCE 1967

1 Jews' right to emigrate is completely forbidden. This
applies even to Jews in Syria who hold foreign passports
2 Jews are forbidden to move more than 3 kilometres
from their place of residence. Those wishing to
travel further must apply for a special permit
3 Identity cards issued to Jews are stamped in red
with the word 'Mussawi' (Jew)
4 Jews are normally subject to a 10 p.m. curfew
5 Jews allowed six years elementary
schooling only
6 Jewish houses in Kamishliye are marked in red
7 Jews barred from jobs in the public service,
in public institutions or in banks
8 Government and military personnel are forbidden
to purchase from Jewish shops
9 Foreigners may not visit the Jewish quarter
unescorted
10 Jews forbidden to own radios or telephones,
or to maintain postal contact with outside world
11 No telephones are installed in Jewish homes
12 The possessions of deceased Jews are confiscated
by the Government. Their heirs must then pay for the
use of the property. If they cannot, it is handed
over to the Palestinian Arabs
13 Only two Jewish schools open in Damascus. Their
directors and most of their teachers are Muslims.
Exams usually ordered to be held on the sabbath

© Martin Gilbert 1975

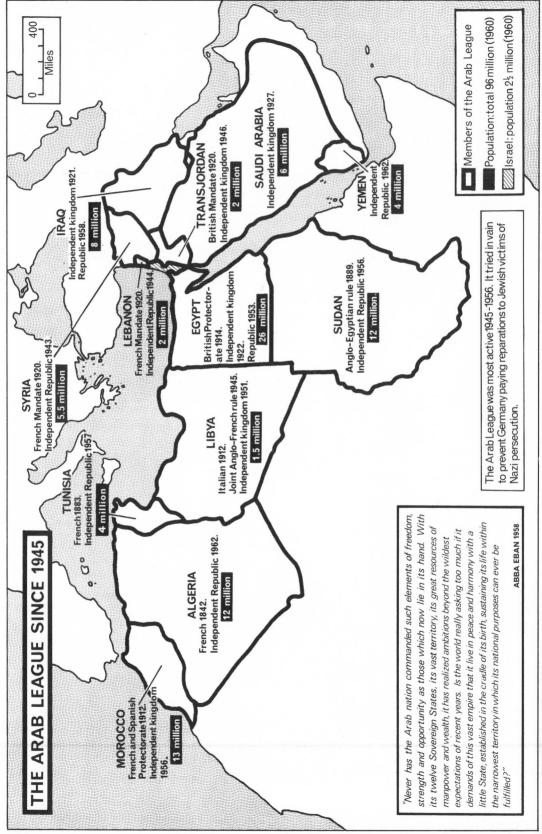

THE ARAB LEAGUE SINCE 1945

0 400 Miles

SYRIA
French Mandate 1920.
Independent Republic 1943.
5.5 million

IRAQ
Independent kingdom 1921.
Republic 1958.
8 million

TRANSJORDAN
British Mandate 1920.
Independent kingdom 1946.
2 million

SAUDI ARABIA
Independent kingdom 1927.
6 million

YEMEN
Independent
Republic 1962.
4 million

LEBANON
French Mandate 1920.
Independent Republic 1944.
2 million

EGYPT
British Protector-
ate 1914.
Independent kingdom
1922.
Republic 1953.
26 million

SUDAN
Anglo-Egyptian rule 1889.
Independent Republic 1956.
12 million

LIBYA
Italian 1912.
Joint Anglo-French rule 1945.
Independent kingdom 1951.
1.5 million

TUNISIA
French 1883.
Independent Republic 1957
4 million

ALGERIA
French 1842.
Independent Republic 1962.
12 million

MOROCCO
French and Spanish
Protectorate 1912.
Independent Kingdom
1956.
13 million

Members of the Arab League

■ Population: total 96 million (1960)

▨ Israel: population 2½ million (1960)

The Arab League was most active 1945–1956. It tried in vain to prevent Germany paying reparations to Jewish victims of Nazi persecution.

"Never has the Arab nation commanded such elements of freedom, strength and opportunity as those which now lie in its hand. With its twelve Sovereign States, its vast territory, its great resources of manpower and wealth, it has realized ambitions beyond the wildest expectations of recent years. Is the world really asking too much of it if it demands of this vast empire that it live in peace and harmony with a little State, established in the cradle of its birth, sustaining its life within the narrowest territory in which its national purposes can ever be fulfilled?"

ABBA EBAN 1958

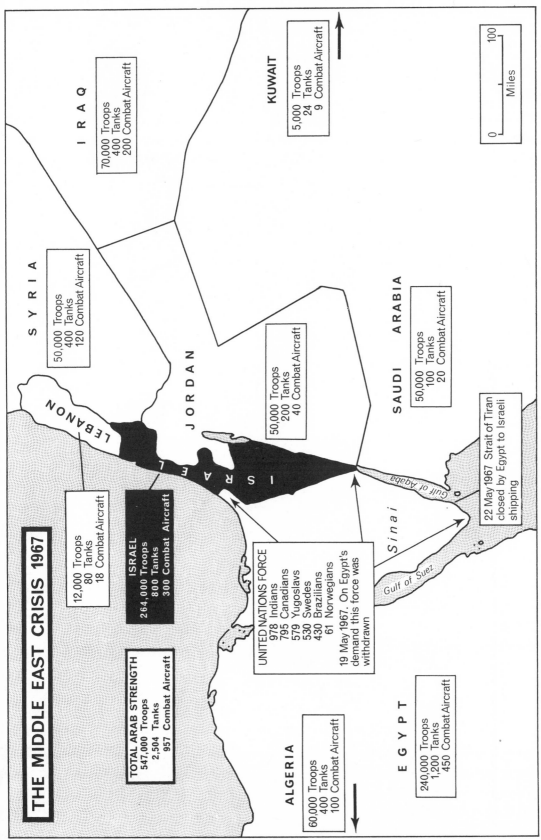

THE MIDDLE EAST CRISIS 1967

ALGERIA

60,000 Troops
400 Tanks
100 Combat Aircraft

EGYPT

240,000 Troops
1,200 Tanks
450 Combat Aircraft

TOTAL ARAB STRENGTH
547,000 Troops
2,504 Tanks
957 Combat Aircraft

12,000 Troops
80 Tanks
18 Combat Aircraft

ISRAEL
264,000 Troops
800 Tanks
300 Combat Aircraft

UNITED NATIONS FORCE
978 Indians
795 Canadians
579 Yugoslavs
530 Swedes
430 Brazilians
61 Norwegians

19 May 1967. On Egypt's demand this force was withdrawn

22 May 1967 Strait of Tiran closed by Egypt to Israeli shipping

LEBANON

SYRIA

50,000 Troops
400 Tanks
120 Combat Aircraft

JORDAN

50,000 Troops
200 Tanks
40 Combat Aircraft

SAUDI   ARABIA

50,000 Troops
100 Tanks
20 Combat Aircraft

IRAQ

70,000 Troops
400 Tanks
200 Combat Aircraft

KUWAIT

5,000 Troops
24 Tanks
9 Combat Aircraft

Sinai

Gulf of Suez

Gulf of Aqaba

0   100
Miles

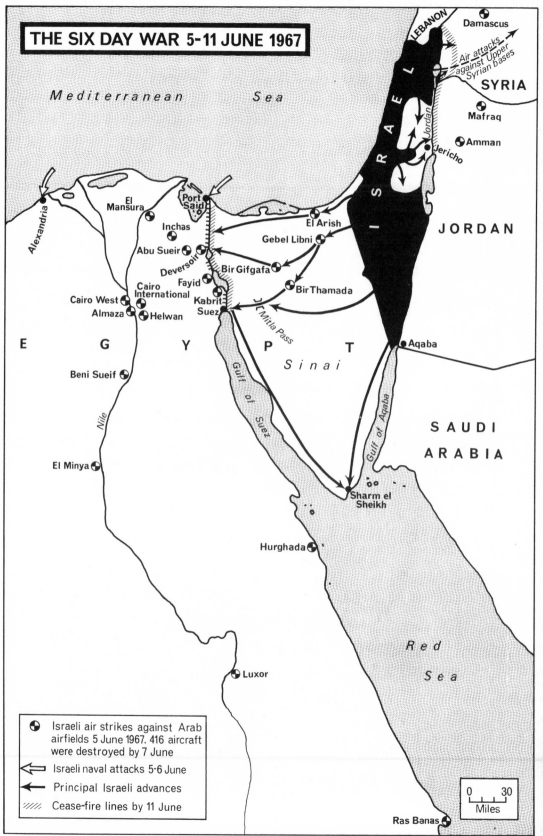

THE SIX DAY WAR 5-11 JUNE 1967

Mediterranean   Sea

LEBANON

Damascus

Air attacks against Upper Syrian bases

SYRIA

Mafraq

Amman

Jericho

I S R A E L

Jordan

JORDAN

Alexandria

El Mansura

Port Said

El Arish

Inchas

Gebel Libni

Abu Sueir

Deversoir

Bir Gifgafa

Cairo International

Fayid

Bir Thamada

Cairo West

Kabrit

Almaza

Helwan

Suez

Mitla Pass

Aqaba

E   G   Y   P   T

Beni Sueif

Sinai

Gulf of Suez

Gulf of Aqaba

SAUDI

ARABIA

El Minya

Nile

Sharm el Sheikh

Hurghada

Luxor

Red

Sea

Ras Banas

Israeli air strikes against Arab airfields 5 June 1967. 416 aircraft were destroyed by 7 June

Israeli naval attacks 5-6 June

Principal Israeli advances

Cease-fire lines by 11 June

0   30

Miles

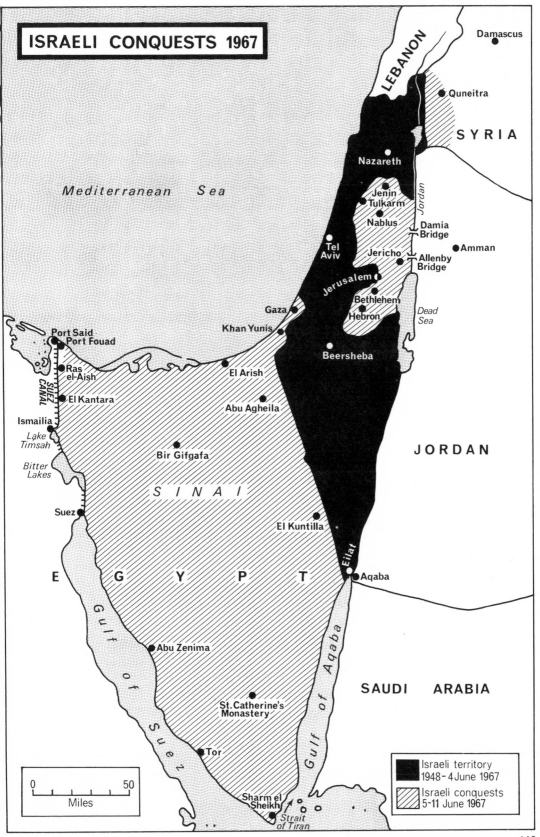

ISRAELI CONQUESTS 1967

Damascus

Quneitra

SYRIA

LEBANON

Mediterranean Sea

Nazareth

Jenin
Tulkarm

Nablus

Damia
Bridge

Jordan

Amman

Tel
Aviv

Jericho

Allenby
Bridge

Jerusalem

Bethlehem

Hebron

*Dead
Sea*

Gaza

Khan Yunis

Beersheba

Port Said
Port Fouad

Ras
el-Aish

Suez Canal

El Kantara

El Arish

Abu Agheila

JORDAN

Ismailia

*Lake
Timsah*

*Bitter
Lakes*

Bir Gifgafa

S I N A I

Suez

El Kuntilla

Eilat

Aqaba

E G Y P T

Abu Zenima

Gulf of Suez

Gulf of Aqaba

SAUDI   ARABIA

St. Catherine's
Monastery

Tor

Sharm el
Sheikh

*Strait
of Tiran*

■	Israeli territory 1948 – 4 June 1967
▨	Israeli conquests 5-11 June 1967

0   50
Miles

119

THE OCTOBER WAR, 6-24 OCTOBER 1973

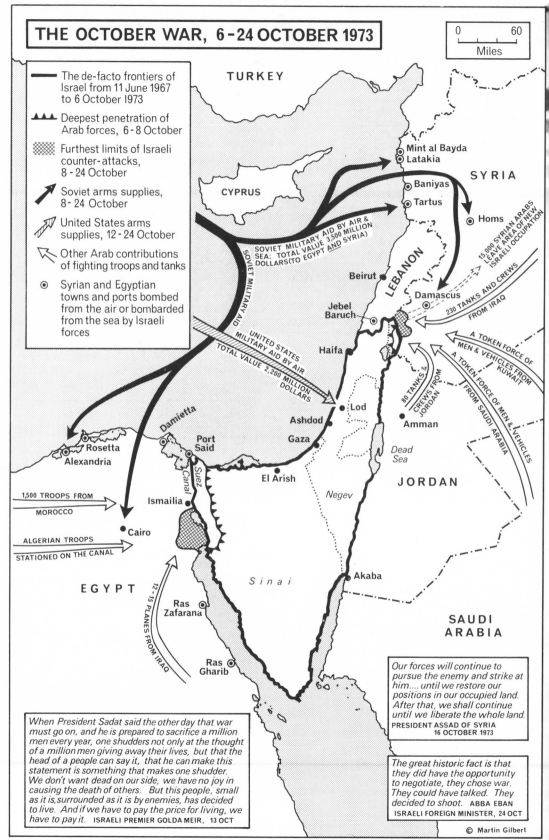

0   60
Miles

Legend:

— The de-facto frontiers of Israel from 11 June 1967 to 6 October 1973

▲▲▲ Deepest penetration of Arab forces, 6-8 October

▨ Furthest limits of Israeli counter-attacks, 8-24 October

➤ Soviet arms supplies, 8-24 October

⇗ United States arms supplies, 12-24 October

⇖ Other Arab contributions of fighting troops and tanks

⊙ Syrian and Egyptian towns and ports bombed from the air or bombarded from the sea by Israeli forces

TURKEY

CYPRUS

SYRIA

Mint al Bayda
Latakia
Baniyas
Tartus
Homs

LEBANON

SOVIET MILITARY AID BY AIR & SEA; TOTAL VALUE 3,500 MILLION DOLLARS (TO EGYPT AND SYRIA)

SOVIET MILITARY AID

15,000 SYRIAN ARABS LEAVE AREA OF NEW ISRAELI OCCUPATION

Beirut

Damascus

230 TANKS AND CREWS FROM IRAQ

Jebel Baruch

UNITED STATES MILITARY AID BY AIR TOTAL VALUE 2,200 MILLION DOLLARS

Haifa

A TOKEN FORCE OF MEN & VEHICLES FROM KUWAIT

A TOKEN FORCE OF MEN & VEHICLES FROM SAUDI ARABIA

Damietta
Port Said
Ashdod
Lod
Gaza
Amman

80 TANKS & CREWS FROM JORDAN

Rosetta
Alexandria

El Arish

Dead Sea

JORDAN

Negev

1,500 TROOPS FROM MOROCCO

Ismailia

Cairo

ALGERIAN TROOPS STATIONED ON THE CANAL

Suez Canal

Sinai

Akaba

EGYPT

Ras Zafarana

12-15 PLANES FROM IRAQ

SAUDI ARABIA

Ras Gharib

Our forces will continue to pursue the enemy and strike at him.... until we restore our positions in our occupied land. After that, we shall continue until we liberate the whole land. **PRESIDENT ASSAD OF SYRIA 16 OCTOBER 1973**

When President Sadat said the other day that war must go on, and he is prepared to sacrifice a million men every year, one shudders not only at the thought of a million men giving away their lives, but that the head of a people can say it, that he can make this statement is something that makes one shudder. We don't want dead on our side, we have no joy in causing the death of others. But this people, small as it is, surrounded as it is by enemies, has decided to live. And if we have to pay the price for living, we have to pay it. **ISRAELI PREMIER GOLDA MEIR, 13 OCT**

The great historic fact is that they did have the opportunity to negotiate, they chose war. They could have talked. They decided to shoot. **ABBA EBAN ISRAELI FOREIGN MINISTER, 24 OCT**

© Martin Gilbert

120

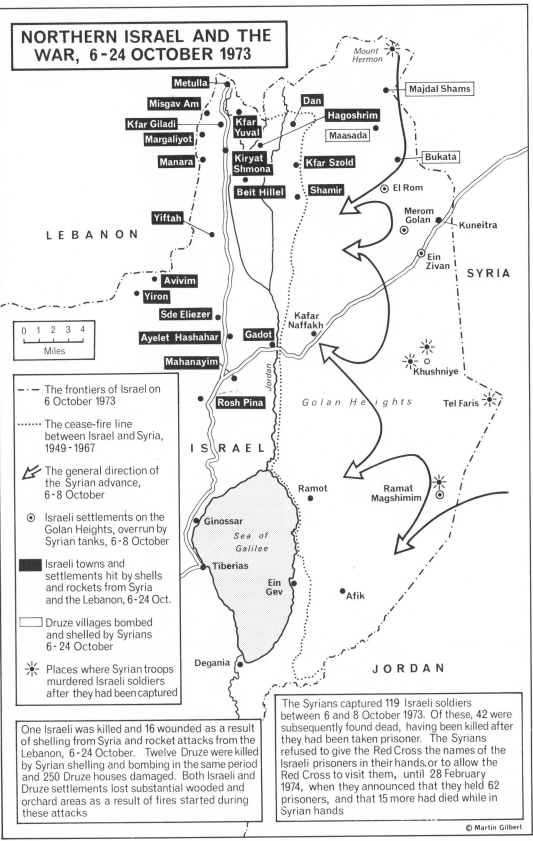

NORTHERN ISRAEL AND THE WAR, 6-24 OCTOBER 1973

Mount Hermon

Metulla

Misgav Am

Kfar Giladi

Margaliyot

Manara

Kfar Yuval

Dan

Hagoshrim

Maasada

Kiryat Shmona

Kfar Szold

Beit Hillel

Shamir

Majdal Shams

Bukata

El Rom

LEBANON

Yiftah

Merom Golan

Kuneitra

Ein Zivan

SYRIA

Avivim

Yiron

Sde Eliezer

Ayelet Hashahar

Gadot

Kafar Naffakh

Khushniye

Mahanayim

Jordan

Golan Heights

Tel Faris

Rosh Pina

ISRAEL

Ramot

Ramat Magshimim

Ginossar

Sea of Galilee

Tiberias

Ein Gev

Afik

Degania

JORDAN

0 1 2 3 4
Miles

– · – The frontiers of Israel on 6 October 1973

· · · · · · The cease-fire line between Israel and Syria, 1949 - 1967

The general direction of the Syrian advance, 6 - 8 October

⊙ Israeli settlements on the Golan Heights, overrun by Syrian tanks, 6 - 8 October

Israeli towns and settlements hit by shells and rockets from Syria and the Lebanon, 6 - 24 Oct.

Druze villages bombed and shelled by Syrians 6 - 24 October

Places where Syrian troops murdered Israeli soldiers after they had been captured

One Israeli was killed and 16 wounded as a result of shelling from Syria and rocket attacks from the Lebanon, 6 - 24 October. Twelve Druze were killed by Syrian shelling and bombing in the same period and 250 Druze houses damaged. Both Israeli and Druze settlements lost substantial wooded and orchard areas as a result of fires started during these attacks

The Syrians captured 119 Israeli soldiers between 6 and 8 October 1973. Of these, 42 were subsequently found dead, having been killed after they had been taken prisoner. The Syrians refused to give the Red Cross the names of the Israeli prisoners in their hands, or to allow the Red Cross to visit them, until 28 February 1974, when they announced that they held 62 prisoners, and that 15 more had died while in Syrian hands

© Martin Gilbert

Bibliography

The following bibliography is strictly selective. It consists of some eighty books which I myself have found useful while gathering material for the maps.
In addition to the books listed below, I have made frequent use of a number of general reference works, of which the most valuable were:

Isodore Singer (Managing Editor), *The Jewish Encyclopaedia*, 12 vols., New York, 1901–1906, the most comprehensive of all encyclopaedias on Jewish affairs.

Y. L. Katzenelson (Editor), *Yevreyskaya Entsiklopediya*, 16 vols., St. Petersburg, 1906–1913. An essential source for all problems of Russian Jewry.

Isaac Landman (Editor), *Universal Jewish Encyclopaedia*, 10 vols. (New York, 1939–1943). The most recent complete multi-volume encyclopaedia of Jewish history.

Cecil Roth (Editor-in-Chief), *The Standard Jewish Encyclopaedia*, one volume (New York, 1962). The fullest single volume work of reference.

Israeli Department of Surveys and the Bialik Institute, *Atlas of Israel* (Jerusalem, 1956), contains an excellent bibliography of over a thousand cartographic sources relating to Israel.

General works on Jewish History

Nathan Ausubel, *Pictorial History of the Jewish People* (New York, 1954)

Salo W. Baron, *A Social and Religious History of the Jews* (New York, 1952–1960)

Edwyn R. Bevan and Charles Singer (editors), *The Legacy of Israel* (Oxford, 1927)

Max I. Dimont, *Jews, God and History* (New York, 1962)

Max L. Margolis and A. Marx, *A History of the Jewish People* (Philadelphia, 1964)

James William Parkes, *A History of the Jewish People* (London, 1962)

Cecil Roth, *A Short History of the Jewish People* (London, 1959)

Cecil Roth, *Personalities and Events in Jewish History* (Philadelphia, 1961)

Biblical and Classical Periods

W. F. Albright, *New Horizons in Biblical Research* (London, 1966)

M. Avi-Yonah, *Map of Roman Palestine* (Oxford, 1940)

Daniel-Rops, *Israel and the Ancient World* (Paris, 1943; London, 1949)

Luc Grollenberg, *Atlas de la Bible* (London, 1956)

James Hastings, *Dictionary of the Bible* (London, 1963)

Jean Juster, *Les Juifs dans l'empire romain* (Paris, 1914)

Harry J. Leon, *The Jews of Ancient Rome* (Philadelphia, 1960)

Benjamin Maisler, *Historical Atlas of Palestine* (Jerusalem, 1942)

W. O. E. Osterley, *The Jews and Judaism During the Greek Period* (London, 1941)

John William Parkes, *Jesus, Paul and the Jews* (London, 1936)

George Adam Smith, *Historical Geography of the Holy Land* (London, 1894)

John Stirling, *An Atlas of the Life of Christ* (London, 1954)

John Stirling, *An Atlas Illustrating the Acts of the Apostles and the Epistles* (London, 1954)

Yigael Yadin, *Masada* (London, 1965)

Yigael Yadin, *Bar-Kokhba* (London, 1971)

Medieval Period

Marcus Nathan Adler, *The Itinery of Benjamin of Tudela* (London, 1907)

George K. Anderson, *The Legend of the Wandering Jew* (Providence, 1965)

Salo Baron, *The Jewish Community; Its History and Structure* (Philadelphia, 1942)

Herbert Ivan Bloom, *The Economic Activities of the Jews of Amsterdam* (Williamsport, 1937)

Claude Reignier Conder, *The Latin Kingdom of Jerusalem 1099–1291* (London, 1897)

D. M. Dunlop, *The History of the Jewish Khazars* (Princeton, 1954)

Louis Finkelstein, *Jewish Self-Government in the Middle Ages* (New York, 1924)

Walter Joseph Fischel, *Jews in the Economic and Political Life of Medieval Islam* (London, 1937)

Solomon Grayzel, *The Church and the Jews in the Thirteenth Century* (New York, 1966)

Julius H. Greenstone, *The Messianic Idea in Jewish History* (Philadelphia, 1906)

Henry Kamen, *The Spanish Inquisition* (London, 1965)

Robert S. Lopez and Irving W. Raymond (eds.), *Medieval Trade in the Mediterranean World* (New York, 1955)

Leon Nemoy, *Karaite Anthology* (New Haven, 1952)

Abraham A. Neuman, *The Jews in Spain* (Philadelphia, 1944)

James William Parkes, *The Conflict of the Church and the Synagogue* (London, 1934)

David Philipson, *Old European Jewries* (Harrisburg, 1894)

L. Rabinowitz, *Jewish Merchant Adventurers* (London, 1948)

Cecil Roth, *The History of the Jews of Italy* (Philadelphia, 1946)

Cecil Roth, *A History of the Marranos* (Philadelphia, 1942)

Cecil Roth, *A History of the Jews in England* (Oxford, 1941)

Cecil Roth, *The Jews of Medieval Oxford* (Oxford, 1951)

Steven Runciman, *A History of the Crusades* (Cambridge, 1951)

Abba Hillel Silver, *A History of Messianic Speculation in Israel* (New York, 1927)

Joshua Starr, *Jews in the Byzantine Empire 641–1204* (Athens, 1939)

Joshua Starr, *Romania, the Jews of the Levant After the Fourth Crusade* (Paris, 1949)

William Charles White, *Chinese Jews* (Toronto, 1942)

Louis Wirth, *The Ghetto* (Chicago, 1928)

Modern Period

Reuben Ainsztein, *Jewish Resistance in Nazi-Occupied Eastern Europe* (London, 1974)

Karl Baedeker, *Austria-Hungary* (Leipzig, 1905)

Salo Baron, *The Russian Jew Under Tsars and Soviets* (New York, 1964)

Norman Bentwich, *They Found Refuge* (London, 1956)

Randolph S. Churchill and Winston S. Churchill, *The Six Day War* (London, 1967)

Israel Cohen, *A Short History of Zionism* (London, 1951)

Israel Cohen, *Contemporary Jewry* (London, 1950)

Israel Cohen, *Vilna* (Philadelphia, 1943)

Israel Cohen, *My Mission to Poland 1918–1919* (London, 1951)

Norman Cohn, *Warrant for Genocide* (London, 1967)

Moshe Dayan, *Diary of the Sinai Campaign* (London, 1966)

S. M. Dubnow, *History of the Jews in Russia and Poland* (Philadelphia, 1916–20)

Abba Eban, *Voice of Israel* (London, 1958)

Lloyd P. Gartner, *The Jewish Immigrant in England 1870–1914* (London, 1960)

Martin Gilbert, *The Jews of Arab Lands: Their History in Maps* (London, 1975)

Martin Gilbert, *The Jews of Russia and the Soviet Union: Their History in Maps* (London, 1976)

Louis Greenberg, *The Jews in Russia: The Struggle for Emancipation* (New Haven 1944 and 1951)

Philip Guedalla, *Napoleon and Palestine* (London, 1925)

Vladimir Jabotinsky, *The Story of the Jewish Legion* (New York, 1954)

Leo Jung (ed.), *Jewish Leaders 1750–1940* (Jerusalem, 1964)

Roderick Kedward, *The Dreyfus Affair* (London, 1964)

Mordechai E. Kreinin, *Israel and Africa* (New York, 1964)

Harry S. Linfield, *Statistics of Jews 1931* (New York, 1931)

Vivian David Lipman, *Social History of the Jews in England 1850–1950* (London, 1954)

Macmillan (publishers), *Atlas of the Arab World and the Middle East* (London, 1960)

Raphael Mahler, *A History of Modern Jewry 1780–1815* (London, 1971)

Arthur D. Morse, *While Six Million Died* (London, 1968)

Alfred Nossig, *Materialen Zur statistik der Judischen Stammes* (Vienna, 1897)

Edgar O'Ballance, *The Arab-Israeli War 1948* (London, 1956)

F. J. Pietri, *Napoléon et les Israélites* (Paris, 1965)

James William Parkes, *Arabs and Jews in the Middle East: a Tragedy of Errors* (London, 1967)

J. H. Patterson, *With the Judaeans in the Palestine Campaign* (London, 1922)

Leon Poliakov, *Harvest of Hate* (New York, 1954)

Malcolm J. Proudfoot, *European Refugees 1939–52* (London, 1957)

Peter George J. Pulzer, *The Rise of Political Anti-Semitism in Germany and Austria* (New York, 1964)

Gerald Reitlinger, *The Final Solution* (London, 1953)

Emmanuel Ringelblum, *Polish-Jewish Relations during the Second World War* (Jerusalem, 1974)

Adolf Rudnicki, *Ascent to Heaven* (London, 1951)

Harry Sacher, *Zionist Portraits* (London, 1959)

Joseph B. Schechtman, *On Wings of Eagles* (New York, 1961)

A. J. Sherman, *Island Refuge* (London, 1974)

Yuri Suhl (ed.), *They Fought Back* (London, 1968)

Christopher Sykes, *Cross Roads to Israel* (London, 1965)

M. U. Schappes, *A Documentary History of the Jews in the United States 1654–1875* (New York, 1950)

Leonard Stein, *The Balfour Declaration* (London, 1966)

Arieh Tartakower and Kurt R. Grossman, *The Jewish Refugee* (New York, 1944)

Chaim Weizmann, *Trial and Error* (London, 1952)

Israel Zangwill, *Children of the Ghetto* (London, 1892)